DATA MANAGEMENT FOR LIBRARIES

Understanding DBMS, RDBMS, IR Technologies & Tools

DATA MANAGEMENT FOR LIBRARIES

Understanding DBMS, RDBMS, IR Technologies & Tools

By

V.J. Suseela

V. Uma

Ess Ess Publications

New Delhi

DATA MANAGEMENT FOR LIBRARIES

Understanding DBMS, RDBMS, IR Technologies & Tools

ISBN: 978-81-933597-1-6

First Published 2017

Published by:
Ess Ess Publications
4831/24, Ansari Road,
Darya Ganj,
New Delhi-110 002.
INDIA
Phones: 23260807, 41563444
Fax: 41563334
E-mail: info@essessreference.com
www.essessreference.com

Cover Design by *Patch Creative Unit*

Printed and bound in India.

I dedicate this book to
our uncle and a scholar librarian
Late Sri D.J. Narayana Rao, (Retd.)
(Dr. V.S.K.M. Library - Andhra University)
For his encouragement in
LIS professional activities & writings

Contents

Acknowledgements

The book entitled **Data Management for Libraries: Understanding DBMS, RDBMS, IR Technologies & Tools** is meant to offer practical perspective and understanding of concepts for the effective implementation of automation in libraries and the management of data and databases. We are indebted to our organization, the "University of Hyderabad" and working department "Indira Gandhi Memorial Library (IGM Library), Hyderabad, India", which has given us an opportunity to work in ICT environment and also provided exposure to handle our database and to work with data.

We express our deep sense of gratitude to Professor V. Viswamohan, Department of Library and Information Science, Osmania University, Hyderabad, India for kindly agreeing to write foreward for our book, in spite of his busy schedule due to various official assignments as well as professional commitments.

The book would not have taken a shape without the technical guidance of Mr. Santha Kumar, the Service engineer, VTLS Software Pvt. Ltd., India. He has provided clarifications and guidance from time to time in handling the database and also so kindly agreed to screen the RDBMS areas of this book, especially the ORACLE part. He did the verification within reasonable time that has given us enough confidence to incorporate the practical zone of RDBMS in our book.

We are grateful to our publishers Ess Ess Publications, New Delhi particularly Shri Sumit Sethi for publishing our book in short span of time.

We are thankful to our senior colleague Dr. N. Varatharajan, University Librarian, IGM Library for his encouragement in writing this book.

We have been deriving consistent support and inspiration from several LIS professionals, senior colleagues, and academicians directly or indirectly from our organization/ department and also from outside institutions. We are thankful to one and all for their encouragement to this professional endeavor.

Finally, we greatly acknowledge the moral support and the appreciation we received from our family members all through the making of this book.

V.J. Suseela
V. Uma

Preface

Library and information professionals are primarily involved in the processes of acquiring, disseminating and retrieving the information or documents and also preserving for future generations. Thus they require compiling the information (metadata) about information/data or documents in the form of 'records' and maintaining them as 'files' or 'databases'. Databases are collections of similar records with a relationship between the records. The information explosion, proliferation of documents and e-publishing as well as digitization activities resulted in exorbitant increase of publications, library collections and digital documents and also related records. Ultimately these developments influenced the size and structure of library databases.

- Libraries have been developing their databases by computerizing their bibliographic records in coordination with the technical departments of their parent organization or acquiring the commercially available tailor-made software and maintaining the same in library/institution servers or availing cloud services.
- The design, type and model of database vary according to the nature of records, the information as well as search needs of library users, which requires the understanding of the structure of different types of records, files, the way of integration, models, creation

and maintenance of databases in their respective storage spaces.

- Additionally, most of the libraries are involving in the digitization activities of their copyright free/permitted books, theses/dissertations and project reports etc. Further, they are making these digital documents available to users through their websites and also web OPAC over the internal and public networks.
- Moreover, libraries are acquiring wide variety of innumerable scholarly resources in electronic form and providing online access to their institutional users. Majority of these electronic databases are maintained in the remote servers of the vendors/publishers of electronic resources in order to retrieve the right information to users from these databases. Some of these information material – electronic books, journals, serial publications and reference sources are subscribed by institutions/consortia on perpetual access basis and thus forming part of the permanent collection of the library along with digitized and print documents. The bibliographic formats, retrieval methods are invariably different from the print ones.
- User's information needs have been changing faster and unpredictable in the era of quickly transforming information types, formats and modes of dissemination. Similarly libraries need to support the top and middle managements with the information as required. Libraries need to import records of perpetually available e-books, journals and other material into their databases to make them visible and searchable through web OPAC. Further, the libraries also need to share export or send the records periodically in different formats (PDF/XML/MARC/RTF etc.) to support and participate in centralized resource sharing activities of consortia for compiling tools like union catalogues, journals lists etc.

Most of the tailor-made LIS software packages are facilitating some reports at individual modules level or through a separate reports modules. The librarian's tasks of maintaining their bibliographic records and related techniques were different before the automation period and less complicated compared to the present day. Libraries will be in a position to customize these module based reports to certain extent only, while many more reports need to be extracted from database directly. LIS professionals need to practically handle the data needs of his users, management and centralized agencies.

The creation and maintenance of databases for libraries require some basic understanding about different types of records, structure of files, the ways of integration, varied models on which the databases are mounted in their respective storage spaces etc. Further the professionals need to possess the skills of retrieving information or documents and build the awareness of technologies as well as tools among themselves and users.

ORGANIZATION OF THE BOOK

The chapters of the book cover the basic concepts of databases, DBMS/RDBMS functioning at the backend of all the LIS operations help in building databases that are to be handled by the libraries in the current scenario for the effective retrieval of information.

CHAPTERS

1. Data in Libraries: an Overview
2. Database Concepts
3. Database Management Systems (DBMS)
4. DBMS/RDBMS Software
5. Data Management for Libraries (DBMS/RDBMS Applications)
6. Library Databases
7. Information Retrieval and DBMS Approach

8. Approach to Online Information (Strategies and Tools)
9. Emerging Trends in Library Data Management

The book is organized in 9 chapters with detailed contents (Contents), introduction to the book preface, Vocabulary before the beginning of chapters and bibliography at the end of book. Chapters commence briefly describing the types and nature of data to be handled by the libraries end after discussing the impact of emerging trends in data management in libraries.

Chapter 1 : describes the significance of acquiring and organizing abundant data accumulates in library servers, explaining its sources of acquisition. The complex relations among various data elements of integrated library bibliographic databases are discussed in relation to the database design, organization, data formats and record structures in relation to the various modules in integrated library system. Further, the role of standards in designing the library databases was discussed emphasizing the bibliographic as well as search/retrieval standards. Finally the chapter ends explaining the advantages of shifting libraries from file processing systems to DBMS/RDBMS while cautioning about the limitations in implementing the technology.

Chapter 2 : explains the basic concepts required to understand the advanced program of database management. While defining the concepts, it draws the contrast between the closely related terms - data, information and knowledge. Further, the detailed applications of different data types including - textual to metadata, usage data to big-data are presented. The elaborate description of databases and their categories are given in this chapter to show the different existing practices of data handling. The databases are varied structurally. Those data structures are called as database models. The popularly used models - Entity-Relationship (E-R) Data Model, Hierarchical Data Model, and Network Model to the latest advanced relational database models (RDBMS) and Object relational database models (ORDBMS) are illustrated in this chapter.

Chapter 3 : explains the concept of database management in detail describing its characteristics, objectives, components, database formats and the logical steps involved in database development process. The most significant aspect of database management is the database design. The chapter gives the logical and physical aspects of database design with the details of file organization and indexing. Archiving part of DBMS i.e. data warehousing and the essential concepts related to data security are explained in connection with web security. The implementation and administration aspects of DBMS development are added pointing out the advantages and limitations of DBMS software packages.

Chapter 4 : introduces the significance of implementing DBMS in managing data in organizations explaining the evolution and development (File Systems to DBMS, RDBMS) of DBMS Software. In this chapter the important features of popular DBMS/RDBMS Software in managing the data are mentioned for FILEMAKER, dBASE, FOXPRO, IBM DB2, MS ACCESS, Microsoft SQL Server, MySQL, PostgreSQL and ORACLE.

Chapter 5 : relates the database management programs for libraries in real sense with DBMS/RDBMS applications reflecting the significance of DBMS/RDBMS applications for libraries. Some of the DBMS applications or functions related to libraries with respect to the creation of databases, records, modification, deletion etc. are illustrated with four popular DBMS/RDBMS software – DBASE, MS ACCESS, MySQL and ORACLE.

Chapter 6 : reflects a variety of internal as well as external databases handled by the libraries. The chapter features the most important library database i.e. bibliographic databases (including multilingual) and the structural of bibliographic database and records drawing the contrast between DBMS features of general and bibliographic databases. The external databases such as electronic databases, aggregators integrated databases, optical disk databases, online databases and bibliographic search databases, online full text databases, statistical data and multimedia databases.

Chapter 7 : reveals information retrieval systems, their objectives, components, functional features explaining bibliographic item representation in the context of developing and implementing DBMS/RDBMS. The impact of DBMS approach on automation of IRS and its scope are discussed. The IRS concepts such as - retrieval, recall, relevance and precision are explaining its limitations and issues. The most important part in the online information retrieval systems are the technological advancements in integration of resources, federated technologies, semantic web, XML (extensible markup language), ontologies, web mining / data mining techniques.

Chapter 8 : unveils various approaches to online information, search strategies commencing from the formulation of query, search techniques, methods, search criteria and construction, and tools to search for information viz. online catalogues, bibliographic search databases, search engines and meta search engines, directories, document delivery services, citation databases, discovery services.

Chapter 9 : is the concluding chapter overviews the emerging trends in data management in libraries including cloud services impact, specialized databases like multimedia, digital and spatial databases and finally new forms of data – digital data, usage data and big data, etc.

Dr. V Vishwa Mohan
Professor, Head and Chairman,
BoS Coordinator, PGDDIM
Department of Library & Information Science
Osmania University HYDERABAD 500 007
Email- profvmohan@gmail.com
Cell: +91 9949 701 855

Foreword

At its basic form, a library is a collection of data. Whether it is numerical, factual, full-text, bibliographic data or metadata, a library contains various types of data in different forms and formats. Therefore, it goes without saying that database management is the most basic and primary operation in any library. Of course, during the pre-digital era, handling of data was not done directly in the libraries as the professionals in the field dealt with gross or macro form of the data in the form of printed materials. In the electronic and/or digital era, there is proliferation of data in digital form, so all types of data assume the digital form in digital libraries and information systems. Even the conventional libraries or the hybrid libraries when automated by using the Information Technology, they also deal with different types of data in digital form. In other words, data in digital form seems to be pervasive. As a result, at present, such data needs to be handled with the help of database management tools and techniques.

Library as a system consists of inter-dependent and interrelated sub-systems. The sub-systems of a library, designated as acquisition system, cataloging system, circulation system, serials control system, etc. are all inter-dependent and interrelated. All these systems, primarily share common data that is the bibliographic data of the holdings of the library. Of course, besides bibliographic data there will be some more data that are also shared by different systems, and these data are related to the users and other resources in the library. It is the bibliographic data that forms the primary and huge amount of data that becomes crucial for all systems in the library. Whatever may be the type of data, basically in any system all the subsystems share and require the primary or commonly required data. It is in view of this a relational database management system (RDBMS) proves to be more effective and economical. Therefore, RDBMS has occupied central stage in almost all systems that tend to be integrated systems.

The typical problem related to database management systems in the present Library and Information Systems is that they deal with almost all types of data thereby they deal with all types of databases, viz. numerical databases, factual (descriptive) databases, full-text databases, bibliographic databases, and knowledge bases. The typical nature of these databases is that most of them contain fields with variable field lengths. Therefore, designing and developing these databases needs specific formats and standards compared to the databases that belong to institutions such as banks, educational institutions, industries, etc. Knowledge of management of all these databases, that are unique to a library or information system, proves to be essential on the part of today's Library and Information professionals. A lucid and comprehensive book on this subject proves to be crucial at this juncture.

The book should essentially be lucid because, the professionals in this field may not be well versed with computing technologies in general and database management systems in particular. At the same time a professional from computer science or software engineering needs to be thoroughly familiar with the intricacies, conventions involved in library management in general and library housekeeping operations in particular. Therefore, such a work needs to be simple and clear for both library professionals and software developers in other words people who deal with database designing, development and management.

There have been a number of efforts to develop standards for bibliographic databases, such as MARC, UNIMARC, CCF, ISO 2709, RDF for standardizing the format of the bibliographic record structure, description, designation and tagging of data fields and elements and so on. Standardization is imperative to facilitate information exchange in the networked environment. The problem does not end here, in fact it begins. There will be a need for developing standards for information retrieval from these databases. Moreover, the information retrieval systems should be in a position to meet various approaches of the users. They should have provision for field search, Keyword searching, Search with Phrase(s), search with Boolean logic operators, Truncated searching, Free-text searching, etc. It is in view of this, standards such as z39.50 are developed for information retrieval.

A work on database management in libraries and information systems should incorporate chapters on all these aspects so as to be exhaustive and comprehensive. This work contains chapters on:

1. Data in Libraries: an Overview
2. Database Concepts
3. Database Management Systems (DBMS)
4. DBMS/RDBMS Software
5. Data Management for Libraries (DBMS/RDBMS Applications)
6. Library Databases
7. Information Retrieval and DBMS Approach
8. Approach to Online Information (Strategies and Tools)
9. Emerging Trends in Library Data Management

A work of this kind will not only be useful to the library and information professionals, but also useful to the students of library and information science.

— **Prof. (Dr.) V. Vishwa Mohan**

List of Tables

List of Figures

Abbreviations, Terms & Definitions

AACR : Anglo American Cataloguing Rules

ACID complaint : Atomicity, Consistency, Isolation, and Durability. It is a set of properties that guarantee that database transactions are processed reliably

ALA : American Library Association

ANSI : American National Standards Institute found in 1918. ANSI is a voluntary organization composed of over 1,300 members including all the large computer companies that creates standards for the computer industry.

ASCII : American Standard Code for Information Interexchange. ASCII is a standard that assigns letters, numbers, and other characters within the 256 slots available in the 8-bit code. The ASCII decimal (Dec) number is created from binary, which is the language of all computers.

Bibliographic Database Management Systems : is a database of bibliographic records, an organized digital collection of references to published literature, including journal and newspaper articles, conference proceedings, reports, government and legal publications, patents, books, etc. containing rich subject descriptions in the form of keywords or abstracts

BIOSIS : is bibliographic database service with abstracts and citation indexing. Now it is part of Thomson

Reuters Web of Knowledge suite. Content was originally integrated from the BIOSIS Company before the merger in 2004 into Web of Knowledge.

Boolean Operators : Simple words (AND, OR, NOT or AND NOT) applied as conjunctions in searching multiple concepts with varied relations. AND to combine the concepts, OR to expand the retrieval, AND NOT to exclude unwanted retrieval.

Browsing : exploring World Wide Web by following one interesting link to another, intentionally but without a planned search strategy. To look at many things in a list to select an interesting piece of information, if any available.

CAS (Chemical Abstracts Service) : CAS is rooted in the publication Chemical AbstractsTM (CA), a journal of the American Chemical Society first published in 1907. The purpose of CA was to help scientists benefit from the published work of their colleagues around the world by monitoring, abstracting and indexing the world's chemistry-related literature.

CASE (Computer-aided Software Engineering) Tools : CASE tools are set of software application programs, which are used to automate SDLC (System Development Life Cycle) activities of any organization - such as Analysis tools, Design tools, Project management tools, Database Management tools, Documentation tools etc. These tools accelerate the development of project until the reach of target and also helps to uncover flaws before moving to next stage of development.

CCC : Classified Catalogue Code devised by Dr. S.R. Ranganathan

Citation : In the context of Information science, it is mentioning of the reference to a book, paper, or author, broadly any scholarly work as a mark of acknowledgement especially when an author/s use them in their own work.

Client : it is a computer or piece of software or equipment that is connected to a server (= a large central computer) from which it gets information and sends the updates (additions, deletions and modifications) back to server.

Column : In the context of DBMS, it is the field or subfield of record in a database

Compound Key : A compound key consists of more than one field to uniquely identify a record. A compound key is distinguished from a composite key because each field, which makes up the primary key, is also a simple key in its own right.

Composite Key : A compound key consists of more than one field to uniquely identify a record. This differs from a compound key in that one or more of the attributes, which make up the key, are not simple keys in their own right.

Data : Data is a distinct piece of information. Data can exist in a variety of forms i.e. numbers or text on pieces of paper, as bits and bytes stored in electronic memory, or as facts stored in a person's mind.

Data Administrators : Persons responsible for the overall information resources of an organization

Data Definition Language (DDL) : provides the meanings to describe the data to the DBMS. This includes - data elements and their attributes; records and relationships between records. The use of the DDL results in a "Schema" which gives complete picture of the database and the rules by which it is to be accessed and updated.

Data Dictionary : a facility that enables programmers, system analysts and end-users to document an application as well as its supporting databases. It simplifies the paperwork involved in designing application system largely

Data Manipulation Language (DML) : provides the syntax to be used in any standard programming language to navigate the database and thus find the records required.

Database : an organized collection of logically related data to meet the information needs of organizational users.

DBMS Manager : The central program of the DBMS provides the ability to store, update and retrieve data. It also provides the ability to design the database and modify the same as and when desired.

DBMS : software to define, create, maintain and to provide controlled access to the data base and to the repository.

DELNET : (Developing Library Network) has been established with the prime objective of promoting resource sharing among the libraries through the development of a network of libraries. It aims to collect, store, and disseminate information besides offering computerised services to users, to coordinate efforts for suitable collection development and also to reduce unnecessary duplication wherever possible

Descriptor : a word or expression used to describe or identify to retrieve information e.g. author or title or subject keyword

DIALOG : Dialog is one of the earliest online global information service existing since 1966. It owned by ProQuest, who acquired it from Thomson Reuters in mid-2008.

DOI : Digital object identifier. It is a serial code used to uniquely to identify objects, especially the electronic documents such as journal articles. This system began in 2000

DOS : Disk operating system. The operating systems that are operated by using the command line devised by Microsoft.

End Users : are the people using the DBMS at operational level to add, delete and modify the data and the people who receive information

Entity : a unit of data i.e. a single person, place, or thing about which data can be stored.

ERIC : is an online library of education research and information, sponsored by the Institute of Education Sciences (IES) of the U.S. Department of Education.

ETL : is short form of three database functions - extract, transform, load, that are combined into one tool to pull data out of one database and place it into another database. ETL is used to migrate data from one database to another.

- Extract is the process of reading data from a database.
- Transform is the process of converting the extracted data from its previous form into the form it needs to be in so that it can be placed into another database.
- Load is the process of writing the data into the target database.

Exporting and Importing Data : The import and export of data is the automated or semi-automated input and output of data sets between different software applications. Formatting data in a way that it can be used by another application. The application that exports data will create a file in a format that another application understands, enabling the two programs to share the same data. The reverse process of exporting is importing. Importing refers to the ability of an application to read and use data produced by a different application.

Field : in the context of database management systems, a space allocated for a particular item of information. Fields are the smallest units of information one can access.

File : A collection of data or information that is saved with filename. The information will be stored in a computer must be in a file

Filters : A program that sets a certain type of data as input, transforms it in the specified manner while providing output.

Foreign key : is generally a primary key from one table that appears as a field in another where the first table has a relationship to the second. In other words, if we had a table A with a primary key X that is linked to a table B, where X was a field in B, then X would be a foreign key in B.

Freeware : copyrighted software given away for free

by the author. Although it is available for free, the author retains the copyright.

Firmware : software (programs or data) that has been written onto read-only memory (ROM). Firmware is a combination of software and hardware.

FTP : file transfer protocol is the protocol for exchanging files over the Internet.

GIST : Global Information Systems Technology. It is India's leading Subscription Agent and represents global STM publishers in India

GUI : Graphic user interface

Hashed Algorithm : A hash value (or simply hash) is a number generated from a string of text. An algorithm is a formula or set of steps for solving a particular problem. It turns messages or text into a fixed string of digits, usually for security or data management purposes. Hashed algorithm producing hash values for accessing data or for security. The key in public-key encryption is based on a hash value. This is a value that is computed from a base input number using a hashing algorithm.

Hashed File Organization : In this file organization, hash function is used to calculate the address of the block to store the records. The hash function can be any simple or complex mathematical function. The hash function is applied on some columns/attributes – either key or non-key columns to get the block address. Hence each record is stored randomly irrespective of the order they come. Hence this method is also known as direct or Random file organization. If the hash function is generated on key column, then that column is called hash key, and if hash function is generated on non-key column, then the column is hash column.

Hashed Index : Hashed indexes maintain entries with hashes of the values of the indexed field. The hashing function collapses embedded documents and computes the hash for the entire value but does not support multi-key (i.e. arrays) indexes.

Host Language Interface : enables programs written in the Standard Computer Program Languages to access and manipulate data in the database. Instructions are coded into the program as a part of the DML and translated by the host language interface into chunks of code. Thus a link is established between the application program and the DBMS.

HTML : stands for Hyper Text Markup Language. HTML is a markup language for describing web documents (web pages). A markup language is a set of markup tags. HTML documents are described by HTML tags. Each HTML tag describes different document content.

Hyperlinks : A hyperlink is a word, phrase, or image that can be clicked on to jump to a new document or a new section within the current document. Hyperlinks are found in nearly all Web pages, allowing users to click their way from page to page. In computing, a hyperlink is a reference to data that the reader can directly follow either by clicking, tapping or hovering.

Hypertext : Hypertext is text with hyperlinks to other texts. The term was coined by Ted Nelson around 1965.

Hypermedia : Hypermedia, an extension of the term hypertext, is a nonlinear medium of information which includes graphics, audio, video, plain text and hyperlinks. This contrasts with the broader term multimedia, which may include non-interactive linear presentations as well as hypermedia.

Indicator : Measurable variable used as a representation of an associated (but non-measured or non-measurable) factor or quantity

IR : Information retrieval. It is the activity of obtaining information resources relevant to an information need from a collection of information resources.

IRS : Information retrieval system. It is a device which aids access to documents specified by subject, and the operations associated with it. A retrieval system stores units of information, which is interlinked. The user retrieves specific unit/s of information applying the appropriate terms and methods.

ISBN : International Standard Book Number

ISI : it has several expansions. In this context, it is Institute of Scientific Information, Philadelphia, USA. Now this institution is called as Thomas Routers.

ISO 2709 : is an ISO (International Standards Organization) standard for bibliographic descriptions, titled Information and documentation—format for information exchange.

ISSN : International Standard Serial Number

JAVA : Java is a set of computer software and specifications developed by Sun Microsystems, which was later acquired by the Oracle Corporation that provides a system for developing application software and deploying it in a cross-platform computing environment. Java is used in a wide variety of computing platforms from embedded devices and mobile phones to enterprise servers and supercomputers. Java applets run in secure, sandboxed environments to provide many features of native applications and can be embedded in HTML pages.

KWIC : Keyword in-context. The term KWIC was first coined by Hans Peter Luhn. A KWIC index is formed by sorting and aligning the words within an article title to allow each word in titles to be searchable alphabetically in the index.

KWOC : key-word out-of-context

LAN : Local area networks

Library 2.0 : second generation libraries. The libraries termed in the same context as web 2.0

Licensed users : subscribed or registered (at price or free of cost) users

MARC : Machine readable catalogue

MATHSCINET : is a bibliographic search database published by American Mathematical Society.

MEDLARS : Medical Literature Analysis and Retrieval System Online is a bibliographic database of articles from academic journals covering life sciences and biomedical sciences, medicine, nursing, pharmacy, dentistry, veterinary medicine, and health care

MIS : Management information system refers to a computer-based system that provides managers with the tools to organize, evaluate and efficiently manage departments within an organization.

Module : In software, a module is a part of a program. A single module can contain one or several routine processes. These modules are one or more independently developed, but integrated by means of a program. In hardware, a module is a self-contained component.

MS DOS : Microsoft Disc Operating System

Navigation : A type of text-based web site containing links of different categories and sub-categories. Navigation allows moving from the major categories of information to sub-categories.

NEXIS : LexisNexis Group is a corporation providing computer-assisted legal research as well as business research and risk management services. During 1970s, LexisNexis pioneered the electronic accessibility of legal and journalistic documents. The company has the world's largest electronic database for legal and public-records related information by the year 2006.

Normalization : In the context of DBMS/RDBMS, normalization is the process of organizing the columns (attributes) and tables (relations) of a relational database to minimize data redundancy. Normalization involves decomposing a table into less redundant (and smaller) tables without losing information, and then linking the data back together by defining foreign keys in the old table referencing the primary keys of the new ones. The objective is to isolate data so that additions, deletions, and modifications of an attribute can be made in just one table and then propagated through the rest of the database using the defined foreign keys.

OAI-PMH : The Open Archives Initiative Protocol for Metadata Harvesting (OAI-PMH) is a low-barrier mechanism for repository interoperability. Data Providers are repositories that expose structured metadata via OAI-PMH. Service Providers then make OAI-PMH service requests to harvest that metadata.

OCLC : The Online Computer Library Center (OCLC) is "a non-profit, membership, computer library service and research organization dedicated to the public purposes of furthering access to the world's information and reducing information costs" .It was found in 1967 as the Ohio College Library Center. OCLC and its member libraries cooperatively produce and maintain WorldCat, the largest online public access catalog (OPAC) in the world.

OLAP (On-line Analytical Processing) : is characterized by relatively low volume of transactions. Queries are often very complex and involve aggregations. In OLAP database there is aggregated, historical data, stored in multi-dimensional schemas (usually star schema). OLAP applications are widely used by Data Mining techniques.

OLTP (On-line Transaction Processing) : is characterized by a large number of short on-line transactions (INSERT, UPDATE, and DELETE). The main emphasis for OLTP systems is put on very fast query processing, maintaining data integrity in multi-access environments and an effectiveness measured by number of transactions per second. In OLTP database there is detailed and current data, and schema used to store transactional databases is the entity model.

OPAC : Online public access catalogue also called as OPAC

OPAC 2.0 : Online public access catalogue also called as OPAC in the context of web 2.0

Open Access : Open access (OA) refers to online research output available free to access without restrictions.

Open Office : is the leading open-source office software suite for word processing, spreadsheets, presentations, graphics and databases

Open Source : Open-source software (OSS) is computer software with its source code made available with a license in which the copyright holder provides the rights to study, change, and distribute the software to anyone and for any purpose. Open-source software may be developed in a collaborative public manner.

ORDBMS : An object-relational database (ORD), or object-relational database management system (ORDBMS), is a database management system (DBMS) similar to a relational database, but objects, classes and inheritance are directly supported in database schemas and in the query language.

OS : Operating System. It is a set of integrated programs that help to run the computer system to execute its operations.

Output File : a computer file that contains data generated as a result of computing operations or a program. Output files are in various formats depending on the system.

Phrase : A phrase is a group or words that express a concept and used as a unit within a sentence.

POPSI : Postulate based permuted subject indexing is a pre-coordinate indexing system development by G. Bhattacharyya. It uses the analytico synthetic method.

POSTGRESQL : An open source object-relational database system.

PRECIS : Preserved Context Index System. PRECIS, designed by Derek Austin (1984), is a development of chain indexing which was used for the subject analysis of material in the British National Bibliography and British Catalogue of Music from 1984.

Primary Key : A primary key is a main reference key for the table and used throughout the database to establish relationships with other tables. The primary key must contain unique values, must never be null and uniquely identifying each record in the table.

Query : A query is a request for information from a database.

Query Language : helps to communicate with DBMS (like the English language) to access data that will be displayed on the terminal easily and quickly. This is especially helpful for those with a minimum computer knowledge. The query syntax is generally simple. Example: "DISPLAY EMPLOYEE - NAME, EMPLOYEE-ADDRESS. IF SALARY >10000.

RAM : Random Access Memory

Random Access : In the context of DBMS, the random access (direct access) is the ability to access an item of data at any given coordinate in a population of addressable elements

Raw Data : Unprocessed data

RDA : Resource Description and Access, is the new cataloguing standard that will replace AACR2. It was published in 2010 and the Library of Congress has announced full implementation of RDA since the year 2013.

RDBMS : Relational Database Management Systems

RDF : Resource Description Framework (RDF). RDF is a standard model for data interchange on the Web. RDF has features that facilitate data merging even if the underlying schemas differ, and it specifically supports the evolution of schemas over time without requiring all the data consumers to be changed.

Record : in the context of DBMS is a basic data structure consisting of more than one or a collection of fields, may be of different data types, typically in fixed number and sequence.

Report Writer : closely associated to the query

language. The query language enable display to the terminal, the 'report writer' produces the output or hard copy (paper) reports. Report Writer saves time and money for both the user and the programming staff

Repository : the centralized knowledge base for all data definitions, data relationships, on- screen /report formats.

Row : in the context of DBMS, it is a record comprising of several fields.

RPM : RPM Package Manager (RPM) is a powerful and mature command-line driven package management system capable of installing, uninstalling, verifying, querying, and updating UNIX software packages.

RSC : Royal Society of Chemistry. RSC publishes full text databases of journals, bibliographic databases

Schema : A database schema is the skeleton structure that represents the logical view of the entire database. It defines how the data is organized and how the relations are associated.

SCOPUS : a citations cum bibliographic search database published by Elsevier

SDI : refers to tools and resources used to keep a user informed of new resources on specified topics. SDI services pre-date the World Wide Web, but appearing now in recent forms as topic alerts from publishers/aggregators databases and gateways.

SDLC : SDLC stands for Software Development Life Cycle. SDLC is the process consisting of a series of planned activities to develop or alter the software products. In the context of DBMS the process applies in database development.

Search Engine : A web search engine is a software system that is designed to search for information on the World Wide Web.

Secondary Key : A table may have one or more choices for the primary key. One is selected as the primary key and the remaining choices are known as secondary keys or alternative keys.

Secondary Storage : A secondary storage device refers to any volatile storage device that is internal or external to the computer i.e. beyond the primary storage that enables permanent data storage. A secondary storage device is also known as an auxiliary storage device or external storage.

Server : In information technology, a server is a computer program that provides services to other computer programs (and their users) in the same or other computers. In computing, a server is a computer program or a device that provides functionality for other programs or devices, called "clients".

SQL : SQL is a standard language for accessing databases. SQL is a database computer language designed for the retrieval and management of data in relational database. SQL stands for Structured Query Language.

Subfield : Sub-fields are the sub-units of information containing in field.

System Developers : professionals to direct the system analysts and programmers to design application programs etc.

Table : it is a framework of database in DBMS/ RDBMS, consists of columns, and rows for storing the data.

Temporality : Different multimedia data types have different requirements. For example, some multimedia data types such as video, audio, and animation sequences have temporal requirements that have implications on their storage, manipulation and presentation, but images, video and graphics data have spatial constraints in terms of their content.

Timesharing : is a technique which enables many people, located at various terminals, to use a particular computer system at the same time. Time-sharing or multitasking is a logical extension of multiprogramming, wherein the processor's time is shared among multiple users simultaneously.

Tuple : A single row of a table, which contains a single record for that relation is called a tuple

UKMARC : MARC format adopted by the British Library, UK initially when MARC was designed in USA. Now it is not in use as the MARC21 superseded.

UNIMARC : Universal Bibliographic format was first created and proposed by IFLA in 1977 to harmonize the geographical variations arouse in initial MARC formats such as US MARC, UK MARC, Canadian MARC etc.

UNIX : UNIX is a computer Operating System which is capable of handling activities from multiple users at the same time. This is a secured operating system used in server.

URL : Uniform Resource Identifier (URI) is the web addresses that refer to objects on the World Wide Web.

Usage log : The log created in data servers at every access of data or application either by clients (staff) or by users.

User interface : to facilitate client interaction as well as user interaction

VFP : Visual FoxPro is a data-centric, object-oriented, procedural, programming language produced by Microsoft. It is derived from FoxPro (originally known as FoxBASE) which was developed by Fox Software beginning in 1984.

VMS : VMS (Virtual Memory System) is an operating system from the Digital Equipment Corporation (DEC) that runs in its older mid-range computers.

CP/M : CP/M-86 was a version of the CP/M operating system that Digital Research (DR) made for the Intel 8086 and Intel 8088. The system commands are the same as CP/M-80.

W3C : The World Wide Web Consortium (W3C) is an international community where member organizations, a full-time staff, and the public work together to develop Web standards. This consortium is led by web inventor Tim Berners-Lee and CEO Jeffrey Jaffe,

Web 2.0 : is the second stage of development of the Internet, characterized especially by the change from static web pages to dynamic or user-generated content and the growth of social media.

Web of Knowledge : Web of Science (previously known as Web of Knowledge) is an online subscription-based scientific citation indexing service maintained by Thomson Reuters that provides a comprehensive citation search.

WWW : The World Wide Web is an information space where documents and other web resources are identified by URLs, interlinked by hypertext links and can be accessed via the Internet through browsers. The World Wide Web was invented by English scientist Tim Berners-Lee in 1989.

(***Source:*** Internet, Books and Articles)

1

Data in Libraries: An Overview

1.1. LIBRARY DATA

Libraries maintain information resources in different forms - books, periodicals, newspapers, magazines maps, music scores and computer files etc. in various forms i.e., textual, numeric, images, electronic and multi-media. Knowledge embodied in such forms is shared among individuals, groups or institutions. Libraries as storehouses of information resources play a significant role in disseminating information, acquiring such resources through purchases, subscription or through consortia and also by way of digitization activities as illustrated in figure 1.1.

Library manages the data so acquired, by providing bibliographic information about their collection. Library enables access to such information embodied in documents in any form to reach the users either through its catalogue or through ILL from external sources.

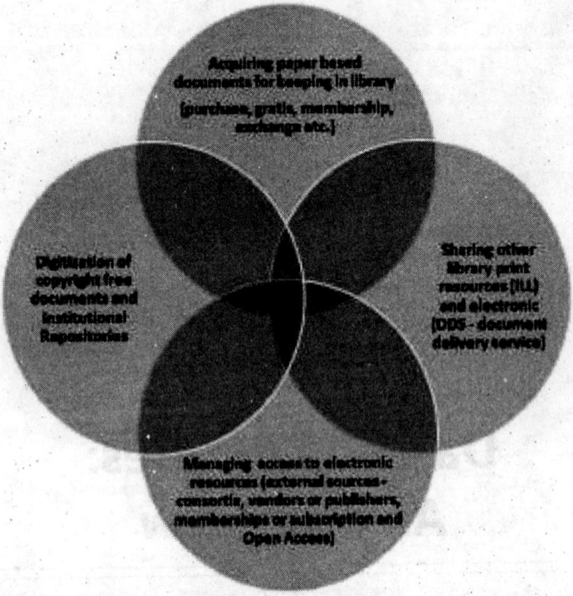

Fig. 1.1. Library Acquisition of Information/Data/Documents

The data management in automated environment is effective and less complex than in print environment with integrated library application software. The objective of an integrated library system (ILS) is to build and manage the library database by creating, storing and updating records of all types of documents, patrons and processes by way of integrated library operations. The database management systems especially the RDBMS are mainly designed and built around library application software became suitable for libraries, permitting two-way interactions of user/staff interface with library database.

1.2. INTEGRATED LIBRARY SYSTEM (ILS)

An integrated library system (ILS), is also known as library management system (LMS). It is meant for planning and organizing resources for a library. In an automated environment, some LIS software work directly on the operating system of the computer or server, but most of the recent integrated library systems, operate on RDBMS software installed in servers over the OS. The RDBMS is designed for managing two types of interaction between the library database and graphical user interfaces (one for patrons, one for library staff). The library application software functions at the outer layer of the library information systems. The Information about information or documents will be created, stored in library data server and made available to clients (library staff working at different modules and levels) for updating the database and users for retrieving the information through OPAC (online public access catalogue).

The pre-requisites of maintaining integrated library systems are – the data server (preloaded Operating System, DBMS/RDBMS software and Application software (LIS software package that supports the data entry in a standard MARC format/ISO2709 exchangeable formats), network (LAN) to connect the staff clients for contributing data from different modules in the system.

The architecture of NewGenLib ILS software comprising several applications to run integrated programs in three layers (*http://www.verussolutions.biz/technology.php*) and the details of components are given in the following table.

Table : Three layers of ILS-components

Presentation Layer: SWING based GUI client - Java Runtime Environment 1.4.2 (Free ware). Java Web Start based Applet JDOM for XML messaging (open source) Java Help 2.0 for help (free ware) Jasper Reports (open source) Hibernate (open source) Java Mail (Free Ware) Jakarta POI (open source) Open Office 2.0 – form letters (open source).
Application Server Layer: Servlets and JSPs - Tomcat web server (open source) Struts frame work Enterprise Java Beans - Jboss Application Server 3.2.1 (open source) JDOM (open source) XCQL – CQL parser(open source)
Database Layer: EJB - Entity beans (Container Managed Persistence); the SQL used: Porting from one database to another is much easier Postgresql (open source) database server is the default database server used

The three layered architecture is shown in figure 1.2.

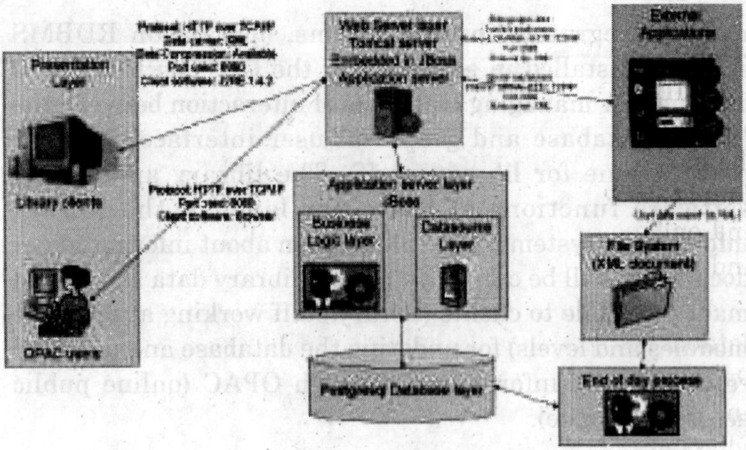

Fig. 1.2. Integrated Library Database System
(*Source : http://www.verussolutions.biz/technology.php*, accessed on 12.3.2016)

1.3. INTEGRATED LIBRARY DATABASE - DESIGN AND ORGANIZATION

Apart from individual libraries, several other agencies also involve in creating bibliographic records, viz. national libraries, publishers, abstracting and indexing services, library networks, etc. The agencies distributing the records / information through traditional information channels (sources or tools) have been using computers for generating the bibliographic records and also developing databases to maintain the data to share within and across the systems. The publishers and agencies supplying information in print environment have moved to electronic environment with the use of computers. Thus, the sharable data needs to be in a standard format and transmitted through standard protocols to achieve uniformity, consistency and universal bibliographic control.

- Selection of headings
- Rendering of elements in heading as well as different fields (tags) in the format

- Representation of subject content (vocabulary control)

1.3.1. Data Files

ILS takes care of all library operations by maintaining books database, vendor database, patron database and all the modules by providing seamless integration of data and data is shared across the modules reducing data redundancy and enhancing data security. This feature of data security and indexing features are mainly because of RDBMS.

The data in an ILS environment is stored in a series of databases called files. In RDBMS the files are called tables. Data in relational DBMS is arrayed in a series of columns and rows. The description of bibliographic data in a database will be hierarchically organized as –

- Databases
  - — Files
    - Records
      - — Fields or data elements
        - Sub-fields
          - — Characters

The data files, records can be accessed via LIS application software through their indexes. The huge data will be indexed for easy access of the staff and users of OPAC. Indexing is the key feature of most of LIS application software. The extent of indexing up to field level or sub field level is an important choice depending on users search requirements, LIS software features and the data sharing capabilities of RDBMS. OPAC is more user centric because of the indexing features which are again due to the RDBMS being built around the ILS software to enhance retrieval functions.

1.3.2. Data Formats

The bibliographic data needs to be input in a standard format to be able to access across the modules of ILS and among the systems. The bibliographic standard format is a chosen pattern or a space to organize or arrange text, words, characters etc. The information can be presented in different formats. They are primarily used for inputting the data, its display and exchange.

- **Internal formats** – for creating, updating, storing and processing data
- **Display formats** – for user's information
- **Exchange formats** – for exchange of records between systems. These exchange formats define physical structure; document/ designators or Tags (codes to designate different data elements (author, title, etc.); and content of record governed by specified rules

1.3.3. Record Structures (Standard Bibliographic Formats)

The data files are in the form of tables, wherein the data of each record will be in a row consisting of two or more fields (columns). The latest MARC format is widely followed by majority of library application software. It is compatible and supports a different variety of bibliographic material. Moreover, it permits the import of MARC records into the internal structure of the database and also export the local records into the MARC exchange format. MARC Records provide framework for bibliographic data, authority data and holdings data.

The MARC record structure for exchange format contains –

Leader	Record directory	Control fields	Variable fields

Leader : contains information about the record. It is a fixed length record. It has 24 characters (0-23) length in MARC format .

Record Directory : index to the data in the record, contains series of entries with variable length fields in a record starting with character 24. Each directory entry has 12 characters. They are in three parts – 'Tag' (3 characters code that defines nature of field), data field with field length of 4 characters. The actual data begins after 3+4 characters and given in 5 characters.

Control fields : contain attributes and data of bibliographic item. The control fields have fixed coded data stored in them. They are numbered as 001 to 008. They signify the following data relating to bibliographic description. (Missing numbers are unassigned)

001 Control number

003 Control number identifier

005 Date and time of latest transaction

006 Additional material characteristics – fixed length data elements

007 Physical description fixed field (repeatable field) – general information

008 Fixed length data elements - general information

Variable fields : contain attributes, data of bibliographic item, and store variable length data. In MARC, unlimited data can be entered in these variable fields and sub-fields. Alpha-numeric data can be recorded. Under each field or tag the first two characters are digits (0 and 1), while the sub field codes are – a, b, c, d . . with separators (delimiters) such as $ or \.

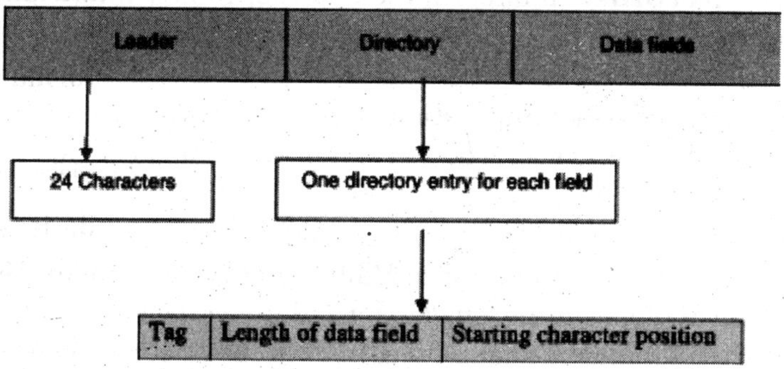

Fig. 1.3. Data structure (ISO- 2709)

The functional setup of data files, records, fields and sub-fields and integral operations in the integrated library database is described in the following section – Modules and Processes.

1.4. INTEGRATED LIBRARY DATABASE - MODULES & PROCESSES

The main files, records processes involved in operating each module in developing library database are detailed below.

1.4.1. Database Management (Administration)

Database management or administration module is distinct from other modules. When the other modules are confined to their individual operations, the administration module monitors the entire integrated library operations. The module manages the default settings for different records, processes, customization of formats, reports, interfaces for users as well as for the staff working at various operations and the generation of the output

1.4.2. Acquisition Sub-System

Files : Library bibliographic records file, currencies & exchange rates file, authority files, in-process file, order history file, invoice data file, financial data file and vendor data file.

Records : bibliographic records, items, languages, locations, vendors, holding records, accounts, budgets, and patrons.

Processes : Suggestions, approvals, orders, receipts, accessioning, invoices, vouchers, claims, order cancellations, accounting, gifts process, reporting

Order record is the prime table for acquisition sub-system. This is connected to Bibliographic file, vendor file, approval file, user file, suggestions file, currency file, budget head and budgets source files, invoice files with respective file_IDs as shown in figure 1.4. In the figure order file consists of data elements - order_id, vendor_id, currency_id, budget head_id, bib_id. This record is connected to bibliographic record with bib_id, which is system generated ID.

1.4.3. Cataloging Sub-System

Files : Library bibliographic records file, authority

files, external records file, holding records, retrospective conversion files, languages and locations.

Records : Bibliographic records, items, languages and locations, authority files (Name, Series, title and subject), holding files.

Processes : Cataloguing, search & retrieval, verification and validation of data, accessing external databases to import bibliographic data and exporting records or data for resource sharing.

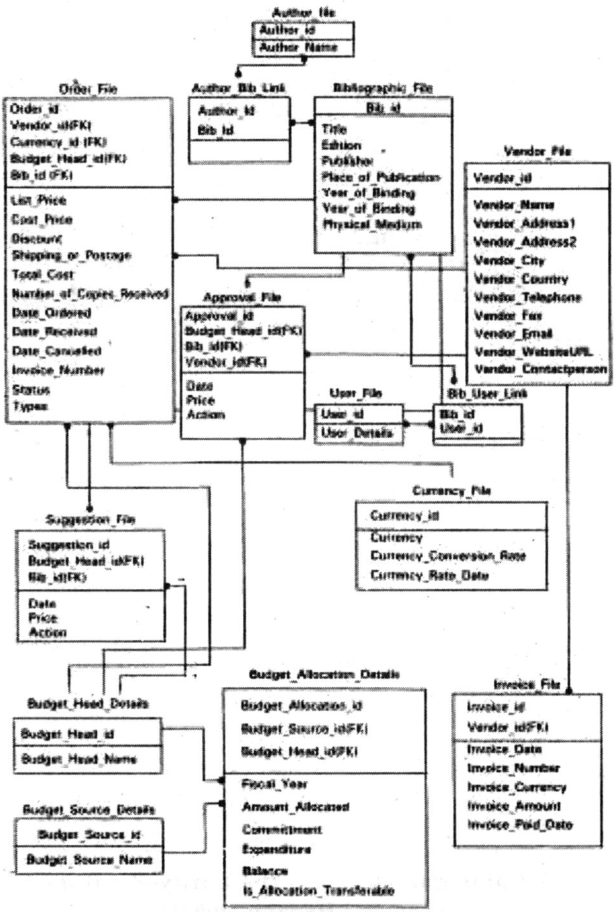

Fig. 1.4. Acquisition Sub-System, the Entity–Relationship (*Source* : Haravu, 2004)

The relationships among entities in acquisition sub-systems connecting fields is illustrated vide figure 1.5 bibliographic file is connected to fixed fields table, keyword table, field table and holdings table by means of respective IDs. For example Bibliographic file consists of data elements - Bib_id, library_id, date_created and date_modified. Similarly the Keyword table comprising of keyword_id and keyword. So the keyword is connected to Bibliographic record by means of 'Keyword_ID'.

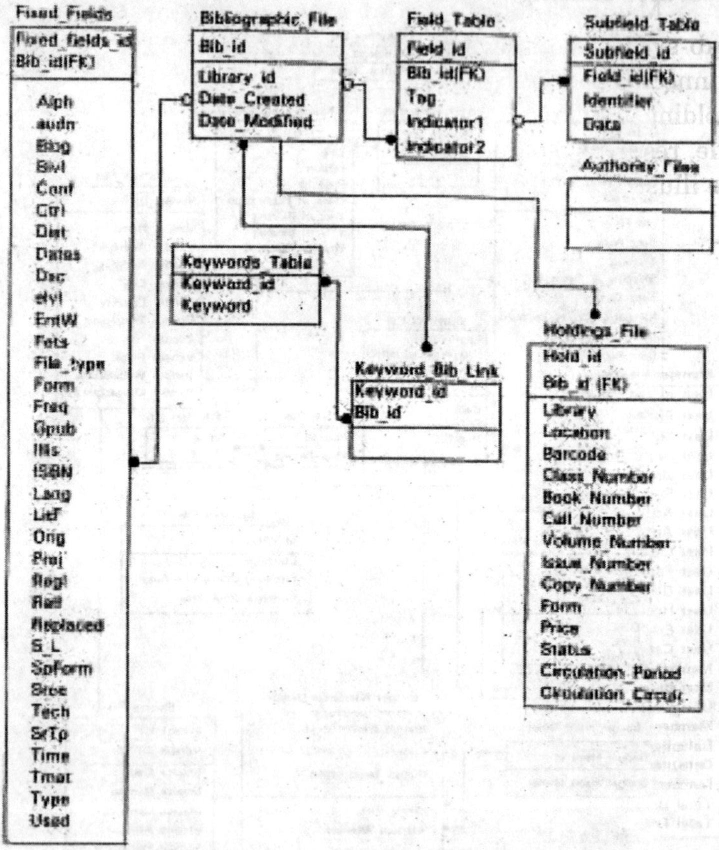

Fig. 1.5. Catalogue Systems - the Entity–Relationship (*Source* : Haravu, 2004)

1.4.4. Circulation Sub-System

Files : patrons with privileges matrix, bibliographic records, items, holdings, transaction log file, transactions file, reservations, fines-audit, holdings.

Records : Bibliographic Records, items, locations and patron records, membership privileges matrix.

Processes : Registration of patrons, check-in, check-out, renewals, holds/reservations, recalls, ILL, overdue notices, fines, tracking transactions, reporting

Member (patron) record is main record in circulation sub-system comprising of several data elements. It is connected to bibliographic file/holding file with bib_id and holding_ids. Further, member file is connected to transaction file, reservations file, reservations queue through their IDs as illustrated in figure 1.6.

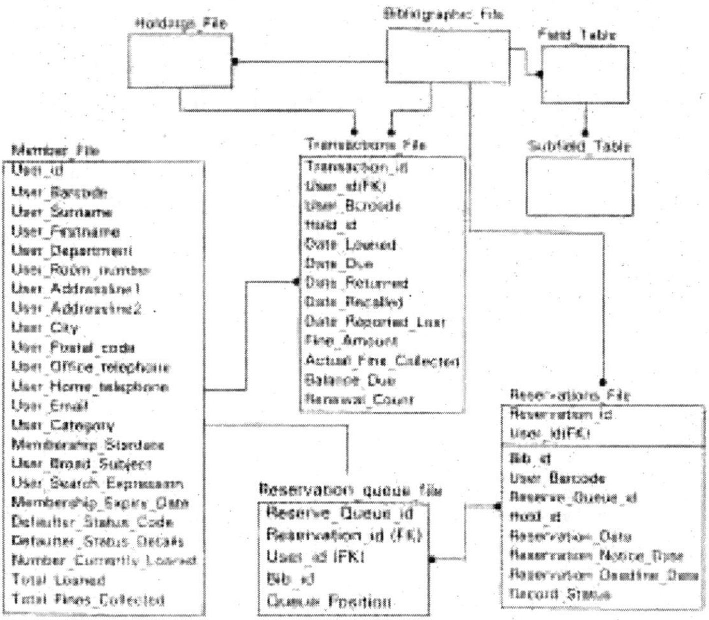

Fig. 1.6. Circulation System, the Entity–Relationship
(*Source* : Haravu, 2004)

1.4.5. Serial Control Sub-System

Files : Serials database, Check-in, non-receipts file, claims, holdings, bindery, locations, acquisition files: currencies and exchange rates file, authority files, in-process file, order history file, invoice data file, financial data file and vendor data file

Records : Bibliographic records, items, languages, locations, vendors, currencies, orders, invoices, vouchers, accounts and patrons

Processes : accessing internal and external database for sharing data, serials data entry, check-in to make holdings, claims for non-receipts, bindery file, and acquisition processes - suggestions, approvals, orders, receipts, accessioning, invoices, vouchers, claims, order cancellations, accounting, gifts process, reporting, etc.

The serial record or serial bibliographic record is the prime record in serial control sub-system, which is mostly joined with holdings record. Though the serial record also a bibliographic record, it is different due to its exclusive features such as – frequency, former title, history, enumeration as well as chronology features, captions and pattern fields, textual holdings location and access fields as depicted in figure 1.7 and 1.8.

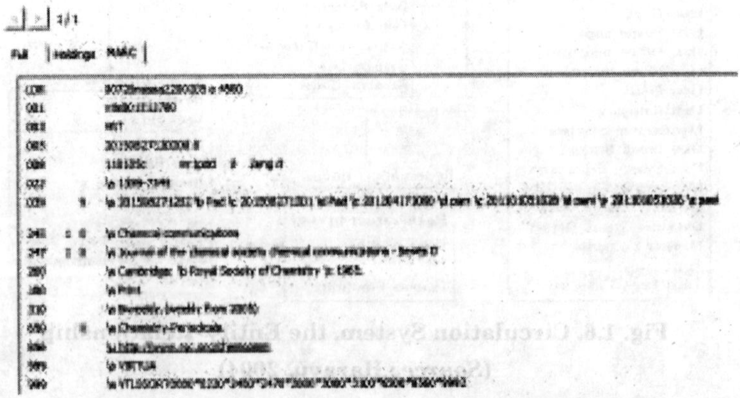

Fig. 1.7. Serial Bibliographic Record (Screenshot)

The serial bibliographic record and holding records are linked by means of 001 tag The acquisition and circulation features and integration of fields in serial control are almost similar to books and other material.

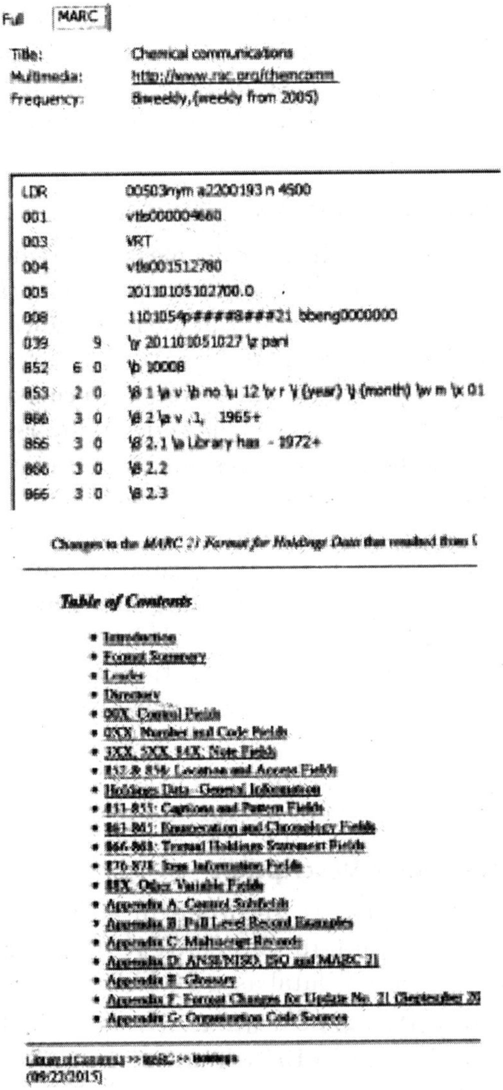

Full MARC

Title: Chemical communications
Multimedia: http://www.rsc.org/chemcomm
Frequency: Biweekly,(weekly from 2005)

LDR			00503nym a2200193 n 4500
001			vtls000004660
003			VRT
004			vtls001512780
005			20110105102700.0
008			1101054p####8###21 bbeng0000000
039		9	\y 201101051027 \z pani
852	6	0	\b 10008
853	2	0	\8 1 \a v \b no \u 12 \v r \i (year) \j (month) \w m \x 01
866	3	0	\8 2 \a v .1, 1965+
866	3	0	\8 2.1 \a Library has - 1972+
866	3	0	\8 2.2
866	3	0	\8 2.3

Table of Contents

- Introduction
- Format Summary
- Leader
- Directory
- 00X Control Fields
- 0XX Number and Code Fields
- 3XX, 5XX, 84X: Note Fields
- 852 & 856: Location and Access Fields
- Holdings Data - General Information
- 853-855: Captions and Pattern Fields
- 863-865: Enumeration and Chronology Fields
- 866-868: Textual Holdings Statement Fields
- 876-878: Item Information Fields
- 88X: Other Variable Fields
- Appendix A: Control Subfields
- Appendix B: Full Level Record Examples
- Appendix C: Multipart Records
- Appendix D: ANSI/NISO, ISO and MARC 21
- Appendix E: Glossary
- Appendix F: Format Changes for Update No. 21 (September 20
- Appendix G: Organization Code Sources

(09/23/2015)

Fig. 1.8. Serial Holding Records (Screenshot)

1.4.6. Information Retrieval (Output)

- Online Public Access Catalog (OPAC) System
- Defaults and Customized Reports

Since libraries need to focus on the retrieval of information, share and exchange of the bibliographic data, it should adopt international standards for structuring the bibliographic records to key-in the data. The formats might vary according to the type of information material and evolving with the increasing requirements as well as complexities.

1.5. STANDARDS IN DATABASE DESIGN

To standardization generally means to create or modify all entries to confirm to a single pattern or format (Kochtanek and Matthews, 2004). Standards create uniformity in the design of products as well as services that results in increase of efficiency in an information system in terms of time and cost. In libraries, creation of bibliographic records in a standard format fetch easy accessing the data by users with the same skill irrespective of the location, type of the library. The standardization facilitates the common language, stability, cooperation, automatic regulation and minimizing the cost of any project, by avoiding duplication of work, resources and time. The rationale behind standardization for library records is inter-institutional cooperation and resource sharing. The standards relevant to libraries, data management and data retrieval were categorized as – bibliographic (including metadata) standards, communications, search/retrieval and markup standards.

1.5.1. Bibliographic Description

Several efforts are recorded in standardization of bibliographic format in the context of designing and developing the library databases for library users.

- Anthony Panizzi formulated a set of 91 rules to catalogue books in British museum

- CC Jewette developed 39 rules, to maintain uniformity and consistency in the catalogue in 1850.
- CA Cutter in 1876 developed rules for dictionary catalogue including choice of headings
- Anglo American Cataloguing Rules (AACR) was formulated in collaboration with American Library Association, Library Association in the year 1968
- International Conference on Cataloguing Principles (1961) in Paris – recommended for standardization of headings and a study on impact of the use of computing equipment on cataloguing rules.
- IFLA (1971) program for the development of International standard bibliographic description (ISBD). It provided framework for the construction of national and multinational cataloguing codes. ISBD provided a generalized structure for the description of bibliographic items. Eight areas of bibliographic elements requiring description were identified. ISBD specified order and punctuation (separators) for bibliographic elements. Different types of material were included. AACR II was developed based on the specifications of ISBD.
- The significant example of standardization for libraries is MARC record, which was initially called as Bibliographic interchange format designated as NISO Z39.2 - 1994. Internationally this format is known as ISO 2709. The NISO Z39.85-2001 standard addresses the Dublin Core Element Set and defines 15 metadata elements for resource discovery. These fifteen fields of the record according to Dublin Core are –

  1. Title
  2. Author or creator
  3. Subject and key words
  4. Description
  5. Publisher

6. Other contributor
7. Date
8. Resource type
9. Format
10. Resource identifier
11. Source
12. Language
13. Relation
14. Coverage
15. Rights management

- The Library of Congress has put significant effort into the development of MARC (Machine Readable Cataloguing) standard in 1960s and by 70s most of the automation uncertainties began clearing. The impact of IT explosion during 80s was remarkable in stabilizing MARC that lead many libraries to proceed for ILS (Integrated library systems). Personal computers and CD-ROM technologies during 80-90s entered the academic library scenario and began laying emphasis on the user needs.
- Due to greater impact of the technological advancements on libraries, type of the information or data that the library database management needs to handle, the criteria for designing standards also took different orientation towards compatibility and interoperability between equipment or hardware, data type, standards, formats practices, and information retrieval methods etc.
- Resource Description Format (RDF) is the initiative of W3C (World Wide Web consortium to support the applicability and exchange of metadata on the web. It is a standard for designating metadata to perform quality searches on the web. RDF is coded in XML, which forms standardized metadata structure. RDF data model consists of - resources, properties

(characteristics, relations or attributes those describe resources). RDF allows to use certain defined schemas that supports interoperability among different computing systems, formats, structures.

1.5.2. Search and Retrieval – Standards (Z39.58) and (Z39.50)

The significant standards for search and retrieval aspects of the library databases are –

1. Common command language (Z39.58)
2. Information retrieval service definition and protocol specifications for library applications (Z39.50), which is a two way communication/conversation between user (client) and server (database).

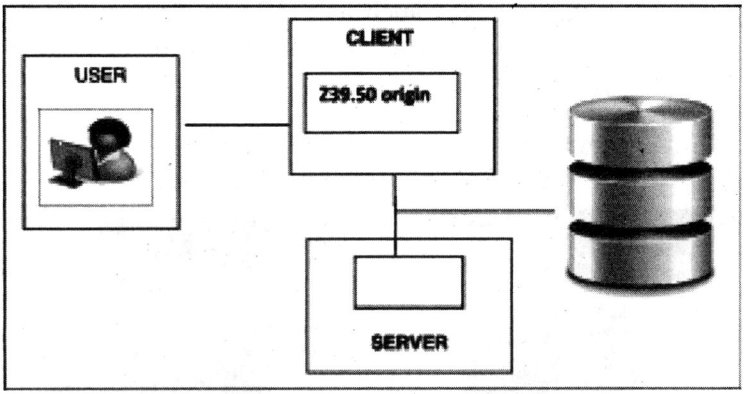

Fig. 1.9. Diagrammatic representation of Z39.50 protocol

Prior to client server computing systems, the data search and retrieval was through command languages. The most popular Dbase, was searchable with commands such as FIND, SEEK, LOCATE etc., but each system will have different capabilities built within the system. So the common command language identifies common set of functions. This Z39.58 facilitated the development of graphical interface and giving users the information about the system specific commands, but vendors were not keen in these practices. Further developments in standardizing search and retrieval aspects of the library databases Z39.50 protocol facilitated the interoperability among the information systems. The following functionalities mentioned by Kochtanek and Matthews (2004) made this protocol very significant in searching and retrieval of library databases.

- Restricting access to authenticated users
- Browsing indexes and thesauri
- Retrieving selected content
- Negotiating the retrieval of large search results (refinement of queries and limiting)
- Removing duplicates from the retrieval set
- Sorting the search results before presentation extending services such as placing orders, updating files, saving search result sets and exporting data in MARC format

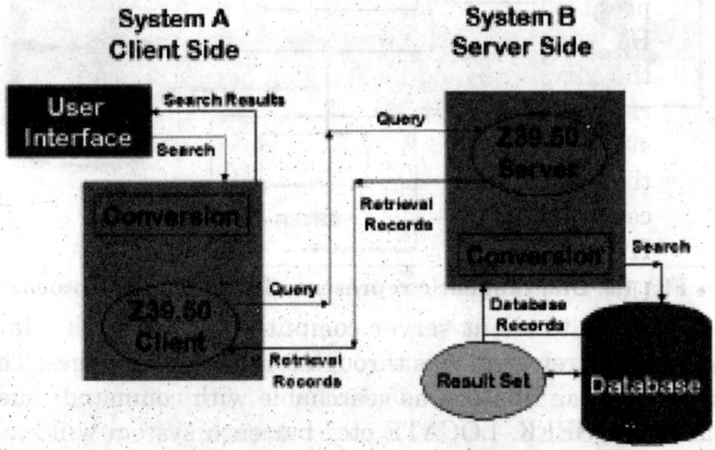

Fig. 1.10. Z39.50 Model of Information Retrieval
(Source: *www.unt.edu/wmoen/Z3950/papers/MoenZ3950.htm*)

Most of ILS software systems have developed Z39.50 compliant client interface to access database and also developed server so that the library can also provide access to its collection.

- SGML (Standard Generalized Markup Language) is a

digital coding system that preserves the logical structure of the text as it is transferred through different OS. SGML documents consists of three layers-structure, content and style, in which structure refers to framework, content description and style refers to the way the document appears on screen. For the web SGML has manifested as HTML.

- HTML (Hyper Text Markup Language) is not the standard, but it is a format developed basing on SGML. The HTML documents began appearing after Tim Berners-Lee created the http (Hyper text protocol). W3C HTML working group is bringing out the developments in HTML versions
- XML (eXtensible Markup Language) standard began from 1998, designed to use of SGML on WWW. It offers extensibility and supports the creativity of the programmers by applying their own stuff, whereas HTML is restricted in such free applications and also the complicated and larger database schemas. HTML rather does not support the applications to verify the structural validity. XML supports Unicode (ISO 10646) the international standard 2-byte character sets that covers almost all scripts. XML is case sensitive, but HTML is not case sensitive.
- Unicode is the standard developed by the Unicode consortium. It provides unique number for each character, irrespective of the language or program. This standard is adopted by all hardware, software companies – apple, HP, Microsoft, IBM, Oracle, SAP, SUN, etc. and also compatible for standards like HTML, JAVA, XML, etc. This standard was even synchronized with ISO 10646 standard (Information Technology: universal multiple Octet coded Character set – UCS).

1.6. LIBRARIES SHIFT TO DBMS (FILE PROCESSING SYSTEMS)

In general sense, the database-management system

(DBMS) is referred as - a collection of such interrelated data or records. In the context of library databases, the system needs to be managed by a set of programs to execute these integral operations ranging from creation, storing the records to retrieving the information from the library bibliographical databases efficiently and effectively. The relational database management systems (RDBMS) are advanced in executing the relations among the sub-fields, fields, records in the file or among the files for the benefit or accessing the data or retrieving information.

Use of computers for data processing, storing and retrieving information; emerging technologies in information industry and library automation initiatives have simultaneously laid impact on the development of library databases. Big hardware companies such as IBM began working with libraries in 1950s. The early focus was on controlling the circulation transactions only. Lavagnino (1997) marked four stages in the evolution of systems relating to the development of data processing, networking as well as computer technologies in libraries.

1. Use of typewriters and adding machines
2. Mainframe & minicomputers, offline batch processing, automating technical tasks etc.
3. Microcomputers, Integrated online systems, OPACs etc
4. Collaborative activities increased between library and external partners such as – computing professionals, vendors, consortia and other libraries. System librarians became knowledgeable in external hardware, software and networking.

As described above, the computers were initially used for scientific/engineering calculations only. With the entry of business applications, computers were used for creating data files, store, manipulate and retrieve larger amount of information. The file processing systems were basically structured linear/ hierarchical, but found less flexible as the business operations were becoming more and more complex.

The situation lead to the development of database systems in the place of file processing systems. These file processing systems remained now for backup of the data. The file processing systems were found disadvantageous in retrieving information.

- Program – data dependency – programs that run the data are interdependent. The data cannot be uniform in all files within or among organizations
- Duplication of data – thus there is every possibility of duplicating data
- Limited data sharing – since data and programs are different with each process, file and organization, the data sharing will not be feasible.
- Lengthy development time - because of non-standard practices, update of present file system is rather difficult as different professionals need to work simultaneously drawing the data from other modules. Thus it is usually preferred to run a fresh program a new file system, which is again involving additional effort, time and cost.
- Excessive program maintenance- of file processing system costs heavily in terms of cost, manpower and time.

Libraries are demonstrated with huge collections of print, electronic or digital books, journals and other material in their physical space as well as virtual. There are internal documents stacked in the physical space of the libraries, while the external electronic resources databases comprising of copy righted content and also the free content through internet. These large files, innumerable records, content are inaccessible, irretrievable and remain stored, if the files (records) are not designed according to the stipulated standards, structurally built on effective model.

It is advantageous for libraries to shift from linear sequential approach of file systems and follow DBMS approach to be able to create and maintain the bibliographic databases and to facilitate random access to information or documents. They need to maintain various interrelated records in the form of databases for effecting the display of information and access to documents or information to users as well as making those records retrievable for various integral operations.

1.6.1. Advantages

The database approach is flexible and fundamentally laying an emphasis on the integration of data, files to share data across the major divisions of the organization. The success of the database approach depends on the type of data, design of database and model of the database management systems. The DBMS approach allows the creation, update of the data by way of modification and deletion in the file. It is considered as advantageous for business as well as other organizations those dealing with the data in abundant quantities such as libraries and information centers. The advantages over the file processing systems are mentioned here.

- Program data independence
- Minimal data redundancy
- Improved data consistency
- Improved data sharing
- Improved productivity of application development
- Enforcement standards
- Improved data quality
- Improved data accessibility and responsiveness
- Reduced program maintenance

1.6.2. Limitations

Some disadvantages or additional risks associated with DBMS approach are mentioned under as a precaution before implementing DBMS approach in any organization.

- New and specialized personnel are required to handle

the latest products

- Installation management costs grow with the increasing complexities in the system
- Conversion of data from old file system into DBMS incurs heavy costs
- Need for explicit backup and recovery of data because the organization should not be effected due to loss of data.
- Organizational conflict shared databases usually suffer from the non-standard practices, differential formats and coding.

The abundant data accumulated in library servers and the complex relations among various fields/sub-fields of library bibliographic records require the understanding of their database design, features, structures or bibliographic formats etc. and also the type of database model on which the bibliographic database is structured. The basic concepts, application of DBMS, RDBMS, database design and modelling are explained in relation to library bibliographic database management, execution of several operations and information retrieval mechanisms in forthcoming chapters.

2

Database Concepts

2.1. CONCEPTS

Libraries deal with data in abundant quantities and have always been engaged in its processing for the efficient retrieval of information for various purposes. This could be in the form of a list of patrons, or the catalogue of books or an inventory of journals and other information material, directory of experts/institutions, etc. All these forms are in their own sense comprising data of related records. They are different collections of records related to each other within the collection or a cross collections. In this sense the organized collections of interrelated records can be termed as database.

The basic terms often referred while explaining the concept of database are - 'data'; 'database'; 'database management'; and bibliographic database.

2.1.1. Data

Data is individual piece/s of information. In simple way, it can also be referred as 'known facts'. It is the plural of 'datum' or existing knowledge. A datum – a unit of data – is a symbol or a set of symbols which is used to represent some entity. The word 'data' is the traditional plural form of the now-archaic datum, neuter past participle of the Latin dare, "to give", hence means "something given". Wikipedia defines the term 'Data' as a set of values of qualitative or quantitative variables. Data can be collected, measured, reported and analyzed. [https://en.wikipedia.org/wiki/Data#cite_note-]. It is in the form of text and audio-visuals i.e. graphs, images. Webopedia further expanded (http://www.webopedia.com/TERM/D/data.html) the meaning in the context of the computation programs as – 'the data is distinct pieces of information, usually formatted in a special way according to the instructions in programs. Data exists as text, numerals or bits and bytes stored in electronic memory, or as facts stored in a person's mind. The data in files containing binary machine-readable information is distinct from the textual human-readable information (ASCII). For example, the library 'patron' data comprises of patron name, address, phone number etc. along with unique identification number (patron ID) or serial number. Similarly, the essential elements of a book data primarily consist of author, title, edition, publisher, year of publication etc.

It can be mentioned that mere accumulation of 'data' or 'facts' will not serve the purpose of gaining 'knowledge', which is again relied on 'information'. The word 'data' differs from 'information', in the sense that it is 'processed data' that can enhance the knowledge of the 'data' user.

Data vs. Information vs. Knowledge

- Data — Raw facts, No context, Just numbers and text — E.g. Data: 261013
- Information — Processed data, can be interpreted according to the 'context', 'value assigned' etc. It can be summarized, organized and analyzed
    - E.g. The data 261013 can be the date by adding a slash next to each of two digits like 26/10/13; it can even mean amount by adding Rupee symbol such as Rs. 2,61,013, Celsius 45.00, 101.5F

- Knowledge – From the processed data it is possible to have knowledge of finances, weather forecasts and bodily conditions of a human being.

Knowledge refers to the use of information combining experience in varied contexts, while information can be transported, stored or shared. The figure 2.1 illustrates the relation between data, information and knowledge.

Data	**The raw material of information**
	e.g. 98.6° F, 99.5° F, 100.3° F, 101° F, ...
Information	**Data organized and presented in a specified manner.**
	E.g. Hourly body temperature: 98.6° F, 99.5° F, 100.3° F, 101° F, ...
Knowledge	**"Justified true belief" Information that can be acted upon.**
	E.g. If you have a temperature above 100° F, you most likely have a fever

Fig. 2.1. Data vs. Information vs. Knowledge

2.1.2. Types of Data

The data exists both in unprocessed raw form and in the later processed form or formatted according to a specific purpose. The unprocessed raw data refers to the collections of alphabets, numbers and characters. The raw data will become "processed data" after passing through the required stages. In this process 'the data' will be in many visible forms. Thus the data is unstructured or semi structured and structured forms.

[http://www.webopedia.com/TERM/B/big_data.html]

Unstructured Data : It is randomly available (acquired) picked data, it is unclassified or unorganized data.

Semi-structured : It doesn't have fixed data structure but has tags or other types of markers are used to identify certain elements of the data. To maintain semi-structured data even word processing software can be used. Emails have the data elements such as -sender, recipient, date, time and other fields added to the unstructured data of the email message. Content and any attachments, photos or other graphics can be tagged with keywords such as the creator, date, location and keywords, making it possible to organize and locate graphics. XML and other markup languages are often used to manage semi-structured data.

Structured Data : It is considered as advanced over paper based data systems and highly effective for making data entries, storing and managing data for the retrieval of information. The data should be input in each record within the framework of a specified data model. The data type will be clearly defined by selecting whether numeric or currency or alphabetic or name or date or address) and size of the field (specifying number of characters; restricted to certain terms such as Mr., Ms., or Dr., M or F). The data cannot be entered if it was beyond the frame work of data model. The structured data can be found in spread sheets, relational databases and managed by Structured Query Language (SQL)

Metadata : The data about data. The metadata describes the properties or characteristics of the data but do not include that data. Metadata helps to retrieve information from database.

Usage Data : The electronic access to scholarly content directly give measures of their usage. The usage metrics can characterize the usage in several aspects such as usability. The subscribing libraries, organizations and consortia have been relying on these metrics generated by the usage of electronic content to measure the same quantitatively as well as qualitatively. The types of log and also the scope of understanding the information extracted through log files have been increasing due to the innovations in web-server software, browsers and the browsing facilities. The raw log thus formed in database-servers on the usage of web based products including electronic information products is termed as web-server usage logs. The concept of usage as detailed by Kurtz and Bollen (2010) through a service request model is a set of 3 entities - the user; the information system or a service unit that connects the user with resource or collections; and specific resource itself

Publishers/aggregators of e-resources supply this usage log in the form of usage metrics/statistics or reports to subscribing organizations and consortia. Consortia too provide these usage reports to all their member institutions as per database, title and period. Library administrators began relying on usage metrics for decision making during the selection, renewal or cancellation of expensive databases. The word 'metrics' means 'measure'. They are labeled as usage metrics, since the log files reflect the real usage of electronic documents in terms of counts. The numerical characteristics of usage metrics tend to attribute data explicitly in some specific managerial applications for exercising decisions and also for creating user centric devices, since the usage data is reflecting the objective information regarding usefulness, usage of e-resources in several facets, users as well as using environment. Thereby a number of inferences can be drawn paving way towards user research. The format, content and the distribution of web usage metrics depends on the type of information, format of the document, purpose and the way of accessing the document or database and also the standards followed by the publishers or vendors.

The incredible efforts of ARL E-Metrics Projects in May 2000 to standardize the log data and subsequent initiation of COUNTER (Counting Online Usage of Networked Electronic Resources) in 2002 tend to devise codes of practice like COUNTER and SUSHI (Standardized Usage Statistics Harvesting Initiative). Thereby it is possible to know - What is being used (content: full text, abstracts, table of contents); Who is using it (user: by IPs or user ID); How is the database used (activity: explained vide sessions, searches, and linking); When is the content being used (by period), and How will the data be presented (format: html, pdf, rtf etc)

Big-data : Big data is recent term used to refer the large massive data accumulated in the data servers as a result of accessing electronic resources in both structured and unstructured form. This large sets of data is *called* big data). This data is now being used very effectively for decision making, to enhance the operational efficiencies, cost reduction and to minimize the loss in e-commerce operations with accurate analyses. The popular industry analyst Doug Laney a way back in 2001 described the big data with three Vs volume, velocity and variety, which was later updated with some more important characteristics like variability and complexity. This accumulated data in large quantities will be processed (collecting, organizing and analyzing) by analysts, who understands the data and discover patterns of use of the product to suggest the users or organizations with a useful information.

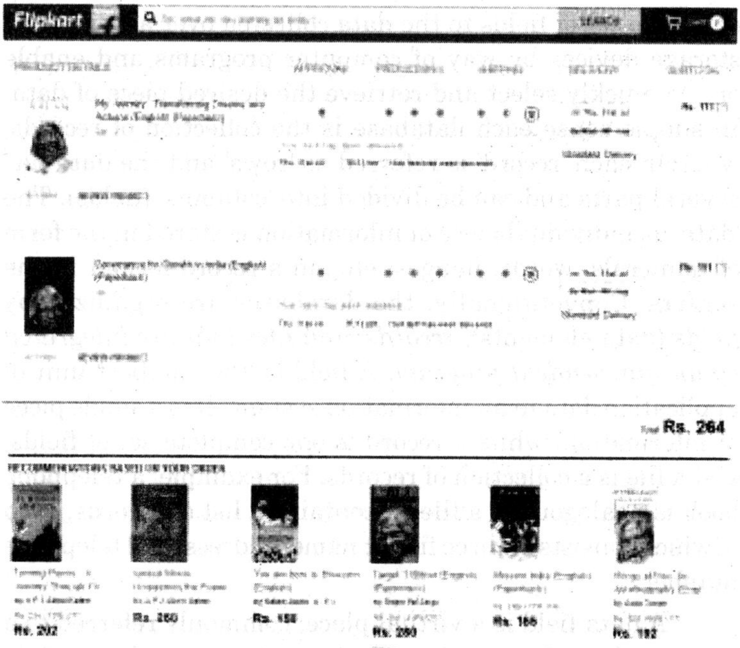

Fig. 2.2. Big data Applications e.g. Flipkart (Screenshot)

Several e-commerce websites have been providing the

most useful data to registered users, book selectors based on their previous searches indicating relevant other material also suggesting them to review. This will be done by matching the concepts / terms used during the searches with the descriptors of other related material. This will help the users/ book selectors to discover unknown items and will have opportunity to review them for their tasks, e.g. Amazon.

2.1.3. Database

A database (file) may be described as "a collection of interrelated data stored together as records which are independent and disabling unwanted redundancy to serve one or more application in an optimal fashion". The concept of database is evolved from a mere collection of interrelated organized information to a system that runs a file consisting of simple set of fields to the data collected over a number of storage devices by way of computer programs and enable one to quickly select and retrieve the desired piece of data. In simple sense each database is the collection of records; wherein each 'record' is referred as 'rows' and the data has several parts and can be divided into 'columns' (fields). The 'data' as individual piece of information is stored in the form of numerals, words, images, etc., in a record format in the servers. Conventionally, the databases are organized by *fields* (data elements), *records,* and *files that are integrated by an independent program.* A field is 'the smallest unit of application data in an information system'. It is a single piece of information, while a record is one complete set of fields; and a file is a collection of records. For example, a telephone book is analogous to a file. It contains a list of records, each of which consists of three fields: name, address, and telephone number.

A data field is a virtual place, commonly referred to a column where data can be stored in a data entry form, while each record can be considered as a row. In an example of patron file – each patron is entered as a separate record and consisting of several fields to enter Patron unique identification number (Patron ID), patron name, type of patron, class or designation or occupation, organization, address in several fields, phone number, email, borrowing eligibility etc. as illustrated vide the following screenshot.

Table 2.1. The Elementary (Data) Structure of a Patron Database (Screenshot)

Patron _Id	*Patron_Type*	*Patron_ Barcode*	*Patron*
3584	Alumni & others	2KSIP-11	Kiefer, Jason, MR.
3528	Alumni & others	C003	Kanaka Durga, V.V.
73	Faculty	0527	Sivasankar Reddy, A.
81	Faculty	0539	Rahmath Ali Khan Yousuf Zai
91	Faculty	0560	Chandrasekhar Reddy, K.
98	Faculty	0753	Prof.Rajaram, G.
102	Faculty	0764	Girija, P.N
155	Faculty	1134	Jnaneshwara Bhikshu, N.
162	Faculty	1180	Satish Deshpande
166	Faculty	1218	Ruma Purkait
188	Faculty	1293	Bendre, S.M
213	Faculty	1363	Lalitha Guruprasad, K.
214	Faculty	1364	Anita, Jagota
219	Faculty	1369	Nagarjuna, B.
6153	Faculty	1574	Vasuki, Belavadi
7442	Faculty	1594	Sri Kanaka Durga, Ptcha
7378	Faculty	1622	Rajagopal, S
12305	Faculty	1727	Rajiv Velicheti
9483	Faculty	1759	Vineet Padmanabhan Nair, C

The database concept refers to the following important elements –

- Collection, storing, organization and integration of data
- Interrelation among the data fields
- The ability to retrieve against different logical orders.

- Avoiding the data redundancy which is repetition of the same data elements or elements across different records.
- Maintaining the data independency, means the ability to change logical data definitions and relationships as well as physical structures without major changes in the application programs.

The principle components of a database are data or content, similar records, data process, storage, input devices and output terminals or user interface and the databases vary according to content, purpose, use and range of applicability. The type of database and the structure are considered as significant criteria in handling information in larger databases. The different types of databases are described in databases categorization - section 2.2 and structures are analyzed in database models in section 2.3.

2.2. DATABASES CATEGORIZATION

Databases vary depending on the nature of the content, functioning, discipline, language, format etc. Before computerisation librarians were relying on book registers, loose leaves of paper, and mainly cards for maintaining their data of patrons, books, journals and other material and also circulation transactions. Gradually, they began using computers, communication networks and other peripheral devices to handle textual/numeric data for delivering several information services and products. The databases categorized as per the nature of content are listed here.

1. Numeric Databases : Generally, the numeric databases contain information more in numerals and less of other textual information, e.g. the salary database, weather database, statistical databases, Census etc. These databases may also include simple arithmetic operations to complex numeric operations.

2. Factual Databases : Factual databases generally include directories or indexes of experts, institutions, individuals, companies, statistics etc. Each record contains the facts about them. They do not contain descriptive or analytic elements of documents nor do they contain numeric data. Such database management systems do not provide scope for any numeric or analytic operations. It can be a computerized or printed source that provides direct access to information for analysis and application, e.g. UGC Inflibnet Centre's Vidwan Database, Universities Database etc. Vidwan database provides information about scientists/ researchers and faculty working at leading academic and research institutions in India. Similarly the directory of universities is a database that gives the details of Indian universities.

3. **Full Text Databases :** These databases contain the full text of documents along with a description of the document. In recent times, many publishers are providing full text of their journal/book/monographs content as articles, current issues, chapters, data tables, back volumes or their collections or as a whole. E.g. legal databases like LEXIS, WESTLAW, etc., contain the full text of the law content. These databases are created, marketed and distributed by the publishers, aggregators, and government or non-government organizations. Though these full text databases were initially distributed through Disks (CD-ROMs), very soon they were made available through online systems using internet. These databases containing full text content are also incorporating value added facilities, user centric applications and powerful search engines etc., e.g. DIALOG, Sciencedirect, ProQuest, EBSCOHost, Emerald etc. Now a days, all most all print publishers are bringing out their content online along with print and even without print.

4. **Bibliographic Databases :** Bibliographic databases contain records of bibliographic description of documents that enable the library users or information seekers to retrieve the information about the documents from them. Thus bibliographic records form a great part among all types of databases drawing the attention of the library practitioners as well as designers of database management

systems. Though initially these databases were published only the bibliographic records of articles, chapters, gradually enhanced their scope and features by integrating with the full text content, citations and cited articles.

5. Meta-databases : They are databases of databases. They can also be called as bibliographic search databases as they allow anyone to search for content that is indexed by other databases. SCOPUS, Mathscinet, Web of Science are examples for bibliographic search database. These databases not only provide bibliographic records of articles and chapters etc. but also the full-text links and article citations published in other databases.

According to the range of applications, Hoffer, Prescott and McFadden (2002) categorized databases as –

1. Personal Databases : limited to single user or single personal computer or laptop

2. Workgroup Databases : created, shared and updated by limited group or team working on a common project

3. Department Databases : are designed to support the database needs of a functional group within an organization

4. Enterprise Databases : caters to the needs of all the departments of entire organization. These databases support the operations of all the departments in organization and the data will be used for decision making. The data usually be transmitted across the departments.

5. Internet, Intranet and Extranet Databases : They are external databases maintained by organizations, publishers, providers meant to distribute worldwide over telecommunication networks. Intranet is restricted to users premises only.

Conventionally and the popularly used data types were numeric, character, date, memo (long text) and logical (True or False). Ever since the multi-media capabilities are becoming common in computation allowing the storage and retrieval of data types called 'objects' i.e. graphics, calculations, images, audio-visuals etc., such data types also help in visualizing information contained in databases and in reports. The following categories are identified according to the functions of databases by the experts of database management systems.

1. Operational databases : These databases store data relating to the operations of the organization.

2. End user databases : the end-users like managers at different levels are sharing the information though they are not concerned about the individual transactions found in operational databases.

3. Centralized databases : store the information and application programs at a central computing facility, whereas the users at different locations access the central data base to process the transaction. Data validation, verification will be carried out by the application programs at the central computer centre, and a registration number is allotted by the application programs located at the central facility. The local area office key-in the data without undertaking any processing.

4. Distributed databases : These databases get data from the local operations done at various sites connected in the organization. This is made possible through client-server technology for managing distributed data bases, wherein one component will be interacting with user (client) transmitting the requests to the other component of DBMS, which in turn responds with the database to meet the information needs of the client. In this computer system, the operations are processed simultaneously at client PC (s) level and also Server.

5. Personal databases : These databases are maintained, on personal computers for a limited use of single or few users group or only among a limited number of users, generally working in the same department. These databases are generally subject specific and are user designed. They use simple and less powerful. DBMS packages available on PCs. These DBMS packages may not have all the features of relational DBMS but do have similar features in a limited way.

6. Commercial databases : journal or book publishers or aggregators provide access to these databases directly from their servers to users on subscription or purchase basis. They are external databases as they are remotely maintained and only access is distributed on commercial venture. These are mostly subject specific. These commercial ventures include full text, statistical and bibliographic search cum citation databases.

The structure of a database refers to 'database model'.

2.3. DATABASE MODELS

Database model refers to the underlying the structure of a database. This is collection of conceptual tools for describing data, data relationships, data semantics, consistency and constraints. Techopedia defines a database model as – "the logical structure, representation or layout of a database. It further explains that the database model tells how the data will be stored, managed and also processed within it. It helps in designing a database and serves as blueprint for application developers and database administrators in creating a database". "Data model specifics the rules according to which data are structured and also the associated operations are permitted. It can also be viewed as a technique for the formal description of data, data relationships and user constraints". There are different types of models representing databases their entities, relationships, data flow, tables and more. Each model represents different approaches in handling the information. The main criteria to evaluate the operation of the DBMS models are:

- Date representation
- Structure

- Dynamic v/s predefined relationship
- Physical storage and retrieval
- Data controls

The database models were evolved to represent the data structures and to overcome the functional as well as structural disabilities.

1. Entity-relationship (E-R) data model
2. Hierarchical data model
3. Network data model
4. Relational data model
5. Object-relational data model

2.3.1. Entity-Relationship (E-R) Data Model

Entity-relationship (E-R) data model represents a real world perception about the collection of basic objects called 'entities' and 'relationships among these objects'. The ER model defines the conceptual view of a database. An entity is a real-world object which can be easily identifiable.

- An entity set is a collection of similar types of entities attributed sharing similar values. For example, in a school database, students, teachers, classes, and courses offered can be considered as entities. All these entities have some attributes or properties that give them their identity. For example - A Students set may contain all the students of a school; and teachers set may contain all the teachers and the Books set of a library attributed sharing similar values; the libraries contain similar attributes
- The entities in a database are described as a set of attributes; the figure 2.3 represents the logical structure (schema) of a database designed with E-R data model.

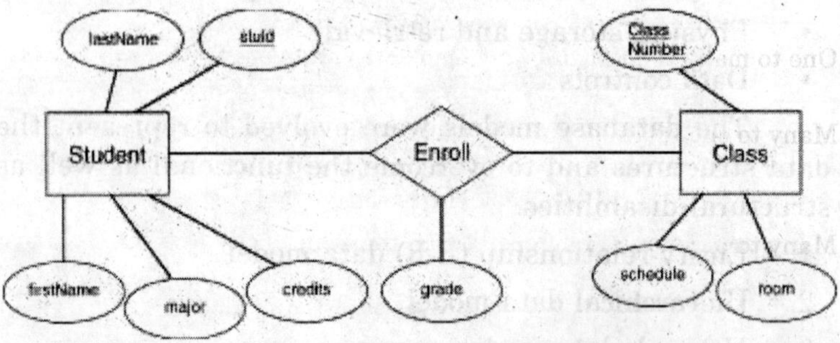

Fig. 2.3. E-R Data Model of Student Enrollment

- Attributes are the properties represented by the entities. The relationship is an association among several entities. The attributes have values. For example, a student entity may have name, class, and credits as attributes and class number schedule, room number etc. are the attributes for class. An enrollment relationship associates a student with their class details, whereas a relationship set is referred to multiple relationships of similar type. Similarly, a book entity will have attributes like - author or authors, title, series, publisher, place and year of publication, subject, etc. Library entity will have attributes such as library name, address, city, country, parent organization etc. The relationship is individual library's book collection.
- The attributes referred to relationships are called descriptive attributes. The number of participating entities in a relationship defines the degree of the relationship. Binary = degree 2; Ternary = degree 3; n-ary = degree.
- 'Cardinality' defines the number of entities in one entity set, which can be associated with the number of entities of other set via relationship set.

One to one relationship:	One entity from entity set A with one from set B and vice versa.
One to many relationship	One entity from entity set A with more than one entities of entity set B.
Many to one relationship	More than one entities from entity set A can be associated with one entity of entity set B
Many to many relationship	More than one entity from entity set A can be associated with more than one entity from B and vice versa.

Figure 2.4 represents entity relational model for 'Library Book Issue/Return System', wherein 3 entities – person, book and librarian are entities (attributes) related to return and loan processes. Persons entity have data elements LibCard ID, Name, Address, whereas Book entity has ISBN, LibID and Librarian has NINO and execute the returns as well as loan operations.

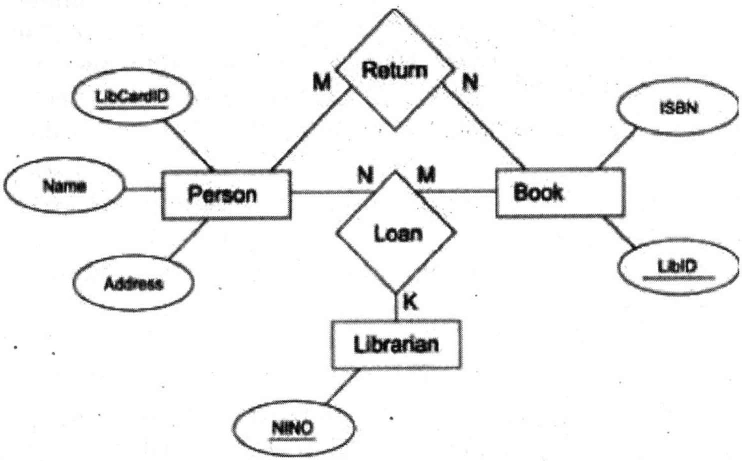

Fig. 2.4. E-R Model for Library Book Issue/Return System (*Source*: http://www.lightenna.com/book/export/s5/111)

2.3.2. Hierarchical Data Model

Hierarchical Database Model postulates the data relation in superior/subordinate approach. This represents a hierarchy of parent and child data segments. To create links between these record types, the hierarchical model uses parent child relationships. IBM's Information Management System (IMS) was based on the hierarchical data model since 1968. IMS is an extremely complex DBMS and is powerful and popular even today.

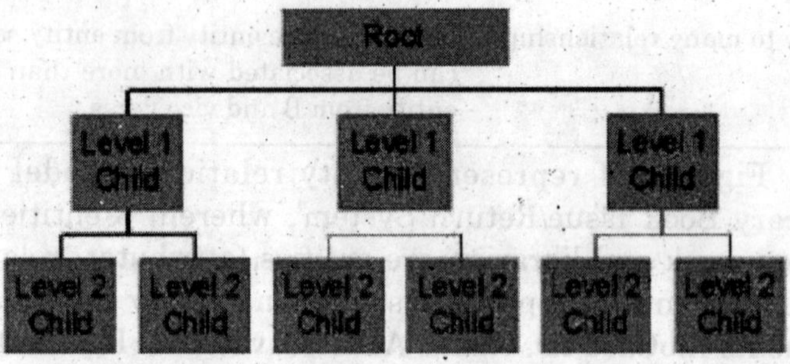

Fig. 2.5. Hierarchical Data Model (General Representation)

The data is in tree structure. The topmost node is the root and the nodes at the bottom are the leaves (child). The structure implies that records can also have repeating information. Each node, except the root, must be connected to one and only one higher-level node. In this structure data follows a series of records. Hierarchical relations may be of two types: One to many and many to many. The above example (figure 2.5) involves 3 generations. One level of hierarchy refers to one "generation". Hierarchical database can be accessed and updated rapidly, because this model structure is like as a tree and the relationships between records are predefined. This type of database structure is that each child in the tree may have only one parent, and any other relationships or linkages between or among children are not possible, even if they make sense from a logical standpoint. The figure 2.6 represents the library book order submodule structured in hierarchical data model, wherein the entities vendors-wise orders are shown and respective invoices.

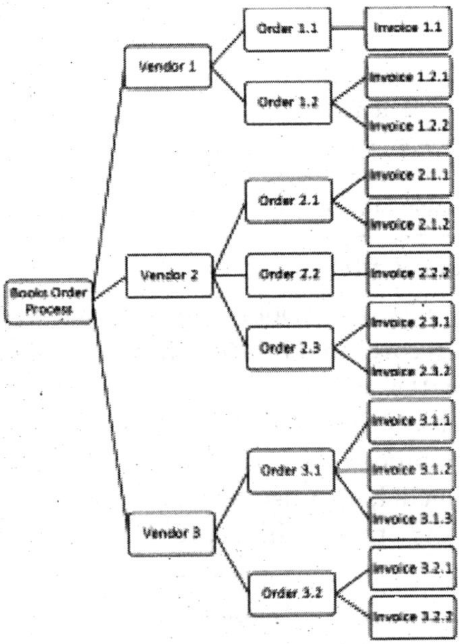

Fig. 2.6. Hierarchical Data Model (Book Order Data)

The hierarchical database model is simple to understand and organize the data and it has its limitations while retrieving the information. The table 2.2 depicts the advantages and limitations of hierarchical database model

Table 2.2. The Advantages and Limitations of Hierarchical Database Model

Advantages	*Limitations*
• Provides a very natural way of modeling	• Unnecessary complexity
• Hierarchical structure form the real world	• Users are forced to devote time and effort in solving problems which are introduced
• Most relationships are one-to-many	• Problems with storage operations such as adding, deleting and updating
• Most data manipulation is routine	• Ad-hoc queries are difficult to handle
• Pre-defined	• Flexibility is less in this database model

- Performance is high,
- Hierarchical databases often outperform relational databases when large amounts of data are processed in a predictable fashion.
- Data inconsistency may result when updating takes place.
- Waste of space is unavoidable

2.3.3. Network Model

In the network model, the data are represented as collections of records and relationships by links. The network model advocates a structure wherein any record can be connected to any other record in the database. In contrast to hierarchical model, the records are less organized in networking model, because any node in this model can be linked with any other as illustrated in the following figure.

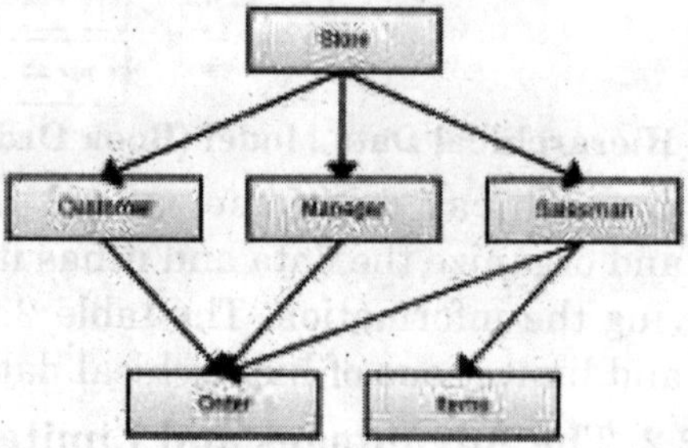

Fig. 2.7. Network Model (General Concept)

The network model was recommended by CODASYL (Conference on Data System Languages) in 1971, where a large number of computer manufacture and large users met and defined database terms. Although the network architecture was ignored by most vendors, the Cullinets IDMS (Integrated DMS) and Cincon systems TOTAL gained popularity to this model. A network has a more general structure than a hierarchy. This is because a given node may have any number of immediate superiors as well as any number of immediate subordinates. There is no restriction in number, it is possible to represent a many-to-many correspondence in a reasonably direct manner. Major advantage over the Hierarchical Data Model, is that symmetric queries require symmetric answers.

This model overcomes most of the difficulties encountered with storage in the hierarchical data model such as adding, deleting and updating records. This model enables strong backup, recovery and integrity features. The network model is very complex in nature, but suited for extensive ad-hoc data access.

Figure 2.8 represents the networked data for a library system, wherein the central library is connected to a school and departmental libraries and the books / journal records created by these libraries in the network are gathered in the central library server. Users/staff access the server from all the places.

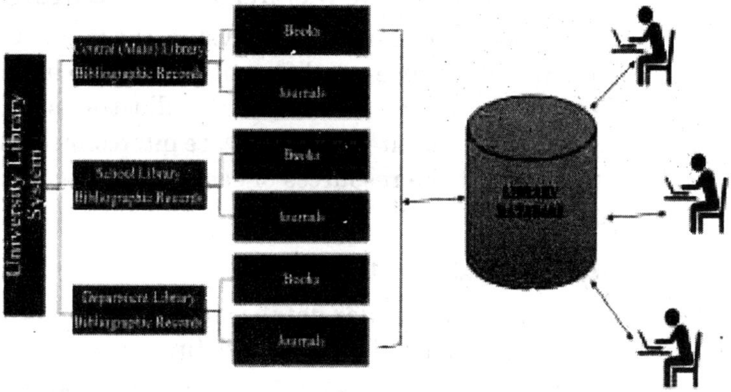

Fig. 2.8. Networked Data for Library System

A tree-structure diagram is the schema for a hierarchical database consists of two basic components: 1. Boxes, represent record types and 2. Lines, to links. A tree-structure diagram serves the same purpose as an entity–relationship (E-R) diagram; namely, it specifies the overall logical structure of the database. A tree-structure diagram is similar to a data-structure diagram in the network model, wherein in the latter, record types are organized in the form of an arbitrary graph, and in the former, record types are organized in the form of a rooted tree.

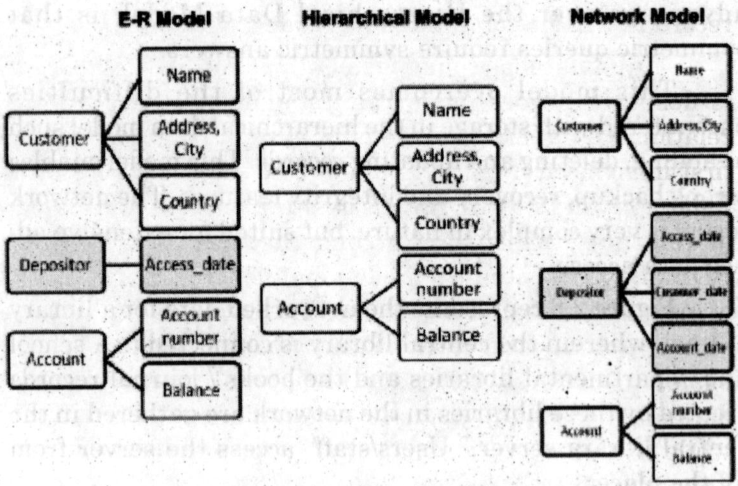

Fig. 2.9. Database Models (E-R, Hierarchical and Network)

In a networked university library system the main and school/departmental libraries or different campuses can be connected alongwith resources. The figure 2.9 illustrates that main library and the associated resources are interconnected. The users can connect the resources of each library location and also together.

2.3.4. Relational Database Model

Currently most of popular databases are based on the relational database model. Techopedia defines a relational database (RDB) as "a collective set of multiple data sets organized by tables, records and columns. RDBs establish a well-defined relationship between database tables. Tables communicate and share information, which facilitates data searchability, organization and reporting." The relational approach is based on the mathematical theory of relations. (RDBMS - relational database management system). A relational database allows the definition of data structures, storage and retrieval operations and integrity constraints. In this model, the data and relations between them are organized as tables in databases,. A table is a collection of records (rows) displayable as 2 dimensional flat files. Each record in a table contains some fields (columns).

Thus database management system (DBMS), which is designed according to relational model, is known as relational database management system (RDBMS). It was first introduced by E. F. Codd, of IBM's San Jose Research Laboratory in 1970. RDBMS is based on mathematical theory of relations, which laid strong theoretical foundation. RDBMSs have become a predominant choice for the storage of information since 1980 and have often replaced the legacy of hierarchical and network databases because they are easier to understand and use. This is called relational database because all the data is stored into different tables, while relations are established using primary keys or other keys known as foreign keys. A Relational Database Management System (RDBMS) is software that:

- Enables to implement a database with tables, columns and indexes
- Guarantees the referential integrity between rows of various tables
- Updates the indexes automatically
- Interprets an SQL query and combines information from various tables

The principle components are its data structure in the form of tables with rows and columns; powerful data manipulation operations using SQL language; and integrity of data. Relational database management systems (RDBMS) are being used for many commercial as well as open source applications to store and manage huge volume of data. The five leading commercial relational database vendors were Oracle, IBM, Microsoft, and SAP including Sybase and Teradata, whereas the 3 important open source databases are MySQL, PostgreSQL, and SQLite. Some definitions are given below in the light of RDBMS.

Database : is a collection of tables, with related data.

Table : is a matrix of data. A table in a database looks like a simple spreadsheet.

Column : (data element) contains data of one and the same kind,

Row : (= tuple, entry or record) is a group of related data

Redundancy : Storing data twice, redundantly to make the system faster.

Primary Key : is unique. A key value cannot occur twice in one table.

Foreign Key : A foreign key is the linking pin between two tables.

Compound Key : (composite key) is a key that consists of multiple columns, because one column is not unique.

Index : An index in a database resembles an index at the back end of a book.

Referential Integrity : makes sure that a foreign key value always points to an existing row.

DBMS packages are very helpful in structuring and organizing information for the purpose of retrieval. The features of the DBMS Software are evolved from time to time with an increasing efficiency towards data control, security and various user centric applications making it advantageous. The relational model uses a collection of tables to represent both data and the relationships among those data, but rejects the structure entirely in favor of two dimensional tables. The Relational tables have the following properties -

- Values are Atomic
- Each row is unique. Two rows from the same table must differ at least in one cell value.
- All rows must be complete.
- Repeating groups are not allowed.
- The sequence of rows is not relevant in this application and insignificant
- Each column represents one attribute and has a unique

name. Column values are of the same kind. The sequence of columns is insignificant

- A domain is the set of all possible values for an attribute.
- A cell represents the data that ties at the interaction of a column and a row. It contains only one value.
- Cardinality is the number of rows in a given table at a specific point of tune (e.g. follows the sequence of numbers 1; 12; 13; 2; 25; 3 . . .)
- Certain fields may be designated as keys, which mean that searches for specific values of that field will use indexing to speed them up.
- RDBs use Structured Query Language (SQL), which is a standard user application that provides an easy programming interface for database interaction

In relational model, information is stored in tables, wherein fields in two different tables take values from the same set, a joint operation can be performed to select related records in the two or more tables by matching values in those fields. In such tables, common attributes (fields) can be linked to match and link the attributes. A difficulty may arise in the case when two or more of underlying domains are actually the same set, so that two or more columns have the same domain name associated with them. The relations existing between tables, records and functional dependencies are classified as follows:

One to One : One table record relates to another record in another table.

One to Many : One table record relates to many records in another table.

Many to One : More than one table record relates to another table record.

Many to Many : More than one table record relates to more records in another table.

Relational tables follow certain conditions to ensure the accuracy and accessibility of the data.

- The rows in a relational table should all be distinct and should not be a duplicate.
- The column values must not be repeating groups or arrays.
- The concept of a null value. Use of a null value to indicate that a value is missing. It does not equate to a blank or zero, because a blank is considered equal to another blank, a zero is equal to another zero, but two null values may not be equal in real context.

When each row in a table is different, it is possible to use one or more columns to identify a particular row. This unique column or group of columns is called a primary key. Any column that is part of a primary key cannot be null. The condition of the database is referred to as entity integrity. The concept of "relation" is illustrated in the following tables of a database. The table 2.3 represents the data about courses, students who have enrolled and the grades they have obtained. The attributes are - Course, StudentId, and Grade.

Tables 2.3. Sample Relations (Students Information) Course, Student Id, Grade

Course	*StudentId*	*Grade*
CS101	12345	A
CS101	67890	B
EE200	12345	C
EE200	22222	B+
CS101	33333	A"
PH100	67890	C+

StudentId-Name-Address-Phone

StudentId	*Name*	*Address*	*Phone*
12345	C. Brown	12 Apple St.	555-1234
67890	L. Van Pelt	34 Pear Ave.	555-5678
22222	P. Patty	56 Grape Blvd.	555-9999

Course-Prerequisite

Course	*Prerequisite*
CS101	CS100
EE200	EE005
EE200	CS100
CS120	CS101
CS121	CS120
CS205	CS101
CS206	CS121
CS206	CS205

Course-Day-Hour

Course	*Day*	*Hour*
CS101	M	9AM
CS101	W	9AM
CS101	F	9AM
EE200	Tu	10AM
EE200	W	1PM
EE200	Th	10AM

Course-Room

Course	*Room*
CS101	Turing Aud.
EE200	25 Ohm Hall
PH100	Newton Lab.

The data in different files is related to each other and can be accessed via application software. Each file will have one or more indexes that can provide access to the data. The relations among different fields, sub-fields, records and files are structured according to RDBMS model.

Data Structures for Relations

The design of data structure depends on the expected mix of queries. These structures will be called "primary index structures." The "secondary index structures, "are additional structures that allow us to answer a greater variety of queries efficiently. When the relational data model is used, the selection of a data structure or appropriate database scheme is very essential. For instance the information about courses is separated as five relations {Course, StudentId, Grade, Prerequisite, Day, Hour, Room} instead of a flat table with 5 columns scheme.

For example, prerequisite information about a course is independent of day and hour information. If prerequisite and day-hour information are combined, then a list of prerequisites for a course in conjunction with every meeting of the course appears and vice versa. Then the data about EE200 if put into a single relation with scheme {Course, Prerequisite, Day, Hour} would appear as presented in following table. From the above example it can be noticed that six tuples are taken, with four components each, to do the work previously done by five tuples, with two or three components each.

Course	*Prerequisite*	*Day*	*Hour*
EE200	EE005	Tu	10AM
EE200	EE005	W	1PM
EE200	EE005	Th	10AM
EE200	CS100	Tu	10AM
EE200	CS100	W	1PM
EE200	CS100	Th	10AM

The figure 2.10 depicts the inter-relational data model for circulation – Issues & Returns sub-module for library system.

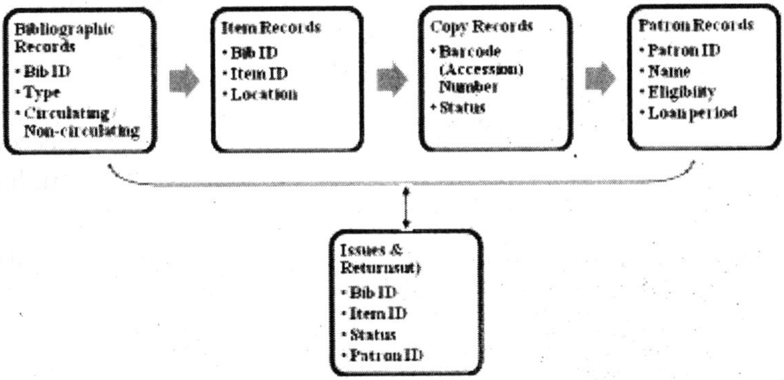

Fig. 2.10. Data model for Library Circulation – Issues & Returns

SQL for Relational Databases

SQL (Structured Query Language) language is used while designing relational databases. The set of basic SQL commands that are working with data on RDBMS are explained with the following illustrations. (https://docs.oracle.com/javase/tutorial/jdbc/overview/database.html.

SELECT statement : a SELECT statement is also called a query, used to get information from a table. It specifies one or more column headings, one or more tables from which to select, and some criteria for selection. The RDBMS returns rows of the column entries that satisfy the user requirement.

1. A SELECT statement such as the following will fetch the first and last names of employees who have company cars:
   - SELECT First_Name, Last_Name
   - FROM Employees (the FROM clause (the second line) gives the table from which the columns will be selected)
   - WHERE Car_Number IS NOT NULL (The WHERE clause in a SELECT statement provides the criteria for selecting values.

The first name and last name are printed for each row that satisfies the requirement because the SELECT statement (the first line) specifies the columns First_Name and Last_Name.

FIRST_NAME	*LAST_NAME*
John	Washington
Florence	Wojokowski

2. SELECT * (means "SELECT all columns.") and FROM Employees

   The following code produces a result set that includes the whole table because it asks for all of the columns in the table Employees with no restrictions (no WHERE clause).

3. SELECT First_Name, Last_Name FROM Employees and WHERE Last_Name LIKE 'Washington%'

   - SELECT First_Name, Last_Name
   - FROM Employees
   - WHERE Last_Name LIKE 'Washington%'

   The keyword LIKE is used to compare strings, and it offers the feature that patterns containing wildcards can be used. In this example the percent sign (%) at the end of 'Washington' signifies any value containing the string will satisfy this selection criterion. So 'Washington' or 'Washingtonian' would be matches, but 'Washing' would not be.

4. The other wildcard used in LIKE clauses is an underbar (_), which refers to any one character. WHERE Last_Name LIKE 'Ba_man' would match 'Barman', 'Badman', 'Balman', 'Bagman', 'Bamman', and so on.

   The WHERE clause uses the equal sign (=) to compare numbers. It selects the first and last name of the employee who is assigned car 12.

   - SELECT First_Name, Last_Name

- FROM Employees
- WHERE Car_Number = 12

5. The next code fragment selects the first and last names of employees whose employee number is greater than 10005:
   - SELECT First_Name, Last_Name
   - FROM Employees
   - WHERE Employee_Number > 10005
6. WHERE clauses can get rather elaborate and retrieved with multiple conditions. The following queries with WHERE clause in two conditions; this query selects the first and last names of employees whose employee number is less than 10100 and who do not have a company car.
   - SELECT First_Name, Last_Name
   - FROM Employees
   - WHERE Employee_Number < 10100 and Car_Number IS NULL
7. A distinguishing feature of relational databases is that it is possible to join from more than one table and get data. Suppose that after retrieving the names of employees who have company cars, one wanted to find out who has which car, its license plate number, mileage, and year of car. Then information stored in another table, 'Cars' need to be connected to table 'Employees' by means of a common column that appears in both tables to relate them to each other.

Car_Number	*License_Plate*	*Mileage*	*Year*
5	ABC123	5000	1996
12	DEF123	7500	1999

This column, which must be the primary key in one table, is called the foreign key in the other table. In this case, the column that appears in two tables is Car_Number, which is the primary key for the table

'Cars' and the foreign key in the table 'Employees'. If the 1996 car with license plate number ABC123 were wrecked and deleted from the Cars table, then Car_Number 5 would also have to be removed from the Employees table in order to maintain what is called referential integrity. Otherwise, the foreign key column (Car_Number) in the Employees table would contain an entry that did not refer to anything in the Cars table. A foreign key must either be null or equal to an existing primary key value of the table to which it refers. This is different from a primary key, which may not be null. There are several null values in the Car_Number column in the table Employees because it is possible for an employee not to have a company car.

8. The following code asks for the first and last names of employees who have company cars and for the license plate number, mileage, and year of those cars. Note that the FROM clause lists both the Employees and Cars tables because the requested data is contained in both tables. Using the table name and a dot (.) before the column name indicates which table contains the column.

   - SELECT Employees.First_Name, Employees.Last_Name, Cars.License_Plate, Cars.Mileage, Cars.Year
   - FROM Employees, Cars
   - WHERE Employees.Car_Number = Cars.Car_Number

This returns a result set that will look similar to the following:

FIRST_NAME	*LAST_NAME*	*LICENSE_ PLATE*	*MILEAGE*	*YEAR*
John	Washington	ABC123	5000	1996
Florence	Wojokowski	DEF123	7500	1999

Common SQL Commands used in Relational databases

SQL commands are divided into categories. DML and DDL

- **Data Manipulation Language (DML) commands** - deal with data, either retrieving it or modifying it to keep it up-to-date.
  - **SELECT :** used to query and display data from a database. The SELECT statement specifies which columns to include in the result set. The vast majority of the SQL commands used in applications are SELECT statements.
  - **INSERT :** adds new rows to a table. INSERT is used to populate a newly created table or to add a new row (or rows) to an already-existing table.
  - **DELETE :** removes a specified row or set of rows from a table
  - **UPDATE :** changes an existing value in a column or group of columns in a table
- **Data Definition Language (DDL) commands.** DDL commands create or change tables and other database objects such as views and indexes.
  - **CREATE TABLE :** creates a table with the column names specifying the type of data in each column. Data types vary from one RDBMS to another, so a user might need to use metadata to establish the data types used by a particular database. CREATE TABLE command is normally used less often than the data manipulation commands because a table is created only once, whereas adding or deleting rows or changing individual values generally occurs more frequently.
  - **DROP TABLE :** deletes all rows and removes the table definition from the database.
  - **ALTER TABLE :** adds or removes a column from

a table. It also adds or drops table constraints and alters column attributes

'schema': The set of schemes for various relations in a database is called the **'schema'** of the database. Example: Their schemes and meanings are:

1. {StudentId, Name, Address and Phone}. The student whose ID appears in the first component of a tuple has name, address, and phone number equal to the values appearing in the second, third, and fourth components, respectively.
   - In the context of databases, a **tuple*** is one record (one row). A row is not a tuple. Tuples* are unordered sets of known values with names. ...assuming of course that x, y, and z are all integers.

     (x=1, y=2, z=3)(z=3, y=2, x=1)(y=2, z=3, x=1)

     A row** is an ordered set of known or unknown values with names (although they may be omitted). Therefore, the following comparisons return false in SQL:

     (1, 2, 3) = (3, 2, 1) ; (3, 1, 2) = (2, 1, 3)
2. {Course, Prerequisite}. The course named in the second component of a tuple is a prerequisite for the course named in the first component of that tuple.
3. {Course, Day, Hour}. The course named in the first component meets on the day specified by the second component, at the hour named in the third component.
4. {Course, Room}. The course named in the first component meets in the room indicated by the second component.

The important operations performed on relations and functions were - insert, delete and lookup.

1. Insert (t,R). Add the tuple 't' to the relation R, if it is not already there.
2. Delete(X,R). Here, X is intended to be a specification

of some tuples. It consists of components for each of the attributes of R, and each component can be either - a value, or the symbol ", which means that any value is acceptable. The effect of this operation is to delete all tuples that match the specification X. For example, if we cancel CS101, we want to delete all tuples of the Course-Day-Hour relation that have Course = "CS101." We could express this condition by delete (("CS101", ", "), Course-Day-Hour)

3. Lookup(X,R). The result of this operation is the set of tuples in R that match the specification X; the latter is a symbolic tuple as described in the preceding item (2). For example, if we wanted to know for what courses CS101 is a prerequisite, we could ask lookup (", "CS101"), Course-Prerequisite). The result would be the set of two matching tuples (CS120, CS101) and (CS205, CS101).

Advantages

Relational Databases have many other advantages, including

- It is the most popularly used data model, because the relational theory is the most comprehensive, cohesive and orderly for a database product
- Easy extendibility, as new data may be added without modifying existing records. This is also known as scalability.
- It is conceptually, the easiest to master and most flexible in retrieval
- It is widely used model as a basis for specific products
- It provides workable applications in short periods of times
- Tables in the relational model are more neutral than structures in the non-relational models
- Logical and physical aspects are more clearly

distinguishable as a consequence of the non-structured nature of tables

- Programmers do not need to navigate data structures (as they do not exist). Navigation needs to be done only in a series of tables with some common attributes
- New technology performance, power and flexibility with multiple data requirement capabilities.
- Data security, which is critical when data sharing is based on privacy. For example, management may share certain data privileges to access and block employees from other data, such as confidential salary or benefit information.

Limitations

- Problems with performance and data integrity
- Not relevant to low-volume, single user environments
- Integrity controls need to be designed into the application program - an unreliable alternative to the built-in enforcement in the Network and Hierarchical systems
- Lack of predefined access paths is highly uneconomical. "Joins" are known to be computer resource eaters.
- Relational models are not well suited for large scale transaction processing.

2.3.5. Object-Relational Data Model

In modern information systems, the object/relational database management systems (ORDBMS) add new object storage capabilities to the relational systems. These new facilities integrate the management of traditional fielded data, complex objects such as geospatial data and diverse binary media such as audio, video, images, and applets. By using encapsulating methods with data structures, an ORDBMS server can execute complex analytical and data manipulation operations to search and transform multimedia and other complex objects. As an evolutionary technology, the object/relational (OR) approach has inherited the transaction and performance-management features of relational as well as the flexible object-oriented models. Database designers can work with familiar tabular structures and data definition languages (DDLs) while assimilating new object-management possibilities.

The description of each of the above models namely is strictly conceptual. In real world implementation is a hybrid frame work of combining the appropriate features containing in any of those models. Depending on the size of the data to be handled and the operations to be undertaken, a choice of the DBMS package needs to be made. In general, the Hierarchical Data Model is considered the most restricted in terms of access with predefined relationship through tree structures. Network Model is regarded as fairly non-restrictive or flexible model and Relational Data Model is a non-structured data model which has formed basis for the advancement of object-relational data models and RDBMS of today.

3
DBMS (Database Management Systems)

3.1. DBMS CONCEPTS

Databases are referred as integrated collection of data. Libraries like any other organizations need to constantly add the new data to their databases modify or update or even delete the existing data and also enable users and staff access to data. This is termed as 'Database management' and in short DBMS. In library terms, the 'Database Management' is a controlled approach used for updating the library database and retrieving the information or data in a desired format from the same database. For the purpose, it requires a 'system' that manages the databases in accordance with the varying needs of users. The database management systems (DBMS) can exactly execute these operations for maintaining the database/s with the required software and helps to handle the data in larger quantities. Further, it resolves major issues in handling large data by controlling data redundancy thereby allowing flexibility in accessing data or information during the developmental stages of database.

DBMS is a set of programs or a software package used

to organize and manage data within the database. The DBMS can be thus defined as "a software package used for creation and maintenance of a database and BDBMS is (Bibliographic Database Management System) that performs the task of managing the library bibliographic database within the computer to facilitate the retrieval or access the stored data.

3.1.1. Characteristics

The DBMS functions are distinct from other data file structures. Though the data can be presented in rows / columns in tables or spread sheets, they cannot form the database. These files are containing data or information. A DBMS is not a data or data bank neither a means to access data, or a storing technique or a management information system (MIS) nor even an application. The following characteristics make the databases flexible to manipulate data and sharable to many.

- It is a set of programs and a software package.
- Putting data together in a structured manner so as to facilitate easy access, maintenance of information for quick retrieval.
- A DBMS is designed to structure the database in a way the data can be shared by all its users and facilitating retrieval. Each user will be able to access the database according to their requirements.
- A DBMS does not even eliminate data redundancy totally but reduces considerably if data input is taken care properly.
- The data organization and access/retrieval are two separate but integrated applications. DBMS facilitates users to deal (retrieve) with the data in abstract terms, i.e., without any reference to how the data is actually input, organized or stored.
- The people who works with a database are - database creators, administrators, clients (staff) and database users.

- The information residing in a database can be accessible in a varied formats or through reports. Most of the DBMSs are integrated with report writer program that elicits the data output in .csv or excel or even .doc formats. Presently the reports are being displayed in graphs and charts as many of DBMSs include a graphics component.

3.1.2. Objectives

A primary objective of a DBMS is to structure a database that facilitate to add, delete, modify the contents of the records, in the database and for the easy retrieval of information from the same.

- To avoid unnecessary duplication of data
- To ensure data consistency
- Enable rapid updating
- Facilitate concurrent use by more than one user
- Increasing control over the data
- Increase security of data
- Achieve independence of application programs and data
- Facilitate maintenance of Standards.
- The DBMS must be able to complex data relationships, control of redundancy and, facilitate generality in applications and ease of retrieval

3.1.3. DBMS Components

The major components of conventional DBMS are detailed hereunder -

Database : an organized collection of logically related data to meet the information needs of organizational users.

Repository : the centralized knowledgebase for all data definitions, data relationships, on-screen /report formats.

User interface : to facilitate client interaction as well as user interaction

CASE (Computer-aided software engineering) Tools : CASE tools are set of software application programs, which are used to automate SDLC (System Development Life Cycle) activities of any organization such as —

- The reach of target Analysis tools,
- Design tools,
- Project management tools,
- Database Management tools,
- Documentation tools etc.

These tools accelerate the development of project untill the target is reached and also helps to uncover flaws before moving to next stage of development.

DBMS Manager : The central program of the DBMS provides the ability to store, update and retrieve data. It also provides the ability to design the database and modify the same as and when desired.

DBMS software : aims to define, create, maintain and to provide controlled access to the database and to the repository.

DBMS Support Software : includes the following operations for the efficient functioning of managing data.

- **Load Programs :** Helps to build new databases and reorganize physical storage of existing databases.
- **Unload Programs :** Helps to extract data from database for use in other systems
- **Database and reorganization :** making certain kinds of definitional changes
- **Purge Programs :** Remove unwanted records
- **Validate/Check Programs :** Ensures related records can find each, other successfully and helps prevent redundancy.
- **Database Dumps :** Enable programmers and

database technicians to view data in its raw form.

- **Backup and Recovery Facilities** : Ensures important data is saved until an update cycle is completed successfully and to restore the damaged pans of the database in case of failure. On the whole it removes inconsistencies, validate and regain the data in the event of failure.
- **Exchange Programs** : To import and export data into a standard format for exchange.

Data Administrators : Persons responsible for the overall information resources of an organization

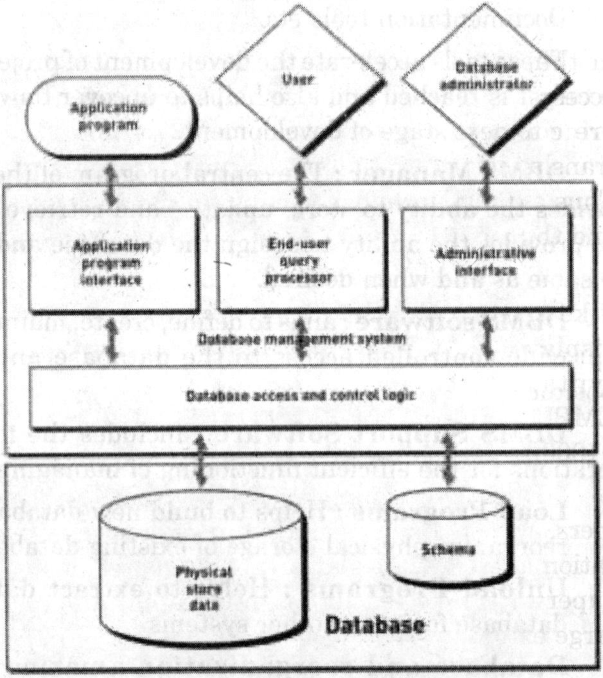

Fig. 3.1. Important Components of DBMS
(*Source* : SatzingerandBurd, 2006)

System Developers : professionals to work with system analysts and programmers to design application programs etc.

End Users : are the people using the DBMS at operational level to add, delete and modify the data and also the people who receive information

Data Definition Language (DDL) : provides the meanings to describe the data to the DBMS. This includes - data elements and their attributes; records and relationships between records. The use of the DDL results in a "Schema" which gives complete picture of the database and the rules by which it is to be accessed and updated.

Data Manipulation Language (DML) : provides the syntax to be used in any standard programming language to navigate the database and thus find the records required.

Host Language Interface : enables programs written in the Standard Computer Programming Languages to access and manipulate data in the database. Instructions are coded into the program as a part of the DML and translated by the host language interface into chunks of code. Thus a link is established between the application program and the DBMS.

Query Language : helps to communicate with DBMS (like the English language) to access data that will be displayed on the terminal easily and quickly. The query syntax is generally simple. Example: "DISPLAY EMPLOYEE - NAME, EMPLOYEE-ADDRESS. IF SALARY >10000.

Data Dictionary : a facility that enables programmers, system analysts and end-users to document an application as well as its supporting databases. It simplifies the paperwork involved in designing application system to a large extent.

Report Writer : closely associated to the query language. The query language enable display to the terminal, the 'report writer' produces the output or hard copy (paper) reports. Report Writer saves time and money for both the user and the programming staff

3.1.4. DBMS Formats

The information can be retrieved from the database in a variety of formats. They are – 1) File formats in which the data is stored as records 2) Query files and 3) Output formats. Database files store data in a structured format that are organized into tables and fields. These database file extensions depend on the software used. The important file extensions for databases are Microsoft Access (ACCDB), Dbase (.DBF); Foxpro (.DBC); Oracle Database configuration file (.ORA). Most of the database management systems constituting a report writer program that generate the report in hard or softcopy. Some DBMSs include even a graphics component that enables the output information in the form of graphs and charts.

3.1.5. Database Development Process

DBMS deals with the structural development of database, organization of data, storage and retrieval of information. The development of database initiates with understanding of content in an information system, information system architecture (ISA), selection of data model and end users. Sowa & Zachman (1992) listed the key components of ISA – data; processes; network, people; events and points in time and reasons. Information engineering is the key concept, which refers to the top-down planning to integrate the individual system components and their relations as per the objectives of the system.

The development of information system is cyclic and dynamic process. This is also called SDLC (Systems Development Life Cycle). Usually teams of information system professionals, database designers, domain experts together participate in developing the system.

The following figure illustrates the logical steps involved in the development of database management systems.

Data Investigation

- Initially at this stage - the nature of data and its use are to be identified

Initiation and Planning

- Planning process initiates with identifying strategic planning factors, objectives and development

Analysis

- Analyzing the situation to determine the requirements, structuring the system to meet these requirements

Data Modeling

- To adopt a conceptual model that reflects the real-world concepts.

Database Design

- Logical database design - transform the conceptual data model into a standard relations based data model and then designing the computer program including input and out put formats, transactions, queries, reports etc.
- Physical database design deals with programs viable to hardware, software including OS and networks

Database Implementation

- The internal or storage format is created as per the DBMS data model. Further the programs written to install and run the database will be tested to assess the performance in the system.

Database Monitoring and Tuning

- Once the database is in operation, it should be subjected to regular monitoring in order to detect any inefficiencies, errors or omissions. Changes in the environment may also be incorporated as the situation warranted.

Development

- Most of the databases implemented in the system lays foundation for subsequent development of the information system.

Fig. 3.2. DBMS Development Process

3.2. DATABASE DESIGN

The database design is the most important step in the process of developing database where its success relies on. Wikipedia defines the term 'design' as "the creation of a plan or convention for the construction of an object or a system". Designing a database requires focus on functions and features of the database before implementation for the better performance of the database. The DBMS is involving in two separate but integrated aspects - files and applications, thus the database design also focus on these two aspects. The Application Design deals with the Interface between the human and the computer whereas the speed of access at the interface is highly dependent on the file design. The File Design is aimed at converting the conceptual model into a physical working model. The purpose of physical database design is to translate logical descriptions of data as per the specifications of storing, retrieving data. The following important factors that are to be considered before designing the file are mentioned here under.

- Operational purpose of the file(creation, storage and retrieval of information)
- Hardware that supports the operational purpose; Operating system (OS) and DBMS Software
- File activity means the frequency of access and the update of the file
- Sorting and indexing requirements
- File access & output requirements
- Cost factor
- Database structure
  - — To select a data type that can represent values, improve data integrity, support data manipulation and minimize storage space.
  - — Number and Name(s) of data fields
  - — Length of the each data field and type of data that each field will contain
  - — Whether there are subfields of a data field
  - — Whether the data field is repeatable
  - — Data volume
  - — Which fields need to be indexed and how to enter the data
  - — Should be able to handle /recover missing data
  - — Usage analysis

3.2.1. Logical Database Design

The logical database design implies transforming the conceptual data model or design into logical data model or logical database design that can be implemented on a selected DBMS according to user needs for data sharing, flexibility and ease of access. Further, the logical design includes input/output formats, those review the performance of programs related to transactions, displays, queries and reports.

3.2.2. Physical Database Design

The physical database design outlines the physical structure of the DBMS process and organization of database in computer storage. It includes programs to process transactions, management information and decision support reports. The information requirements of the physical file and database design are –

- Normalized relations, including volume estimates
- Definitions of each attribute
- The way (where and when) to enter, modify and retrieve data
- Specifying the response time, data security, back up, data recovery and integrity etc
- Description of DBMS applied for implementation.

The following factors influence the effective performance of the physical design of database -

- Selecting the storage format (Data type) that can save storage space
- Selecting data structures (indexes, database architectures)
- Grouping attributes from the logical model to physical structure
- Arranging similarly structured records in secondary memory to enable them to store, update and retrieve effectively
- Primary memory is in hard disks

- Preparing strategies for handling queries against the database

Physical Record is a group of fields stored in adjacent memory locations in DBMS for retrieval purpose. The design of physical record should be able to handle efficient use of secondary storage and sequencing of fields on which the data processing speed depends on. The use of secondary storage is influenced by the size and page of the physical records and its structure. The number of records per page is limiting factor and for the effective use of RAM in the host computer system. Further, it enables the performance of data processing.

3.2.3. File Organization, Indexing and Controls

All the database files in a system are connected and link to one piece of data with another piece by means of pointer. A pointer is a field of data that can be used to locate a related field or record of data.

A physical file is an element of secondary memory allocated for storing records. Most of DBMS store data in OS (operating system files) i.e. a database (named) file is listed in the directory of C drive of the system. The structure of physical storage in ORACLE is table space. There may be several such table spaces in use in information systems. It may be for temporary workspace; database recovery; user transaction etc.

A file organization is a technique for physically arranging records of a file on secondary storage, whereas relational DBMS do not require file organization. The file organization however should consider the following factors – faster retrieval of data; processing data input and maintenance of transactions; efficient use of storage space; data recovery; minimal file reorganization; accommodating growth and data security.

Sequential file : in sequential file organization, the records in a file are in sequence as per the prime key value. There will not be wastage of space. Retrieval of data on prime key is very speedy, but not practical to retrieve at random even on prime key. Other keys require scanning of entire file. Deletion of records create space, (Cancellation of old unsupplied titles and its bibliographic records when deleted by the library leaves a space in the database occupying storage space) thus require reorganizing, whereas addition of records and their modification require file rewriting.

Indexed file : in an indexed file organization, it is no matter the records are stored sequentially or inconsequentially. An index is created that allows the application software to locate individual records by matching the index entry with key value. An index can point to unique records (a primary key index)such as unique ID. The primary index may or may not use primary key. Similarly, the secondary index may or may not use unique field across the rows of the table. The most powerful capabilities of an indexed file organization is the ability to create multiple indexes. Example, libraries maintain author, title subject indexes pointing to the same set of books and journals.

Hashed file organization : is a storage system in which the address for each record is determined using hashed algorithms. Hashed algorithm converts a primary key value into a relative record number/address. Hashed index table – a file organization that uses hashing to map a key into a location in an index. There is a pointer to the actual data record matching the hash key.

3.2.4. Design Features

The design of the database should be structurally, functionally feasible to implement and perform as per the objectives of the system. The figure 3.3 lists the design features in general, structural features, system-wise specifications, technical support features, features for integration and retrieval.

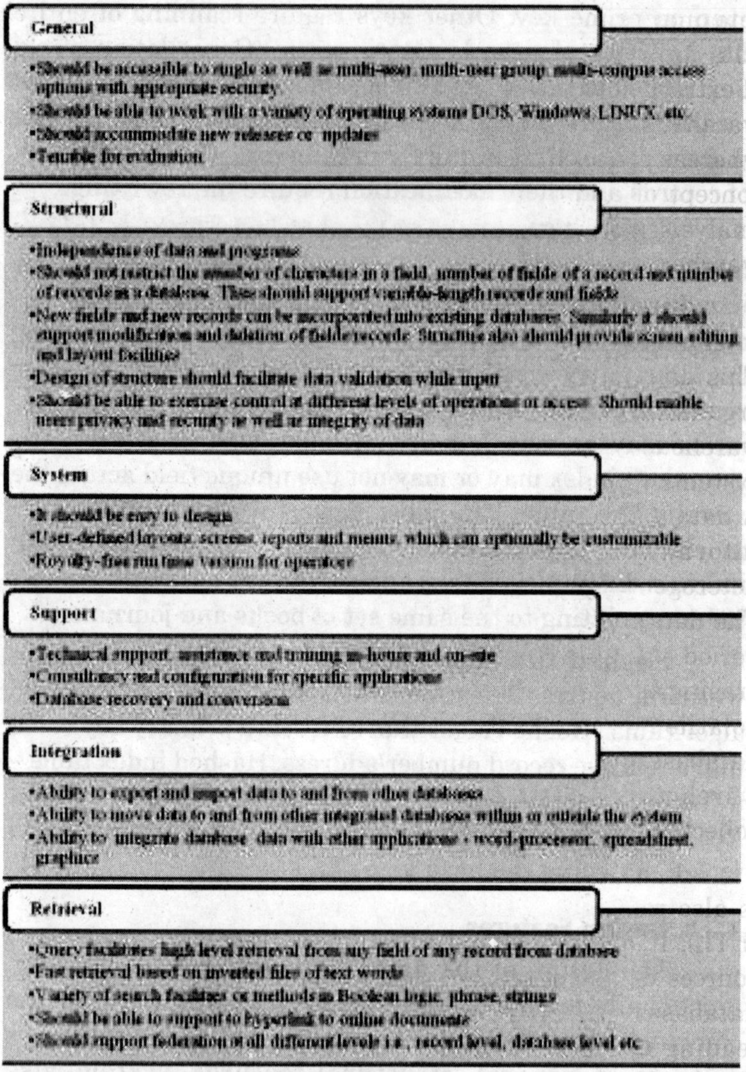

Fig. 3.3. Design Features

3.3. DATA WAREHOUSING

Data warehousing is the process of centralizing or aggregating data from multiple sources into one common repository. This process of compiling and organizing data into one common database should occur for easy retrieval of data for any purpose i.e., data mining which is the process of extracting meaningful data from that database. The data warehousing stage is purely managed by system engineers, whereas the data mining and retrieval is done by users. The concept of data warehousing is now a significant in data analysis and online analytical processing. The word "data warehouse" was first coined by Bill Inmon in 1990.

Inmone defined the term as "a subject oriented, integrated, time-variant, and non-volatile collection of data. This data helps analysts to take informed decisions in an organization". These four characteristics distinguish data warehouses from other data systems like relational database systems, transaction processing systems, and file systems. A data warehouse is 'subject oriented' because it provides information around a subject and 'integrated' from heterogeneous sources (relational databases, flat files etc.). The data collected will be identified with a particular time period –'time-variant' and the newly added data will not be erasing or overwriting on the previous one, so it is also 'non-volatile'. Therefore, the changes occurred in operational databases will not be reflected in data warehouse. The data warehousing has three–tier architecture connecting the collected data to the client as shown in figure 3.4.

1. Extraction and Transformation : This process is also referred as extraction, transformation and loading (ETL). In this process the data collected from the different sources like internal database of the organization, external databases from various departments of the institute, other leading educational libraries in the city, etc. is refined. Further the collected data will be transformed into standard format before loading into the warehouse.

2. Connective Tier : comprising of data source rules, the programs applied for the transformation, the data structure, contents and meta-data.

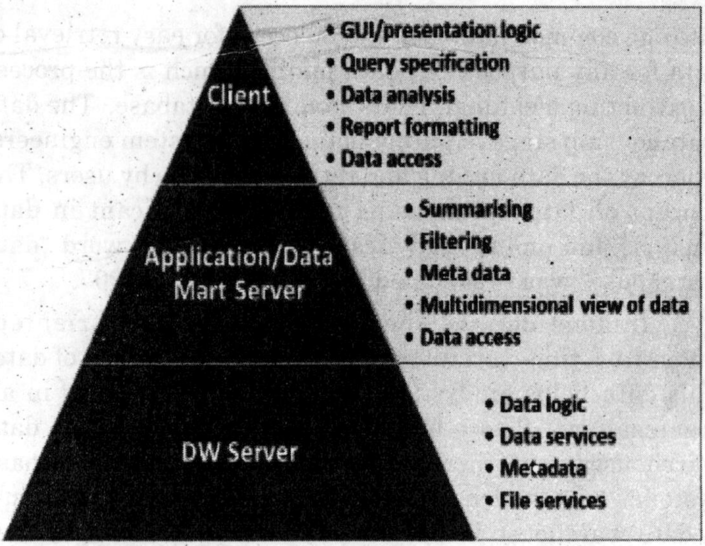

Fig. 3.4. Data warehouse 3 tier operations

3. Data Access and Retrieval Stage : OLAP tool allows user to generate queries while reporting tool helps to produce canned, graphic intensive, sophisticated reports.

A data warehouses gives comprehensive data in a wider perspective and also provide Online Analytical Processing (OLAP) tools to help in interactive and effective analysis of data. The data mining functions such as - association, clustering, classification, prediction can be integrated with OLAP for the effective operations. The data warehouse is also a database, but maintained separately from the operational database. This contains historical data without making frequent updates in it, but helps to integrate the diversity of application systems, to organize, understand, and also use their historical data to analyze for taking strategic decisions. The operational database maintains current data; support concurrent processing of multiple transactions, control and recovery mechanisms; handles the workloads such as searching, indexing, etc., whereas the data warehouse queries are complex. It presents a general form of data.

The operational database systems are called 'online transaction processing' (OLTP) systems as they are covering day to-day operations of an organization, whereas the data warehouse systems can organize and present data in various formats in order to accommodate the diverse needs of varied users. These systems are known as 'online analytical processing' (OLAP) systems. The distinguishing features between OLTP and OLAP mentioned by Sharma (2009) are illustrated in the following figure:

Features	*OLTP* *Operational Database*	*OLAP* *Data warehouse Systems*
Users & system orientation	• Customer-oriented • Used for regular transaction such as issue of books, query processing	• Planning/decision-making oriented • Used by knowledge workers- managers, executives, and analysts.
Data contents	• Manages current data and run the day-to-day business operations of the institution library	• Manages historical data in huge quantities, provide tools for summarization, aggregation, and stores and manages information at different levels of granularity
Database design	• Adopts an entity-relationship (ER) data model and an application-oriented design	• Adopts a star or snowflake model and a subject-oriented database design.
View	• Focuses on the current data within the department, without referring to historical data or data in different organizations	• Spans multiple versions of a database schema, due to the evolutionary process of an organization. Also deal with information that originates from different organizations, integrating from many data stores. The huge volume of data are stored on multiple storage media.
Access Patterns	• Consisting mainly of short, atomic transactions. Such a system requires concurrency control and recovery mechanisms	• Read-only operations (mostly data warehouses store historical rather than up to-date information), although many could be complex queries.

Fig. 3.5. Contrasting features of OLTP and OLAP Systems

Data Warehouse tools and utilities that improve the quality of data are given below - (*http://www.tutorialspoint.com/dwh/dwh_overview.htm*)

- Data extraction includes aggregating the data from multiple heterogeneous sources.
- Data cleaning means locating and correcting the errors in data.
- Data transformation involves converting the data to warehouse format.
- Data loading encompasses sorting, building indices/partitions, checking integrity summarizing, consolidating etc.
- Refreshing is updating from data sources to warehouse.

The significant applications of data warehousing are - information processing, analytical processing, and data mining.

- Information processing of the data stored in it such as - querying, statistical analysis and reporting using crosstabs, tables, charts, or graphs.
- A data warehouse supports analytical processing of the information stored in it by means of basic OLAP operations.
- Data mining supports knowledge discovery by finding hidden patterns and associations, constructing analytical models, performing classification and prediction. These mining results can be presented using the visualization tools.

Data warehousing – Library Applications

Library database operations have gone beyond just maintaining the bibliographic as well the transactional records of books and other conventional and non-conventional material. Moreover libraries are providing their users the online facilities such as searching, reservations, renewals, recommendations and browsing of e-journals and also downloading of full text articles, etc. Since libraries are involved in handling data coming from these various integrated operations and piled up over the period as well as the maintenance of digital resources and digital libraries, the data warehousing concept has become equally significant along with operational databases.

1. Libraries do not require much storage space to maintain their e-catalogue or store their bibliographic cards or even for their circulation transactions. As analyzed by Sharma (2009), the library with 50,000 members, each occupy 200 kilobytes then the storage requirement would be 10 GB. If a circulation record is using 40 bytes per item and if 1000 item borrowing happens per day then the storage requirement would be 40 KB. Over a year this would accumulate to about 10 GB.
2. The emergence of digital libraries with bibliographic records and full text resources, images, multimedia files, having integrated from different sources gave an opportunity to obtain their usage reports through data warehousing applications.
3. A library will be gaining benefit by managing larger databases, data warehousing and applying data mining in instances such as aggregations, electronic referencing and searching through classification of library content. Data warehouses are the accepted for these kind of operations and quickest retrieval of information from large quantities of data.

3.4. WEB (DATA) SECURITY

The data is highly valuable not only in terms of cost of its production or acquisition, maintenance and dissemination but also its research value and use as well as re-use value. Libraries store and maintain their meta-data (about their resources), data resources in their servers or server spaces for their user's access. Thus it is important to secure the stored data from the following threats -

- Unauthorized people's access
- Accidental or intentional destruction
- Natural disasters could damage the information system entirely or partially i.e. OS, Storage units, networks, databases etc.
- Damage due to infection or corruption of information
- Improper handling of database
- Damage of data due to hardware (server, storage or backup devices) problems.
- Loss of data during migration of data to another application software or hardware.
- Virus, malware

In the context of online information processing systems run by libraries as well by the non-library agencies, and the acquisition of web resources, the terms - security, privacy or confidentiality can be perceived in two dimensions – data security, web security. The strategic storage security is essential for maintaining applications, databases, file systems and server operating systems in a secured data environment. Most of the data now is being accessed from World Wide Web through internet. So the web security is considered important in the context of secured data or information systems. Moreover, the recent trends such as - wide spread of digital libraries, the data mining operations in business as well as information industries and other areas, business and research collaboration activities, electronic commerce trends in are gaining more security concerns than ever.

It was necessitated to create more security in certain sensitive zones for the effective and safe usage of web based information viz. encryption, secure protocols, clients, servers, payment systems, to maintain confidentiality, privacy and also for digital rights management.

The secure systems viz. access control, secure operating systems, secure data-management systems, and secure networks are to be maintained to manage electronic as well as digital libraries.

For building secure information systems, it is essential to understand the security requirements; then frame a policy to design an appropriate model and develop the system accordingly and test its functionality as per the requirements.

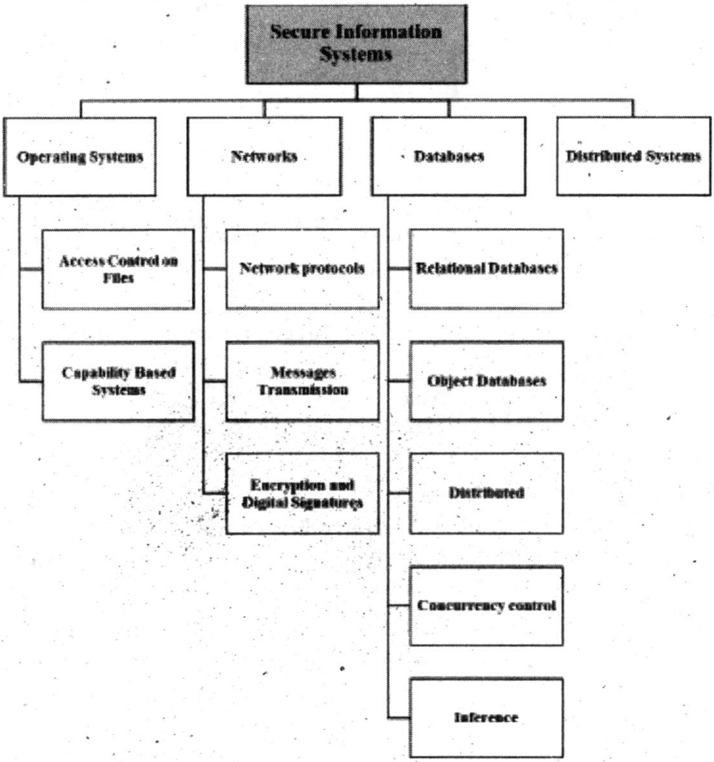

Fig. 3.6. Secure Information Systems
(*Source*: Bhavani Thuraisingham, 2008)

Data Security

Covers data integrity which means the accuracy of data and processes involved to maintain quality of information. The data quality depends on the authenticity, applying the techniques of real-time processing and fault tolerance (ability to recover from faults occurred whether accidentally or maliciously.

Data Security Measures : The popular computer magazine 'computer world' listed few measures to secure the valuable data

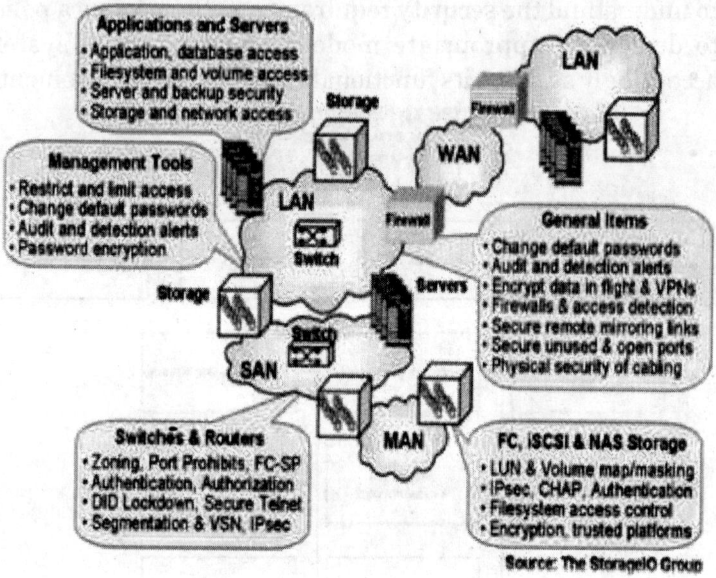

Fig. 3.7. Secured Systems
(*Source* : http://www.computerworld.com/article/2546352/ data-center/top-10-ways-to-secure-your-stored-data.html)

- To implement a tiered data protection and security model that includes multiple perimeter rings of defense to counter the applicable threats. Multiple layers of defense can isolate and protect data.
- To apply both logical and physical securities in the system. The logical security (authorization, authentication, encryption and passwords) also covers securing networks with firewalls, running antispyware and virus-detection programs on servers and network-addressed storage systems, whereas the physical security (restricted access, locks on server, storage and networking cabinets) represents access controls,

design of database allows complex structures.

Control of application of data redundancy is achieved, since the design allows complex structures. As a result, databases developed are more comprehensive than the conventional files. However, fewer data elements that need repetition in different files may be sufficient to satisfy different application.

Changes to data definitions can take place easily without going through the entire process of reprogramming. This is due to the data independence. As a result, system maintenance becomes easier. The system also gets more response to the user's changing needs.

Since DBMS avoids redundancy and duplication of records or entries, it saves storage space, which is important especially in the case of large databases.

It is possible to reduce update errors and elimination of inconsistencies through data validation.

Automated enforcement of relationships between records is possible when an application program is scientifically designed, whereas it is a complex and error-prone procedure in a traditional system.

Data Security

— A DBMS can restrict access (authentication) to certain parts of the database to users and facilitate at specified levels.

— Control of overlapping updates and queries, when more than one user is accessing or updating the database at the same time. If a user is trying to examine the record while another is updating the exactly the same record, DBMS prevent this by alerting user automatically "locked record" or "record in use" and avoid misinformation of data which could occur.

DBMS should facilitate restart and recovery of the data

change of key-code or door-lock combinations regularly, informing only those who need access. Some more precautions like change of default passwords fixed at installation and on an ongoing basis. Likewise, restrict access to management tools to those entitled for these operations.

- To identify the weak links in data-movement processes and correct those deficiencies.
- Application of data-discovery tools can be used to identify sensitive data that may not be adequately protected.
- Data backup should compulsorily be maintained at different location lest there not be any data loss in case of any un-eventualities
- During migration of data electronically to avoid losing tapes it can be transmitted over a public or private networks.
- Data encryption is the popularly followed technology and while implementation it needs the understanding of the level or depth of encryption, considering the potential effect on performance and interoperability of the environment.

Web Security

Web security includes wide range of threats from viruses, Trojan horses to unauthorized intrusions, access control violations, integrity violations, identity thefts, privacy violations, inference problems, privacy violations and insider threats.. Some threats are even categorized as cyber-threats, network threats, operating systems threats, middleware, e-payment systems.

Implementing access controls at different levels will resolve the issue to some extent in case of web databases i.e. individual researcher level, institutional user level, administrator level, super administrator level etc., yet enforcing access control at OS levels are harder as it is at file level. Selecting strong passwords, change of passwords at regular intervals, multi-level verifications, multi-device verifications, installing fire-walls, introduction of biometric verification system, cryptographic verification etc. would arrest some of the threats.

While data encryption is a popular issue, it is just one of many techniques and technologies that can be used to implement a tiered data-security strategy. Steps to secure data involve understanding applicable threats, aligning appropriate layers of defense and continual monitoring of activity logs, are needed in actual data environment.

3.5. DATABASE IMPLEMENTATION

In this implementation phase, the hardware, the DBMS software and application programs should be readily installed. This stage includes coding, testing of database processing programs, debugging, until the software is ready to deliver. Further the documentation, preparation of training materials and installation of actual databases in the real environment will take place in implementation by creating databases, tables, views, user authorizations or converting data etc.

The database contents can be loaded interactively or batch mode, using a variety of methods and devices.

- Customized user programs
- Database interface programs for data related operations
- Conversion programs that can import the data from varied file structures using batch programs or database utility.

The implementation phase is always crucial in the database development. It was usually occupying much time earlier, which has been reducing with the advent of sophisticated application generators and debugging tools. The implementation program is a continuous process of evaluation and betterment.

change of key-code or door-lock combinations regularly, informing only those who need access. Some more precautions like change of default passwords fixed at installation and on an ongoing basis. Likewise, restrict access to management tools to those entitled for these operations.

- To identify the weak links in data-movement processes and correct those deficiencies.
- Application of data-discovery tools can be used to identify sensitive data that may not be adequately protected.
- Data backup should compulsorily be maintained at different location lest there not be any data loss in case of any un-eventualities
- During migration of data electronically to avoid losing tapes it can be transmitted over a public or private networks.
- Data encryption is the popularly followed technology and while implementation it needs the understanding of the level or depth of encryption, considering the potential effect on performance and interoperability of the environment.

Web Security

Web security includes wide range of threats from viruses, Trojan horses to unauthorized intrusions, access control violations, integrity violations, identity thefts, privacy violations, inference problems, privacy violations and insider threats.. Some threats are even categorized as cyber-threats, network threats, operating systems threats, middleware, e-payment systems.

Implementing access controls at different levels will resolve the issue to some extent in case of web databases i.e. individual researcher level, institutional user level, administrator level, super administrator level etc., yet enforcing access control at OS levels are harder as it is at

2. Technical complexity : DBMS requires substantial knowledge and experience. Even minor changes in the design may result in large differences in performance. Most of the technical work needs to be undertaken by the database experts. The application analysts must also have background knowledge of details of physical storage, retrieval, updating, etc.

3. Need for increased staff : Installing DBMS warrants skilled man-power such as a database administrator (DBA) and various technical staff. In-house staff need to be trained but usually technical expert's support is needed to train the staff and direct the implementation of the first DBMS application.

4. Inefficient resource usage : DBMS is generalized in nature. It is designed to operate with reasonable efficiency over a wide range of data structures and applications.

5. Handling large volumes : DBMS need a vast amount of software and its application programs and customization for the best applications in automation. The resource usage becomes inefficient in the case of larger transactions.

When the library shifts from one LIS software to another, if it is built around a compatible RDBMS adhering to standards, the data migration will be easier, secure without incurring any data loss and the bibliographic database is secure. The RDBMS applications for libraries, though incur heavy initial costs, it is highly significant and recommendable, in view of the advantages in handling library data or documents in larger quantities.

facility to minimize damage occurring due to power failures, human errors, and hardware failure or software problems.

- It will improve the data sharing across applications, departments, and organizations.
- The very purpose of DBMS is sharing data between different applications by defining clearly the relationship between data. Complex relationships are easier to implement than with traditional life systems since there is much common data floating between applications. This will not only avoid the redundancy and duplication, but also reduce the storage space.
- Data sharing demands standardization of format through which the data is shared. So the DBMS enforces standards in formats and procedures. Thus improves the quality of data.
- Data accessibility can be improved, when the user interaction or responsiveness increases.
  - — Data is input in machine readable form
  - — The data is structured including logical connections between relational elements
  - — Software is applied for data retrieval
  - — The software is flexible enough to apply selection of variety of data values and conditions.
  - — Ability to develop sophisticated applications

3.7.2. Limitations

DBMS have some demerits along with its merits. The following are a few:

1. High initial costs : The initial costs of selecting, acquiring and installing DBMS software can be high. If new staff needs to be hired, the costs shoot up further. Usually the development of the first application will be a highly expensive program

3.6. DATABASE ADMINISTRATION

After implementation, during the operational phase, the system may require changes and generate maintenance activities. Doke and Swanson (1991) described the following three types of maintenance activities.

1. Corrective maintenance in response to system errors
2. Adaptive maintenance due to changes in the business environment
3. Perfective maintenance to enhance the system

In the process of development, changing operational environment and requirements, obsolete processes and technological advancements might induce revamping the system. The situation results in a great effort, beginning of SDLC and high costs. Computer Assisted Systems Engineering (CASE) helps to produce better operational systems within short span of time at reasonable cost, with their standardized procedures.

3.7. DBMS ADVANTAGES AND LIMITATIONS

In the era of computation, the DBMS approach is considered advantageous for the information processing, storage and retrieval process as their data structures are extremely complex and highly time consuming, when compared to traditional file processing system and also the manual print processes. Continuous research and efforts are made to overcome the limitations that are coming across while implementing the DBMS in real operations. The advantages and limitations in general are described underneath.

3.7.1. Advantages

- The DBMS offers flexibility for structuring data and simultaneously forcing discipline in design. It forces an ordered and consistent file design methodology, as opposed to sequential file system.
- Complex data relationships can be maintained as the

design of database allows complex structures.

- Control of application of data redundancy is achieved, since the design allows complex structures. As a result, databases developed are more comprehensive than the conventional files. However, fewer data elements that need repetition in different files may be sufficient to satisfy different application.
- Changes to data definitions can take place easily without going through the entire process of reprogramming. This is due to the data independence. As a result, system maintenance becomes easier. The system also gets more response to the user's changing needs.
- Since DBMS avoids redundancy and duplication of records or entries, it saves storage space, which is important especially in the case of large databases.
- It is possible to reduce update errors and elimination of inconsistencies through data validation.
- Automated enforcement of relationships between records is possible when an application program is scientifically designed, whereas it is a complex and error-prone procedure in a traditional system.
- Data Security
  - A DBMS can restrict access (authentication) to certain parts of the database to users and facilitate at specified levels.
  - Control of overlapping updates and queries, when more than one user is accessing or updating the database at the same time. If a user is trying to examine the record while another is updating the exactly the same record, DBMS prevent this by alerting user automatically "locked record" or "record in use" and avoid misinformation of data which could occur.
- DBMS should facilitate restart and recovery of the data

4
DBMS/RDBMS Software & Technology

4.1. INTRODUCTION

Database management systems (DBMSs) are highly significant in software development and industry, since the databases, data communications, as well as management systems forms the basis for constructing several core applications in all most all industries, government as well as non-government agencies.

- It handles or programs complex applications in efficient and cost effective way
- It is helpful to share data among multiple applications and multiple users according to some standards by creating specialized user-oriented languages
- It provides standard interfaces for the data communications programs.
- It helps to manage databases without the programming skills
- It will be able to undertake data transfer and other applications from one vendors software to another and even one OS to another with ease

The term 'database management systems software' denotes a set of programs designed for creating databases and managing the information stored in them for sharing retrieval. DBMS, or database software packages are even referred as tools used for structuring and organizing information for the purpose of retrieval. There were several DBMS, RDBMS software, developed for organizing business and industrial data and databases. Blasgen (1982) mentioned in general the services offered by DBMS.

- User view of data – describing the way data appears to user
- Data language – allowing to retrieve, update, insert, and delete data from database
- Transaction management – providing the execution control over the database i.e. determining the level of concurrent users, recovery options and specifying with atomicity of database operations

The advantageous features of the DBMS Software are evolved from time to time with an increasing efficiency towards data control, security and various user centric applications.

4.2. EVOLUTION & DEVELOPMENT OF DATABASE (MANAGEMENT) SYSTEMS

In the initial years, most of the applications were in batch mode using data that was sequentially stored as flat files on magnetic tape. The data or records are maintained as files and were organized in serial way. The disk storage was exceedingly expensive and less integrated and inflexible. During 1960s the decreasing costs of disk storage lead to the emergence of DBMS software for managing data. The early DBMS systems were structured in accordance to the data to be stored or retrieved. Data stored in database records were linked to related data via "pointers". (i.e. hierarchical and network databases). The application software was used only for input and output operations. Thus there was every possibility of data redundancy, duplication, no data independence but access delay. The data was then referred as 'data files' or 'data sets'. The term "database" came in use during late 1960s. Storing data in tables became possible gradually which reduced data redundancy proving more flexible for data access. Recognizing the major role played by DBMS products, the IEEE Annals of the History of Computing published 2 special issues sponsored by the Software Industry Special Interest Group of the Computer History Museum (formerly the Software History Center). They focused on the products, companies, and people who designed, programmed, and sold mainframe DBMS software products during 1960s and 1970s. The second issue was on the relational DBMS products, which were developed during the 1970s and came to prominence during the 1980s and 1990s and so on. The initial DBMSs though were hierarchical and network-based systems as per their structure and retrieval capability. The companies responded to the development of relational DBMSs and continued to focus on RDBMS products applications of query oriented usages and transaction-processing applications.

Database management systems were developed to surpass the limitations of file processing systems applied in computing. Though the personal computers (PCs) do support databases to some extent, its limitations in processing the data tend to development of DBMS products in parallel to the PCs revolution.

- Initially in 1960's, file processing systems were prominent, but some random access files were used to allow the users access to any record without searching serially. By late 60's the efforts began to standardize the database tasks.
- 70's were predominant with first generation DBMS with hierarchical and network data systems. They were popular database models widely used, but it was considered difficult to access data. There was very limited data independence.

- In stage 3 the application programs were isolated from the hardware changes. It facilitated reduction in data redundancy, enabled to retrieve multiple logical files from the same data. 1980s was very important in the evolution of database systems as the relation model developed by E.F. Codd and others in 70s became widespread and achieved commercial acceptance. This model is recognized as 2nd generation DBMS. The structured query language was used for retrieval in this model and thus providing easy of access to nonprofessional users.
- The next stage during 1990s is marked for technological advancements such as client/server computing, data warehousing, internet applications etc. The data was more structured, and also including multimedia. In this decade, object oriented databases were designed to meet the exceedingly complex data. Software provides a logical as well as physical data independence. Moreover, with the invention of microcomputers and integrated circuits the costs of computers came down at the same time more facilities were included increasing the processing speed.
- In 2000s multiple database could be compiled and maintained without raising costs though communications, storage, complexities were increasing. The data privacy and security aspects were becoming significant. There was a consistent development of universal servers and the internet applications. Moreover these databases were designed to provide answers to different forms of queries making the retrieval of information highly easy.

All through the database evolution, apparently there was a greater need to achieve independence between the data and programs; to manage the complex data types and structures; to provide easier access to the users who are unaware of database technologies or skills.

The development of data files to the present stage of databases came through several evolutionary stages of technological advancements as illustrated in figure 4.1.

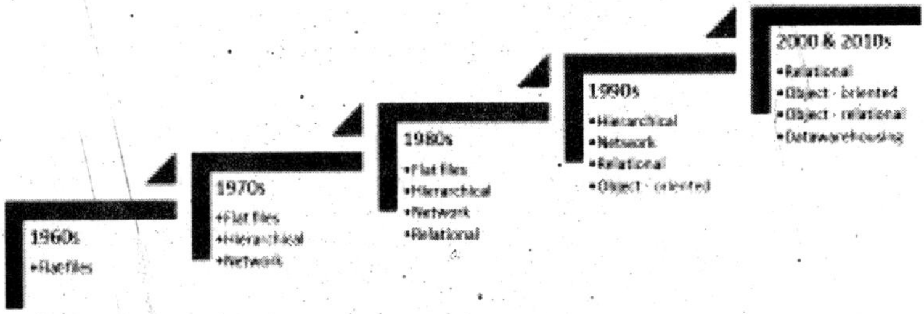

Fig. 4.1. Evolution of Database Systems

There were thousands of database management systems and lakhs of people using them for various purposes over the period of evolution. Some applications are limited for certain types of data operations, while certain software confined for inventories. This kind of software are also used for managing some flexible operations in administration, banking, personnel and accounts divisions, whereas some are designed for meeting the information storage, search and retrieval functions in several disciplines, contexts. Some popular DBMS/RDBMS software are described in the following section.

4.3. POPULAR DBMS, RDBMS SOFTWARE

The popular software widely applied to carryout database management functions partially or completely are - DB2, Dbase, Fox Pro, Microsoft Access, and FileMaker Pro and the server solutions like MySQL, Microsoft SQL Server and Oracle. Each software or tool has been developing its features over the period overcoming its limitations. Most of these packages initially began with DOS programs and now working with the most sophisticated RDBMS environments.

4.3.1 FILEMAKER (http://www.filemaker.com/)

FileMaker Pro is the relational database application

product of FileMaker Inc. FileMaker began as an MS-DOS–based computer program named Nutshell - developed by Nashoba Systems of Concord, Massachusetts, in the early 1980s. It was evolved from a DOS application as Claris, a subsidiary of Apple Inc. and later developed for the Apple Macintosh. Since 1992 it began available for Microsoft Windows, Mac OS, and used in a cross-platform environment. It integrates a database engine with a graphical user interface (GUI) and security features, allowing users to modify the database by dragging new elements into layouts, screens, or forms. Though FileMaker server briefly ran on Linux up to version 7, it currently supports only Windows or OS X servers.

Current versions are: FileMaker Pro 14, FileMaker Pro Advanced 14, FileMaker Server 14, and FileMaker Go 14 for iPhone and iPad. A client version was released for iOS devices in July 2010. It was available in desktop, server, iOS and web-delivery configurations. FileMaker versions are easy to use; supports iPad and iPhone; and share with team; containing built-in reporting tools like - spreadsheet format, make eye-catching charts and easily build custom reports with a step-by-step assistant; data security and integrate with other data sources - such as SQL, ODBC/JDBC, XML, and more.

4.3.2. dBASE dBase http://www.dbase.com/

DBase is a microcomputer database management system (DBMS) that runs on a Windows with wide variety of applications. dBase was originally published by Ashton-Tate for microcomputer operating system CP/M in 1980, and later ported to Apple II and IBM PC computers running DOS. DBase is designed to manipulate relational databases. it was created by Wayne Ratliff and initially named the "Vulcan in 1978 and marketed it as DBase II. Later Ashton-Tate purchased it in 1980s. The subsequent versions of DBase III, III+ and DBase IV were used on 16-bit DOS platforms. Further versions like Visual DBase 5.5 and Visual DBase

5.7 also worked on 16-bit Windows platforms, whereas the Visual DBase 7.0, Visual DBase 7.5, dB2K and DBase Plus versions operate on 32-bit Windows.

A major upgrade was released as dBase III, and ported to a wider variety of platforms, adding UNIX, and VMS. Starting in the mid-1980s, several companies produced their own technically stronger variations on the dBase product and especially the dBase programming language e.g. FoxBASE+ (later renamed FoxPro), Clipper, and other so-called xBase products. The IBM shift toward SQL and Microsoft Windows put pressure on the makers of xBase products to invest in major improvements and to provide new capabilities. In spite of growing pressure to evolve, in the early 1990s xBase products constituted the leading database platform for implementing business applications. Borland purchased Ashton-Tate, Microsoft bought Fox Software, and Computer Associates acquired Nantucket.

Data storage format is widely supported by numerous database management systems for a wide variety of applications. The simple commands similar to natural language for data manipulation influenced many to use this software. Its file format of DBase is .dbf. Its flexible features made this software widely applicable. Techopedia described the following important features of dBase software. (https://www.techopedia.com/definition/1192/dbase)

- A just in time (JIT) compiler, which converts the source language into machine language
- A linker to create DBase applications (.exe files)
- A runtime engine installer for Web servers and machines that need to execute DBase runtime applications
- Preprocessors for reading the program source file and producing preprocessed files as output, which is fed into the compiler
- An integrated development environment with a command window and navigator

- Two-way graphical user interface (GUI) design tools, which possess the ability to switch back and forth between using a GUI design tool and a code editor
- The source code editor allows for the manual editing and entry of codes

4.3.3. FOXPRO https://en.wikipedia.org/wiki/Visual_FoxPro

FoxPro is both a database management system (DBMS) and a relational database management system (RDBMS), originally published by Fox Software and later taken over by Microsoft for MS-DOS, Windows, Macintosh, and UNIX. FoxPro was derived from FoxBase (Fox Software, Perrysburg, Ohio), from dBase III (Borland), then dBase II (Ashton Tate). FoxPro extensively supports multiple relationships between multiple DBF files (tables). However it lacks transactional processing. Visual FoxPro is a data-centric, object-oriented, procedural, programming language produced by Microsoft. It is derived from FoxPro (originally known as FoxBASE) which was developed by Fox Software beginning in 1984 containing the fastest PC-based database engine available at the time. Fox Technologies merged with Microsoft in 1992, after which the software acquired the prefix "Visual" and further features.

- The database engine known as the 'Microsoft Jet Database Engine' was used by Microsoft Access. Though the final version, (FoxPro 2.6) worked on all platforms Mac OS, DOS, Windows, and UNIX: Visual FoxPro 3.0, the first "Visual" version, reduced platform support to only Mac and Windows, and later versions confined their support to Windows only.
- Visual FoxPro originated as a member of the class of languages commonly referred to as "xBase" languages, which have syntax based on the dBase programming language.

- Visual FoxPro, commonly abbreviated as VFP, is tightly integrated with its own relational database engine, which extends FoxPro's xBase capabilities to support SQL query and data manipulation. Visual FoxPro is relatively easy to learn and fast for developing reusable code. Programs can be written to access a FoxPro database or as well as to connect to such databases as SQL Server and Oracle.
- Unlike most database management systems, Visual FoxPro is a full-featured, dynamic programming language that does not require the use of an additional general-purpose programming environment.
- It can be used to write not just traditional "fat client" applications, but also middleware and web applications.

4.3.4. IBM DB2 IBM http://www-01.ibm.com/software/data/db2/

DB2 is a relational database management system (DBMS) from IBM in 1983 to run on the MVS operating system. A distributed version released on OS/2 in 1987 and the subsequent versions on wide variety of UNIX, Linux and Windows platforms. DB2 Editions include the - DB2Workgroup; DB2 Workgroup Unlimited; DB2 Enterprise Server Edition and DB2 UDB Data Warehouse Enterprise Edition (DWE). The DB2 UDB Data Warehouse Enterprise Edition includes business intelligence capabilities such as ET, data mining and online analytics. The DB2 Universal Database (UDB) Enterprise Server Edition (ESE) is one of the popular RDBMS. DB2 has APIs (Application Program Interface) for many languages such as -.NET; CLI; Java; Python; Perl; PHP; C++; C; PL/1; Cobol and Fortran etc.

4.3.5. MS ACCESS Access

Microsoft provides a wizard for creating a database

with MS Access database application. This is relational database management system (RDBMS) opted by small businesses firms for limited users. It can be easily run on a personal computer or server and provides an interface for designing simple databases, reports and data entry forms. This software has ODBC (Open Database Connectivity is a standard application programming interface (API) for accessing database management systems. It has capabilities for connecting to other data sources and take data from external databases and even from spreadsheets.

4.3.6. MICROSOFT SQL SERVER Microsoft https://www.microsoft.com/en-us/server-cloud/

Microsoft SQL Server is a comprehensive database software platform providing enterprise-class data management and integrated business intelligence (BI) tools. Microsoft has made efforts to push its SQLServer to the frontline to compete with Oracle and DB2. As the foundation of Microsoft's comprehensive data platform, SQL Server delivers breakthrough performance for critical applications, using in-memory technologies, faster insights from any data to any user in familiar tools like Excel, and a resilient platform for building, deploying, and managing solutions that span on-premises and cloud.

SQL Server is one of the leading industries with a remarkable performance in SQL Server 2014 and the next generation capabilities in SQL Server 2016. SQL Server 2014 enables high-performance, in-memory security technology across OLTP, transactions, queries data warehousing, analytics, faster transactions and 100x query performance, greater security, scalability, hybrid backup, disaster recovery across on-premises and cloud. It has been a consistent programming model across on-premises and cloud support hybrid infrastructures and scenarios.

4.3.7. MySQL http://www.mysql.com/ http://www.tutorialspoint.com/mysql/

MySQL is developed, marketed and supported by a Swedish company MySQL AB. MySQL is the most popular open source RDBMS software developed for web-based business applications and dynamic websites like e-commerce websites. MySQL is named after co-founder Monty Widenius's daughter 'My'. Many of the world's largest and fastest-growing organizations including Facebook, Google, Adobe, Alcatel Lucent and Zappos rely on MySQL to save time and money powering their high-volume Web sites, business-critical systems and packaged software. MySQL is developed, distributed, and supported by Oracle Corporation. MySQL is featured with the following advantages -

- Released under an open-source license. MySQL can be customizable. The open-source GPL license allows programmers to modify the MySQL software to fit their own specific environments
- MySQL is powerful program can handle a large subset functionality of the most expensive and powerful database packages.
- MySQL uses a standard form SQL data language.
- It works on several operating systems and with many languages including PHP, PERL, C, C++, JAVA, etc.
- Works very quickly with large data sets.
- Compatible to PHP, the most useful for web development.
- Supports larger databases, up to 50 million rows or more in a table.

W3 Consortium describes the features of MySQL as – 'It is database system that runs on a server and ideal for both small and large applications. This software uses standard SQL, complying on a number of platforms.

4.3.8. PostgreSQL http://www.postgresql.org/

PostgreSQL is an open source object-relational database system. It runs on all major operating systems, including Linux, UNIX (AIX, BSD, HP-UX, SGI IRIX, Mac OS X, Solaris, Tru64), and Windows. It is fully ACID compliant, has full support for foreign keys, joins, views, triggers, and stored procedures (in multiple languages). It includes most SQL: 2008 data types, including INTEGER, NUMERIC, BOOLEAN, CHAR, VARCHAR, DATE, INTERVAL, and TIMESTAMP. It also supports storage of binary large objects, including pictures, sounds, or video. It has native programming interfaces for C/C++, Java, .Net, Perl, Python, and Ruby etc. with documentation. Its features are -

- Multi-Version Concurrency Control (MVCC), point in time recovery
- Table spaces, asynchronous replication, nested transactions (save points),
- Online backups
- A sophisticated query planner/optimizer and write ahead logging for fault tolerance.
- It supports international character sets, multi-bit character encodings
- Unicode and it is locale-aware for sorting, case-sensitive and formatting.
- It can handle the larger quantities of data exceeding of 4 terabytes of data and in the number of concurrent users
- Some general PostgreSQL limits are included

Maximum Limit	*Value*
• Database Size	• Unlimited
• Table Size	• 32 TB
• Row Size	• 1.6 TB

• Field Size	• 1 GB
• Rows per Table	• Unlimited
• Columns per Table	• 250 - 1600 depending on column types
• Indexes per Table	• Unlimited

- SQL implementation compliant to international standards - ANSI-SQL: 2008 standard. It has full support for subqueries (including sub selects in the FROM clause), read-committed and serializable transaction isolation levels.
- PostgreSQL has a fully relational system catalogue that supports multiple schemas per database; its catalogue is also accessible through the Information Schema as defined in the SQL standard.
- Data integrity features include (compound) primary keys, foreign keys with restricting and cascading updates/deletes, checking constraints and unique constraints, and not null constraints.
- GiST (Generalized Search Tree) indexing system gets a wide array of different sorting and searching algorithms including B-tree, B+-tree, R-tree, partial sum trees, ranked B+-trees and many others. It also provides an interface which allows both the creation of custom data types as well as extensible query methods with which to search them.
- The events system is an inter-process communication system in which messages and events can be transmitted between clients using the LISTEN and NOTIFIES commands, thus allowing both simple peer to peer communication and advanced coordination on database events.
- PostgreSQL runs stored procedures in more than a dozen programming languages, including Java, Perl, Python, Ruby, Tcl, C/C++, and its own PL/pgSQL, which is similar to Oracle's PL/SQL. PostgreSQL includes a framework that allows developers to define

and create their own custom data types along with supporting functions..

- Best of all, PostgreSQL's source code is available under a liberal open source license: the PostgreSQL License allowing modifications, enhancements, or changes as per the requirements.
- Some ILS packages are working on PostgreSQL for maintaining their database operations e.g. NewGenLib ILS package

4.3.9. ORACLE

The Oracle RDBMS is also called as Oracle. It is produced and marketed by Oracle Corporation. This is an object-relational database management system. Software Development Laboratories (SDL) developed the original version of relational database management software in 1977 by Larry Ellison, Bob Miner and Ed Oates as non-commercial product and later renamed as Oracle and grown beyond the relational database servers. The name Oracle comes from code-name of a CIA-funded project. Oracle is an object-relational database (ORD), or object-relational database management system (ORDBMS), which is similar to a relational database, but with an object-oriented database model.

Oracle revolutionized the database management systems in the field of enterprising, with the release of Oracle Database 10, by introducing the industry's first self-management capabilities built right into the database kernel* (The kernel is a program that constitutes the central core of a computer operating system. It has complete control over everything that occurs in the system). Oracle provides several business intelligence tools, including a multidimensional database management system, database design, query & analysis tools, data mining products and an application server with a close integration to the database server and also Oracle OLAP.

Additionally the company offers application software for enterprise resource planning and customer-relationship management including areas such as financials, human resources, manufacturing marketing, sales and supply chain management. The important functions of ORACLE are described briefly as follows.

Features

- Oracle Server includes a DBMS
- Storing data in the database area
- Data recovery applications using appropriate optimization techniques
- Database Security and tasks allowed for certain users
- Consistency and data protection tasks including archiving & search mechanisms
- Communication and integrity of information, when databases are distributed in a network.

Database Administration (DBA)

The major database administrative functions are given below

- Installation & Creation of database
- Setting clients
- Data Security & Network management
- Storage, Backup and Recovery
- UNIX and Windows Database Administration
- Testing
- Data mining & Analytics

Advantages

- An Oracle RDBMS is an open system and complies with industry standards in force relating to data access languages (SQL).
- Oracle database supports any size from a few bytes to several gigabytes.

- Supports a large number of users access simultaneously minimizing the data access conflicts and guarantees simultaneous data.
- Oracle supports a client / server environment real. It allows dividing processing between the database server and client application programs.
- Oracle offers full safety features to control monitor access to data and its use.
- Oracle behaves identically on all platforms (Windows, UNIX, Macintosh and Mainframe systems).

Open source DBMS such as My SQL and Postgres are used in open source library integrated software like KOHA and NewGenLib for backup recovery and indexing features. ORACLE, the RDBMS platform for larger enterprising databases is used for VTLS the international commercial LIS software. Library databases built by the automated ILS, if structured around advanced RDBMS, it will be undoubtedly advantageous in terms of data organization, data security, recovery of data in the event of failure, data access across modules of ILS and information retrieval by users.

5

Database Management For Libraries (DBMS/RDBMS Applications)

5.1. INTRODUCTION

The concept of database management arises with the computerization of library records and automation of library in-house processes. Prior to computerization, library data related tasks were carried out manually. The processes were independent and not connected. The conventional means of maintaining the records of print publications, library holdings as well as the holdings of other libraries and tools to retrieve the information are presented via figure 5.1.

University of Texas began using a punch card system to manage library circulation in 1936. It allowed only tracking of loans with which the remaining library operations or related data were not affected.

Later the 60s were recognized for initiation and experimentation of library computerization programs with the growth of computer technologies, the advent of MARC standards; the OCLC's launching of bibliographic services with RLG (Research Libraries Group) and the Washington Library Networks.

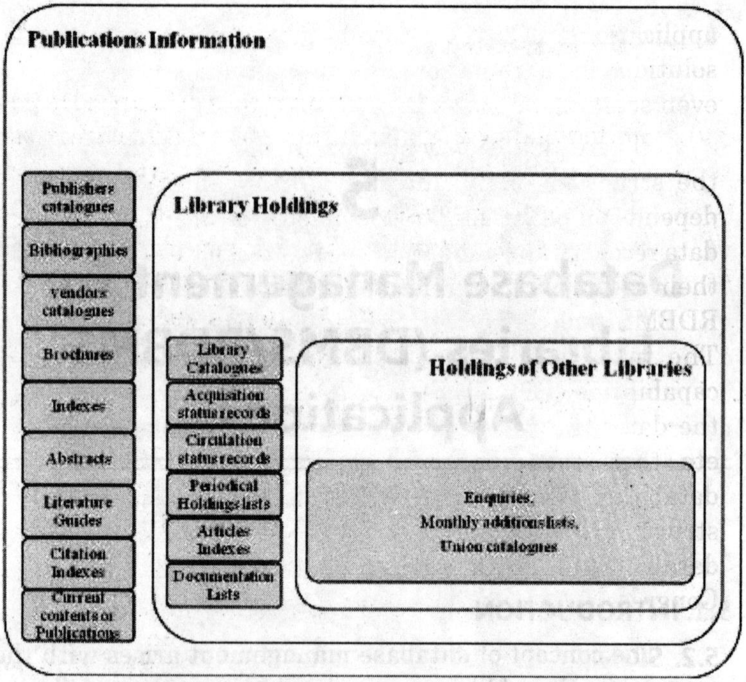

Fig. 5.1. Traditional Information Sources

During 1970s and 1980s, the early-integrated library system were developed with the improvements in computer storage, as well as telecommunications. The hardware and software allowed the connectivity between all major circulation tasks, including overdue notices and gradually integrating with acquisition, cataloguing, reservation of titles, and monitoring of serials, etc. The evolution of Internet greatly influenced Integrated Library Systems, allowing users to access information about resources through OPACs and online web-based portals by 1990s and further progressed during 2000s and onwards. Users could get authentication for OPAC and be able to access their library accounts and reserve or renew books and also access library-subscribed online databases. During 2000s, many commercial ILS emerged increasing the integration of library operations and services. Some open source ILS have launched their operations and began testing. The cloud computing applications in 2010s provided many modern cloud based solutions for automation allowing automated cataloging by even scanning a book's ISBN.

There has been variation in ILS systems as well as the structure of the internal library database's since it depends on processing, retrieval efficiencies, data integrity, data recovery and validation needs. Most of the ILS, structure their catalogue as a relational database using the popular RDBMS such as MySQL Server, PostGreSQL or Oracle etc. The integrated library system built around RDBMS capabilities such as - SQL as query language for searching the database, indexing, data validation and data recovery etc. that strengthen both the ILS and relational model databases. Further, RDBMS enable to import MARC records structured according international standards, into local database server from external databases like Library of Congress, OCLC catalogs (OPACs) and publisher's websites.

5.2. SIGNIFICANCE OF DBMS/RDBMS APPLICATIONS FOR LIBRARIES

Libraries acquire information or documents as per the general and specific requirements of clientele (users). When the information in print was predominant, users were entirely depending on libraries for information and their print based services. They were redundant, slow and error-prone. The approaches to information also were limited to few major keys such as author, title, subject heading etc. through card or book catalogues. So the secondary and tertiary services maintained by external agencies were supplementing the library services by providing users the bibliographic information about the publications in their respective disciplines, especially when individual libraries were not able to procure all of them. Thus, the automation of integrated library operations, development of standards for bibliographic format, advancements in database management technologies such as RDBMS have not only improved the library working environment with utmost precession, minimizing the repetition of tasks and duplication or redundancy as the data entered in a module will be utilized by the other modules in the system for carrying out further operations. To cite an example, the bibliographic record entered through cataloguing module will be utilized by the circulation section to check-out the same (if required) to the patron. The patrons registered through circulation module will be able to recommend books, journals for the library through OPAC. Similarly, the acquisition section will be able to track the catalogue to eliminate duplicates of books, journals etc. and also retrieve the existing bibliographic records to order for additional copies for the library. Further, the library users can search for books, journals and other material and also track the acquisition or availability status of information. The kind of integrated library operations can be attributed to the structure and functioning of relation database systems that coordinate the data within and among the files residing in the library database.

The libraries usually will not be able to survive only with the limited resources they acquire, but relying on several external sources for their information needs, especially on resource sharing activities, which invariably needs a sharable database for each library comprising the bibliographic records in international standard format, to be part of a resource sharing network to share institutional resources across the globe. The world's largest databases offering free bibliographic services are - OCLC, Library of Congress, while other networks DELNET etc. are providing on the basis of memberships. The RDBMS applications are the backbone to such services.

Similarly the libraries need to contribute their holdings in international standard format to the union catalogues hosted by the consortia or any authorized agency. In such instances, it is feasible to retrieve records through DBMS software in MARC / XML format as desired by the agency to directly incorporate into their database.

In addition to the users queries met through online public access catalogue there will be many coming unexpectedly from them. Libraries require to support the management and audit with the information or data in their specified format. The LIS software whether open source or commercial include few default reports at the level of operational module, the remaining customizable reports will be located in reports module. The unforeseen queries for information from the management or audit need to be met from integrated data management system by relating the fields in records of a database.

The advent of electronic medium has been showering innumerable resources through internet, but the scholarly resources and information is being locked up behind IP authentications and only accessible against the library subscriptions or purchases. These electronic publications though not physically housed in libraries, became part of library collections and the relevant information needs to be displayed for users appropriately through library web OPACS or portals providing hyperlinks to the full text files in the respective bibliographic records. The integration or federation at different levels i.e. database, file and record could be possible with technologies built around the relations within and among the databases hosted by the publishers, aggregators and even intermediaries that ultimately reaches end users such as – consortia, institutions, libraries and users. Though these resources are maintained at the remote servers of publishers, and the online access is facilitated to institutional users only against library's or consortia's subscription; certain databases form the permanent collection of the libraries as they are purchased on perpetual basis. The e-books, e-monographs, reference books records and serials are required to be imported from the respective publisher's websites to incorporate in library catalogue. The type of integration of records is possible through effective RDBMS software.

Likewise, though libraries are working with LIS

software packages to build their database through their automated library operations, the backend RDBMS need to be explored to an extent that the users and management of the libraries are supported by the data.

5.3. DBMS SOFTWARE APPLICATIONS

The purpose of computerized library databases is to facilitate retrieval of the information from the library holdings data and beyond i.e. across the published scientic literature. Despite the disadvantages of high costs of installations, management, required technical expertise etc. the libraries, information centres, publishers and vendors have been applying DBMS software for maintaining their databases for the efficient and precise retrieval of information contained in them. Prior to the development of the advanced relational database management systems such as Oracle, MySQL for integrated library operations, libraries have been using initially programs and DOS/command based applications and later Windows based software for executing specific or individual applications. They are used for limited purposes such as serials lists or inventories, duplicates lists, bindery lists, articles indexes, patron's records, financial statements, staff's leave statements, etc. Majority of the software have been evolving through handling the data requirements and complexities in retrieving information over the period. For example, dBase II, III plus, IV versions were widely used by libraries for individual operations. MS Access is found to be used directly by the libraries with smaller collections and also used as a platform to access the tables or data residing in major RDBMS such as Oracle.

The widely applied DBMS products for individual or integrated library operations are detailed hereunder. The popular DBMS packages for individual library operations as well as integrated applications are – dBase, Microsoft Access, the advanced RDBMS software packages such as the MySQL and a commercial ORACLE are described in the context of bibliographic database management systems required for libraries. These RDBMS/ORDBMS are known to construct full-fledged relational database management systems to handle the complex ILS operations.

5.3.1. Dbase

dBASE was one of the DBMS software used offline in microcomputers and personal computers for several applications and also online. Ashton-Tate originally published this software for microcomputer operating system CP/M in 1980, and later ported to Apple II and IBM PC computers in DOS mode. Its file format is the .dbf. The dBase system includes the core database engine, a query system, a forms engine, and a programming language that ties all of these components together.

Its popular variations were FoxBASE+ (FoxPro), Clipper, and other so-called xBase products. Borland purchased Ashton-Tate, Microsoft bought Fox Software, and Computer Associates acquired Nantucket. Despite the emergence of several advancements in parallel products, many initial applications in LIS and inventories were recorded with dBase II, dBase III plus dBase IV etc. in DOS mode. DBase has later evolved into a modern object oriented language that runs on 32 bit Windows. Dbase is still being used to build a wide variety of applications including web apps hosted on a Windows server, Windows rich client applications, and middleware applications. dBase can access most modern database engines via ODBC drivers. DOS versions can still run on the latest Windows/Linux machines using the Virtual Machine (VM)DOSbox, or the later variant dbDOS. In 2015, dBase, LLC. introduced a set of new utilities called dbfUtils. The utilities include: dbfExport(TM) to export data from .dbf files to CSV, Microsoft(R) Excel, and XML, dbfImport(TM) allows users to import CSV, Microsoft(R) Excel, and XML files into a .dbf. dbfCompare(TM) allows 2 .dbf tables to compare differences and gives an easy way to synchronize tables. Finally the new dbfInspect(TM) allows users to deep-dive into the .dbf files and their contents.

For example, the employee database for a company may consist of two files, one for payroll and another for job classification. The two files share an employee identification number or a job title. In the payroll file, there will be one record for each employee. Each record will consist of a number of fields and will probably include the employee identification number, the employee name, the job title, the employee's social security number, and salary.

Creating the Database Structure

A data structure defines each item of data in a database system. The structure defines:

- field name (maximum of 10 characters)
- field type (numeric, character, date, logical, memo)
- field length (specified in characters except for memo, which is variable length)

After creating database structure the screen shows at the bottom 'Input data records now? (Y/N)', If 'y' is selected, the program displays the data entry form for the structure defined to facilitate data entry. As each record is completed, a new data entry form is presented. If 'N' is selected the file will be saved with filename.DBF.

According to varying types of different kinds of data structures are defined

- .DBF database records (CREATE)
- .DBT database memo fields, has same filename as the associated database file (.DBF)
- .FMT entry screen format commands for custom entry forms (CREATE/MODIFY SCREEN)
- .FRM report format (CREATE/MODIFY REPORT)
- .NDX database index pointers (INDEX)
- .PRG program files, sequence of commands (ASCII file; any editor)
- .QRY query file (CREATE/MODIFY QUERY)

- .SCR entry screen format (CREATE/MODIFY SCREEN)
- .TXT normal DOS ASCII text file used for output (COPY TO)
- .VUE view file (CREATE/MODIFY VIEW)

Field Types – popular five types are listed here

- Character - textlength=1 to 254 characters
- Numeric numbers: integer or decimal length=1 to 20 digits used for calculations
- Date in various formats length=8 characters limited calculations possible
- Logical either true (.T.) or false (.F.) length=single character memo text length=variable

Different types of commands are functional in Command Mode for creating database, adding modifying records/database, deleting, copying records or databases and also querying the information. Additionally there are commands applicable with

- [Date and Time Functions]
- [Character Functions]
- [Mathematical Functions]
- [Other Type Functions]
- [Record Pointer Functions]

5.3.2. MS Access

Microsoft Access is a relational database management system (RDBMS), which can be installed in personal computer as a part of the Microsoft Office suite. It can run on a single computer and also in server. It is designed primarily for smaller tasks. Microsoft Access has included a web solution since 2010 and further integrated with, SQL Server since 2013.

The database created in Microsoft Access since 2007 will be saved with *.accdb* extension. Older versions of MS

Access have .mdb or sometimes a .mde extension. Older versions of databases need to be converted to .accdb file.

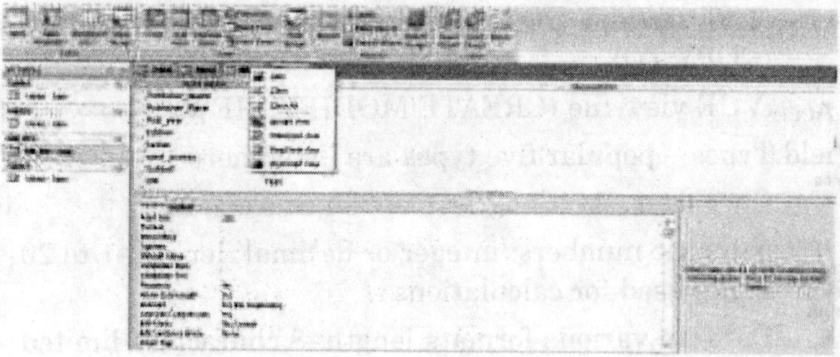

Fig. 5.2. MS Access - Creation of Database and Tables (Screenshot)

The important features of this RDBMS software are

- Like any other package in Microsoft suite, it is also a menu driven to create, update or delete database/s.
- Fields can be configured according to the specification of data in the design mode or through table
- Records can be added, updated and deleted
- Update individual records by creating form
- From the data added to table, Query can be created with required fields.
- Relations can be set to retrieve data.
- The SQL view enables to do many things with database including creating tables. To select SQL View from the Ribbon, select CREATE > Query Design, then select SQL View.
- Accessing external data or databases to import and export data either from excel, PDF, XML file or RTF or ODBC database etc.

Fig. 5.3. MS Access – Export of Data (Screenshot)

Tables can be designed in datasheet view, designer view, and pivotal table /charts.

In MS Access, there are many ways to add data into database. The data entry depends largely on the quantity of data to be added and if any import from other external or internal file.

Datasheet View – direct entry of data into the table. Maintaining even a small database is tedious task especially to update data that's spread across multiple tables.

So, for non-technical users the alternate mode of entry is to create a user-friendly form. Once the form is set up, the data can be entered and submitted for updating the record or database. Access provides a form wizard, which takes the process to building a form.

Step 1 : Create the Database - will create a blank database first which can be saved with desired name.

- By default table 1 will be created, which can be renamed
- From create menu, multiple tables can be created from and renamed

Step 2 : Required fields to be designed

- Defining the characteristics of each field by selecting the pull down menu from data type
- Fixing primary key

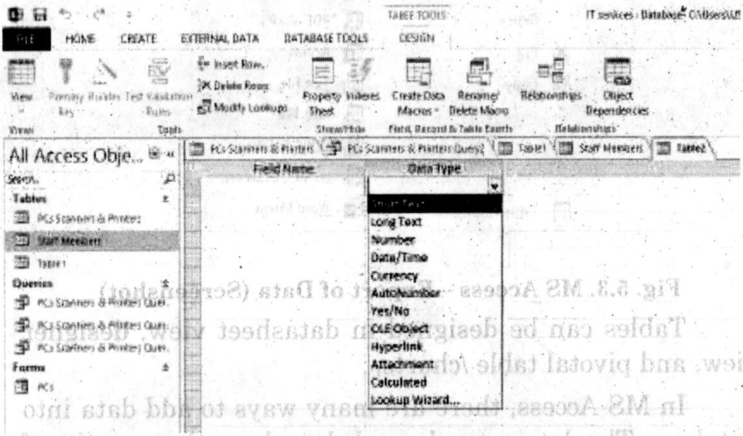

Fig. 5.4. Ms Access – Table Configuration (Screenshot)
http://www.quackit.com/microsoft_access/microsoft_access_2013/tutorial/adding_data.cfm

Field settings	Allow zero length
Size of the field	Indexed Yes/No
Format	Unicode compression
Input mask	IME Mode
Caption	IME sentence mode

Default value
Validation rule
Validation text
Required
Smart tags.

5.3.3. MySQL: (http://www.tutorialspoint.com/mysql/)

MySQL is the world's widely used open-source relational database management system (RDBMS).The SQL phrase stands for Structured Query Language. MySQL was owned and sponsored by a single for-profit firm, the Swedish company MySQL AB, now owned by Oracle Corporation. The MySQL development project has made its source code available under the terms of the GNU General Public License, as well as under a variety of proprietary agreements.

- MySQL is a popular choice of database for use in web applications along with LAMP, which is an acronym for Linux, Apache, MySQL, and Perl/PHP/Python.
- MySQL applications are wide - including TYPO3, MODx, Joomla, WordPress, phpBB, MyBB, Drupal and other software and also in large-scale websites such as Wikipedia, Google, Facebook, Twitter, Flickr and YouTube.
- MySQL supports large databases, up to 50 million rows or more in a table. The default file size limit for a table is 4GB, but it can be increased (if the respective operating system handles it) to a theoretical limit of 8 million terabytes (TB).
- The important feature of MySQL is that it supports most of the LIS software such as KOHA, the latest version of. SOUL 2.0 software, e-Grandhalaya (National Informatics Centre, India) etc. in building up bibliographic database systems.

MySQL Installation on Linux/UNIX

MySQL can be downloaded from provider's (MySQL) website according to the prescribed version and Operating System platform. The recommended way to install MySQL on a Linux system is via RPM. The MySQL RPMs are all built on a SuSE Linux system, but they'll usually work on other Linux variants with no difficulty.

[**The RPM Package Manager (RPM) is a powerful command line driven package management system capable of installing, uninstalling, verifying, querying, and updating computer software packages. It is free software, released under the GNU GPL. RPM is a core component of many Linux distributions, such as Red Hat Enterprise Linux, the Fedora Project etc.* - Refer http://www.rpm.org/]

- The MySQL database server -Manages databases, tables, controls user access, and processes SQL queries.
- MySQL-client - Programs to connect and interact with the server.
- MySQL-devel - Libraries and header files that come in handy when compiling other programs that use MySQL.
- MySQL-shared - Shared libraries for the MySQL client.
- MySQL-bench - Benchmark and performance testing tools for MySQL database server.

Installation Steps are as follows –

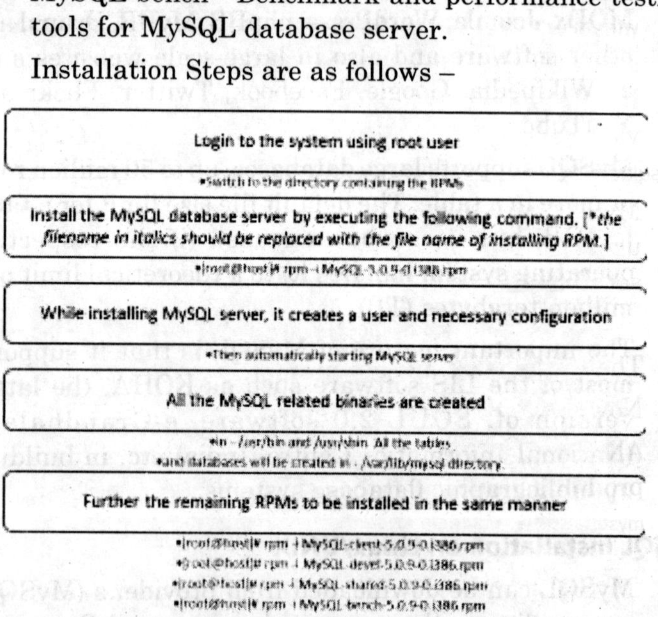

Fig. 5.5. MySQL Installation

MySQL on Windows : Download the installer package, unzip and run 'setup.exe'. Default installer 'setup.exe' will install under C:\mysql. Test the server from the command prompt 'C:\mysql\bin'. Type: ['mysqld.exe – console']

After Installation

Immediately after the installation MySQL will not appear in the start menu and do not show stop process for the server. Therefore to start the server, double click the 'mysqld' executable, the process can be halted by using 'mysqladmin', 'Task List', 'Task Manager', or other Windows-specific means. After installation, the base tables will be initialized and the server starts. This can be viewed by the following means -

- Use the 'mysqladmin' binary to check server version. This is available

```
linux                    - /usr/bin
windows                  C:\mysql\bin.
                         [root@host]# mysqladmin –version
```

- It will produce the following result on Linux. It may vary depending on the installation:

```
mysqladmin  Ver 8.23 Distrib 5.0.9-0, for redhat-linux-gnu on i386
```

- MySQL server can be connected by using MySQL client using 'mysql' command. Password by default will be set to blank.

```
[root@host]# mysql
```

- Then it appears mysql> prompt.
- Now, MySQL server is connected to the client
- All the SQL command can be executed at mysql> prompt as follows:

```
mysql> SHOW DATABASES          +------+
                               Database
                               +------+
                               | mysql  |
                               | test   |
                               +------+
                               2 rows in set
```

Important Tasks (Commands) with MySQL

(From root user access **mysql> prompt)**using mysql 'mysqladmin' binary

Steps	*Task*	*Commands*
1	**Setting Password** MySQL shows blank password for the root MySQL user. After database and client are installed it is needed to set a root password	[root@host]# mysqladmin -u root password "new_password";
2	**Connecting to MySQL Server** After setting root password	[root@host]# mysql -u root -p Enter password:*******
3	**Creating Database** called TUTORIALS create or to delete	[root@host]# mysqladmin -u root -p create TUTORIALS Enter password:****** This will create a MySQL database TUTORIALS.
4	**Selecting Database** called TUTORIALS	[root@host]# mysql -u root -p Enter password:****** mysql> use TUTORIALS
5	Database change	mysql>
6	**Dropping (Deleting) Database** (existing/created) database TUTORIALS	[root@host]# mysqladmin -u root -p drop TUTORIALS Enter password:******

Creating Tables

After creating database, the first important step is to define the fields in a table for overall optimization of database. 1) The data type in field, and 2) the size of field.

1) MySQL uses 3 data types: numeric, date and time, and string types.
   - **Numeric Data Types:** MySQL uses all the standard ANSI SQL numeric data types

- **Date and Time Types:**
  - A date in YYYY-MM-DD format, between 1000-01-01 and 9999-12-31
  - A date and time combination in YYYY-MM-DD HH:MM:SS format, between 1000-01-01 00:00:00 and 9999-12-31 23:59:59
- **String Types:** most of the data stored will be in string format. This list describes the common string datatypes in MySQL.
  - CHAR(M) - A fixed-length string between 1 and 255 characters in length. Defining a length is not required, but the default is 1.
  - VARCHAR(M) - A variable-length string between 1 and 255 characters in length; field length must be defined when creating a VARCHAR field.
  - BLOB ("Binary Large Objects") or TEXT - A field with a maximum length of 65535 characters. BLOBs are used to store large amounts of binary data, such as images or other types of files including TEXT. The difference between these two is that stored data are case sensitive on BLOBs and are not case sensitive in TEXT fields. The length cannot be specified with BLOB or TEXT.
    - TINYBLOB or TINYTEXT - A BLOB or TEXT column with a maximum length of 255 characters. Field length need not be specified with TINYBLOB or TINYTEXT.
    - MEDIUMBLOB or MEDIUMTEXT - A BLOB or TEXT column with a maximum length of 16777215 characters. Field length need not be specified with MEDIUMBLOB or MEDIUMTEXT.
    - LONGBLOB or LONGTEXT - A BLOB

or TEXT column with a maximum length of 4294967295 characters. Field length need not be specified with LONGBLOB or LONGTEXT.

— ENUM - An enumeration, which is a fancy term for the list of items from which the value must be selected (or it can be NULL). For example, if the field requires to contain "A" or "B" or "C", then it should define ENUM as ENUM ('A', 'B', 'C') and only those values (or NULL) could ever populate that field.

The table creation command requires the:

- Name of the table
- Names of fields
- Definitions for each field

E.g. To create table in TUTORIALS database

```
CREATE TABLE table_name (column_name column_type);
tutorials_tbl(
  tutorial_id INT NOT NULL AUTO_INCREMENT,
  tutorial_title VARCHAR(100) NOT NULL,
  tutorial_author VARCHAR(40) NOT NULL,
  submission_date DATE,
  PRIMARY KEY ( tutorial_id )
);
```

It is important to note that –

- Field Attribute NOT NULL is being used because this field should not be NULL. So if any user tries to create a record with NULL value, then MySQL will raise an error.
- Field Attribute AUTO_INCREMENT tells MySQL to add the next available number to the ID field.
- Keyword PRIMARY KEY is used to define a column as primary key. Multiple columns can be used by separating with comma to define a primary key.
- MySQL does not terminate a command until a semicolon (;) is given at the end of SQL command.

Dropping (Deleting) Tables

SQL syntax to drop a MySQL table:DROP TABLE table name;

Selecting and Inserting Query (Insert data in Table, fields)

```
INSERT INTO table_name ( field1, field2,...fieldN )
                VALUES
    ( value1, value2,...valueN );
```

SQL syntax of INSERT INTO command to insert data into MySQL table:

To insert string data types, it is required to keep all the values into double or single quote, for example: - **"value"**.

```
root@host# mysql -u root -p password;
Enter password:*******

mysql> use TUTORIALS;

Database changed
mysql> INSERT INTO tutorials  tbl
   ->(tutorial_title, tutorial_author, submission_date)
   ->VALUES
   ->("Learn PHP", "John Poul", NOW());
Query OK, 1 row affected (0.01 sec)

mysql> INSERT INTO tutorials_tbl
   ->VALUES
   ->("Learn MySQL", "Abdul S", NOW());
Query OK, 1 row affected (0.01 sec)

mysql> INSERT INTO tutorials_tbl
   ->(tutorial_title, tutorial_author, submission_date)
   ->VALUES
   ->("JAVA Tutorial", "Sanjay", '2007-05-06');
Query OK, 1 row affected (0.01 sec)

mysql>
```

The point to be noted here that the arrow signs (->) are not part of SQL command; they are indicating a new line and they are automatically created by MySQL prompt while pressing enter key without giving a semicolon at the end of each line of the command.

Select and Update Query

SQL syntax of SELECT command to fetch data from MySQL table:

```
SELECT field1, field2,...fieldN table_name1, table_name2...
[WHERE Clause]
[OFFSET M ][LIMIT N]
```

- One or more tables can be used separating by comma to include various conditions using a WHERE clause, but WHERE clause is an optional part of SELECT command.
- One or more fields in a single SELECT command.
- Star (*) symbol can specify in place of fields. In this case, SELECT will return all the fields.
- Any condition can be specify using WHERE clause.
- An offset can be used for **OFFSET** from where SELECT will start returning records. By default offset is zero.
- The number of returns can be limited using **LIMIT** attribute.

SQL syntax of UPDATE command to modify data into MySQL table:

```
UPDATE table_name SET field1=new-value1, field2=new-value2
[WHERE Clause]
```

- One or more field can be updated
- Any condition can be specified using WHERE clause.
- Values can be updated in a single table at a time.

The WHERE clause is very useful to update selected rows in a table

Sorting and Indexing Data in fields

Here is generic SQL syntax of SELECT command along with ORDER BY clause to sort data from MySQL table:

```
SELECT field1, field2,...fieldN table_name1, table_name2...
ORDER BY field1,[field2...][ASC [DESC]]
```

- Results can be sorted on any field or on more than one field provided that filed is being listed out.
- ASC or DESC keywords to be applied to get results in ascending or descending order. By default, it's ascending order.
- WHERE...LIKE clause can be used in usual way to put condition.

Exporting data

SELECT...INTO OUTFILE statement exports a query result (a table data) directly into a file on the server host. Syntax:

```
SELECT with INTO OUTFILE filename
```

The default output format is the same as for LOAD DATA, so the following statement exports the tutorials_tbl table into /tmp/tutorials.txt as a tab-delimited, linefeed-terminated file:

```
mysql> SELECT * FROM tutorials_tbl
   -> INTO OUTFILE '/tmp/tutorials.txt';
```

The output format can be changed using options to indicate how to quote and delimit columns and records. To export the tutorial_tbl table in CSV format with CRLF-terminated lines, use this statement:

```
mysql> SELECT * FROM passwd INTO OUTFILE '/tmp/tutorials.txt'
   -> FIELDS TERMINATED BY ',' ENCLOSED BY '"'
   -> LINES TERMINATED BY '\r\n';
```

The **SELECT ... INTO OUTFILE** has the following properties:

- The output file is created directly by the MySQL server, so the filename should indicate the location of file to be written on the server host.
- The output file must not already exist, to prevent clobbering of files
- Should have a login account on the server host to handle this operation
- If the file is created under UNIX, world readable and

is owned by the MySQL server, the file can be read but cannot be deleted.

Exporting Tables as Raw Data (Back up) : The ***mysqldump*** program is used to copy or back up tables and databases. It can write table output either as a raw datafile or as a set of INSERT statements that recreate the records in the table.

To dump a table as a datafile, you must specify a — tab option that indicates the directory, where you want the MySQL server to write the file. For example, to dump the tutorials_tbl table from the TUTORIALS database to a file in the /tmp directory, use the following command:

```
$ mysqldump -u root -p —no-create-info \
        —tab=/tmp TUTORIALS tutorials_tbl
password ******
```

Exporting Table Contents or Definitions in SQL Format : To export a table in SQL format to a file, use a command as follows:

```
$ mysqldump -u root -p TUTORIALS tutorials_tbl > dump.txt
password ******
```

To back up all the databases available on your host, use the following : This method can be used to implement a database backup strategy.

```
$ mysqldump -u root -p —all-databases > database_dump.txt
password ******
```

Copying Tables or Databases to another Host

To copy tables or databases from one MySQL server to another, by using mysqldump with database name and table name.

- The following command will dump complete database into dump.txt file:

```
$ mysqldump -u root -p database_name table_name > dump.txt
password *****
```

- Now, ftp dump.txt file on another host and use the following command. Before running this command, make sure you have created database_name on destination server.

```
$ mysql -u root -p database_name < dump.txt
password *****
```

Importing Data

The way to load data into MySQL database from a previously backed up file is explained below. MySQL provides a LOAD DATA statement that acts as a bulk data loader. E.g. a file reads as dump.txt from the current directory and loads it into the table mytbl in the current database.

```
mysql> LOAD DATA LOCAL INFILE 'dump.txt' INTO TABLE mytbl;
```

MySQL reads the file from the given location. By default, LOAD DATA assumes that data files contain lines that are terminated by linefeeds (newlines) and that data values within a line are separated by tabs. The following LOAD DATA statement specifies that the data file contains values separated by colons and lines terminated by carriage returns and new line character:

```
mysql> LOAD DATA LOCAL INFILE 'dump.txt' INTO TABLE mytbl
-> FIELDS TERMINATED BY ':'
-> LINES TERMINATED BY '\r\n';
```

LOAD DATA takes the columns in the datafile have the same order as the columns in the table. If that's not the case, it can be indicated which table columns the datafile columns should be loaded into. E.g. a table has columns a, b, and c, but successive columns in the datafile correspond to columns b, c, and a. Thus the file like this:

```
mysql> LOAD DATA LOCAL INFILE 'dump.txt'
-> INTO TABLE mytbl (b, c, a);
```

MySQL supports many of the LIS software like KOHA. The reporting systems in KOHA are illustrated through few Screenshots.

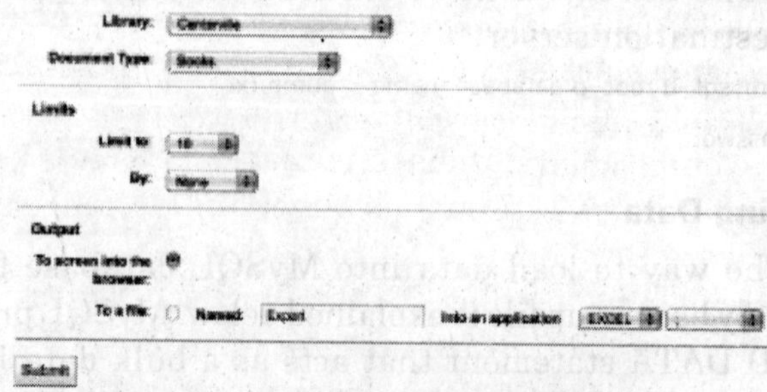

Fig. 5.6. MySQL Reporting (KOHA) Book (Items with no checkout) (Screenshot)

Reports the list of books not borrowed as well as most circulated items.

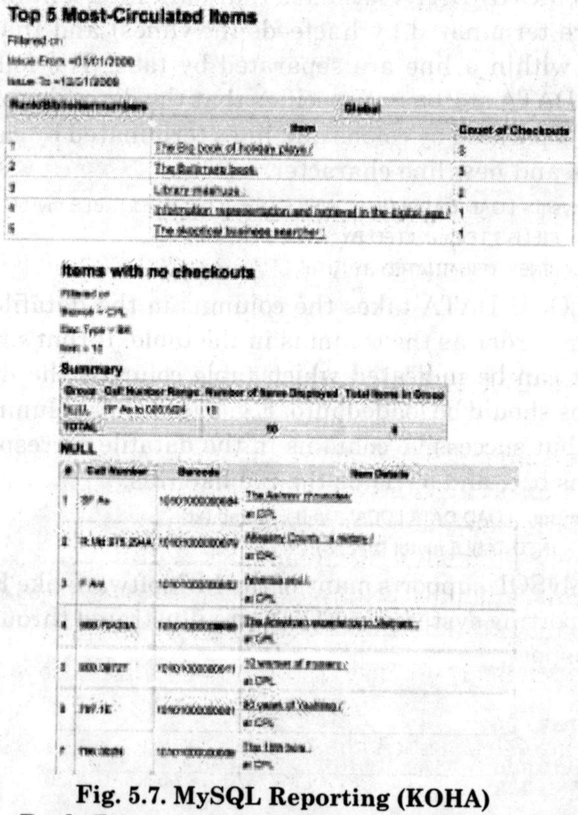

Fig. 5.7. MySQL Reporting (KOHA) Book (Items with no checkout) (Screenshot)

5.3.4. ORACLE

The Oracle RDBMS is also called as Oracle. It is produced and marketed by Oracle Corporation. This is an object-relational database management system. The original version of relational database management software was developed by Larry Ellison, Bob Miner and Ed Oates in 1977 and Software Development Laboratories (SDL) brought out as non-commercial product. This product was later renamed as Oracle and grown beyond the relational database servers. The name Oracle comes from code-name of a CIA-funded project. Oracle is an object-relational database (ORD), or object-relational database management system (ORDBMS), which is similar to a relational database, but with an object-oriented database model.

Oracle revolutionized the database management systems in the field of enterprising, with the release of Oracle Database 10, by introducing self-management capabilities built right into the database kernel*. (The kernel is a program that constitutes the central core of a computer operating system. It has complete control over everything that occurs in the system).Oracle provides several business intelligence tools, including a multidimensional database management system, database design, query and analysis tools, data mining products and an application server with a close integration to the database server and also Oracle OLAP* (*a world class multidimensional analytic engine embedded in Oracle Database 12c).

Additionally the company offers application software for enterprise resource planning and customer-relationship management including areas such as financials, human resources, manufacturing marketing, sales and supply chain management. The important functions of ORACLE are described briefly as follows.

Features

Oracle Server includes a DBMS which controls:

- Storing data in the database area
- Data recovery applications using appropriate optimization techniques
- Database Security and tasks allowed for certain users
- Consistency, data protection tasks including archiving and search mechanisms
- Communication and integrity of information, when databases are distributed in a network.

Database Administration (DBA)

The major functions of database administration are given below

- Installation & Creation of database
- Setting clients
- Data Security & Network management
- Storage, Backup and Recovery
- UNIX and Windows Database Administration
- Testing
- Data mining & Analytics

Advantages

- An Oracle RDBMS complies with industry standards in force relating to data access languages (SQL).
- Oracle database supports any size of database ranging from a few bytes to several gigabytes.
- Oracle offers full safety features to limit and monitor access to data and their use.
- Oracle supports a large number of simultaneous users minimizing the data access conflicts and guarantees data.
- Oracle supports a client/server environment real. It allows dividing processing between the database server and client application programs.
- Oracle behaves identically on all platforms (Windows,

UNIX, Macintosh and Mainframe systems).

Installation & Creation of Database

The Oracle Universal Installer (OUI) is used to install Oracle Database software. OUI is a graphical user interface utility that enables to view the Oracle software that is installed on a machine. It is suggested to install new Oracle Database software, deleting Oracle software that no longer needs to use. One of the installation options is to create a database. If database creation is selected, OUI automatically starts Oracle Database Configuration Assistant (DBCA) to guide through the process of creating and configuring a database and also the additional databases.

Hardware and Software Requirements

Before installing the software, OUI performs several automated checks to ensure that the installing computer fulfills the basic hardware and software requirements for an Oracle Database installation. The requirements may vary depending upon the type of computer and OS (operating system). The minimum requirements are shown below -

- Oracle Database 12c downloaded software
- Having a general knowledge of product installation
- Minimum of 1 GB of physical memory
- Installation of appropriate service packs and/or patches
- Sufficient paging space and Use of appropriate file system format

Installation Step (typical)

There are two types of Oracle Database installations: basic (typical) and advanced. The typical one enables to quickly install the software with minimal input. The advanced installation enables to perform a custom installation. The important typical installation steps are listed below.

- Logon to the computer as a member of the

administrative group that is authorized to install Oracle Database software and create a database.

- The Autorun feature of the Disk opens to select a Product to install window automatically.
- If the software is downloaded from the Oracle Website, the instructions on the site to invoke the Oracle Universal Installer. The Security updates need to be configured as specified on the window - email address and Oracle Support password etc. to receive security issue notifications via email.
- The Download of software updates requires to be configured.
- Next to "Create and configure a database."
- In the 'system class window' – option to select **Desktop Class** or **Server Class** is required depending on the type of system being used.
- For typical installation, **Server Class** should be opted with basic configuration

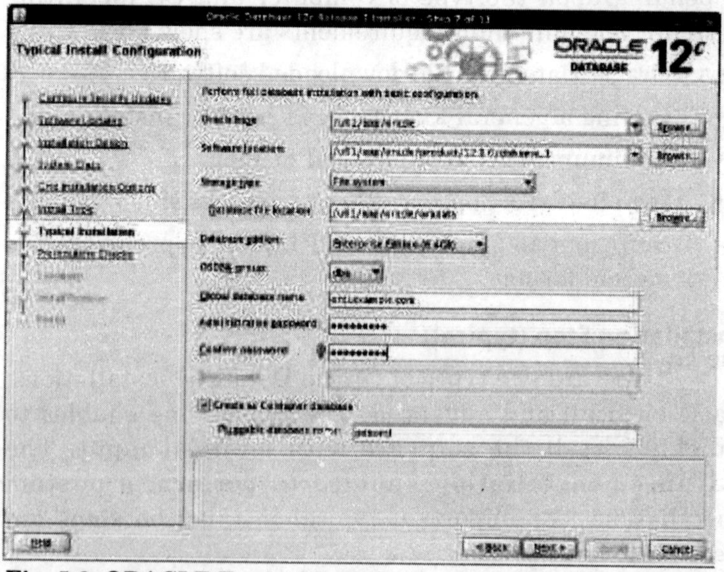

Fig. 5.8. ORACLE Typical Installation Process (Screenshot)

- Next step is to **Create Inventory**.
- **Summary window** (appears to perform the prerequisite checks before proceeding to install

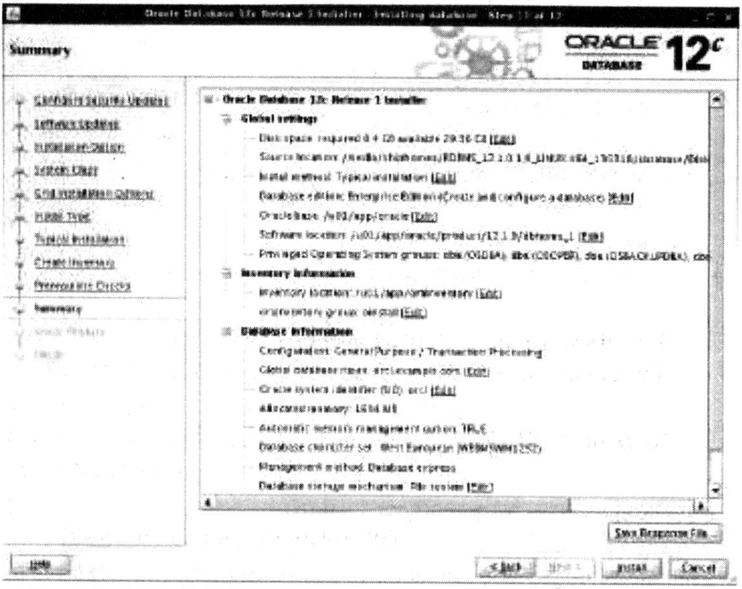

Fig. 5.9. ORACLE Typical Installation Process (Screenshot)

- The Execute Configuration Scripts window appears.
  - Open a terminal window and log in as the root user.
  - Execute the scripts as instructed.
  - Close terminal window.

After executing the scripts in terminal window, return to the Execute Configuration scripts window and click OK

- The Database Configuration Assistant creates the database.
- After the Database creation click "Password Management" to unlock accounts, after the installation process completes.
- The Finish window appears indicating the installation of Oracle Database software and creation of the

database was successful. Click Close to exit the Oracle Universal Installer.

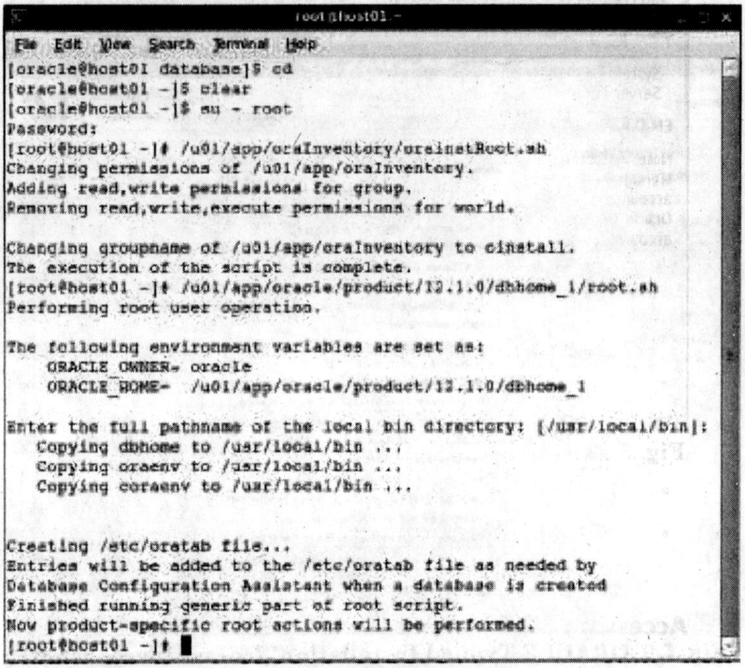

Fig. 5.10. ORACLE Typical Installation Process (Screenshot)

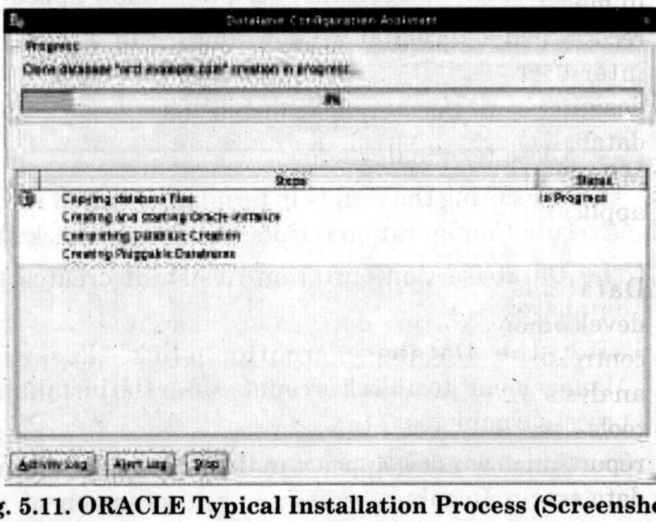

Fig. 5.11. ORACLE Typical Installation Process (Screenshots)

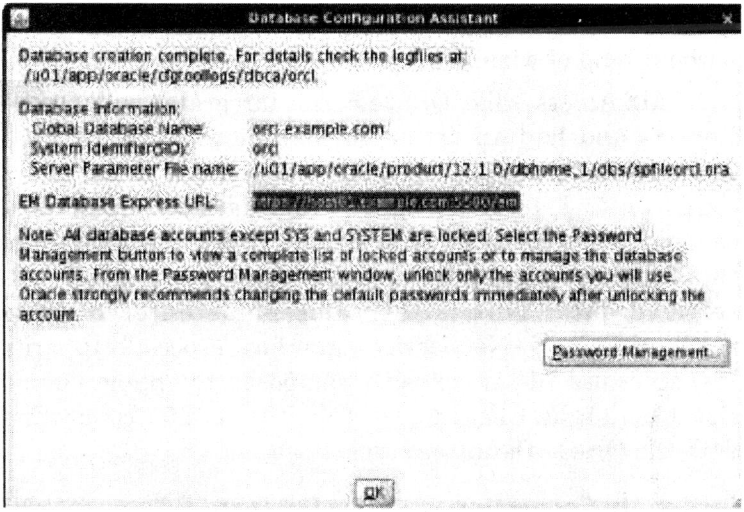

Fig. 5.12. ORACLE Typical Installation Process (Screenshots)

- c > oracle
- Need to copy the file tnsnames.ora from database folder to config folder from Oracle Middleware

Accessing Bibliographic Data on Oracle through MS Access

In a Library bibliographic database, the data is spread in many interrelated tables. Each table consists of multiple records (rows) and attributes (columns). Each record in these interrelated tables is linked by means of a commonly designated field (tag)containing unique data. The library database built on Oracle RDBMS can be accessed through MS Access owing to connectivity features and front end applications.

Ms Access : MS Access is RDBMS (Relational DataBase Management System), helps in database development, sorting data, frontend applications (forms to control the data, reports, and sophisticated queries), and data analysis and data manipulation.Microsoft Access database tools – provide facility to create forms for data manipulation, reports, queries (SQL statements. MS Access has options to data export or import between many data sources (not only database tables). These functions can also be used with or without help of wizards.

MS Access is like Oracle Forms integrated with Oracle Reports and had an option to connect with any ODBC* (*Microsoft Open Database Connectivity) ready database (built on Oracle or MySQL), with data import/export capabilities". ODBC drivers require TNS (*the location of the Oracle database from which the ODBC driver will retrieve data. This is the same name entered while configuring Oracle Net Services) interface, especially to verify tnsnames.ora file is correctly composed to enable Oracle Database 11gR2 Client to use TNS interface for connecting with the Oracle Database server.

Setting Up Connection to Oracle Database

Open MS Access

- Select "Blank database"
- Mention the Name of the database (existing)
- Click "Create" button -> Click on External Data ->Click on ODBC Database
- Select to "link to the data source by creating to linked table"

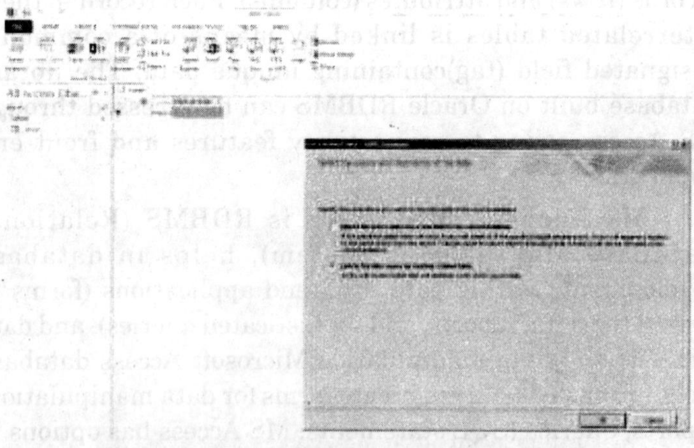

Fig. 5.13. Setting Up Connection to Oracle Database through MS Access (Screenshot)

- Select the "name of the database"

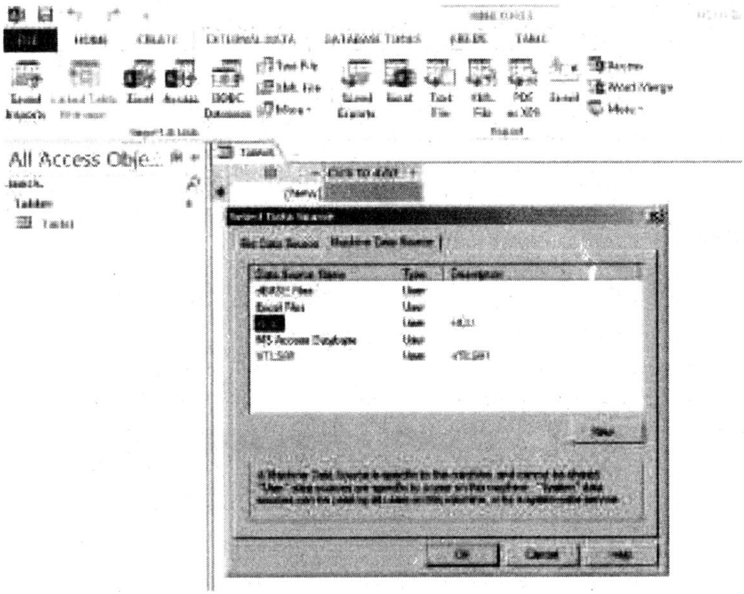

Fig. 5.14. Accessing Oracle Database through MS Access (Screenshot)

- Give password and click on OK

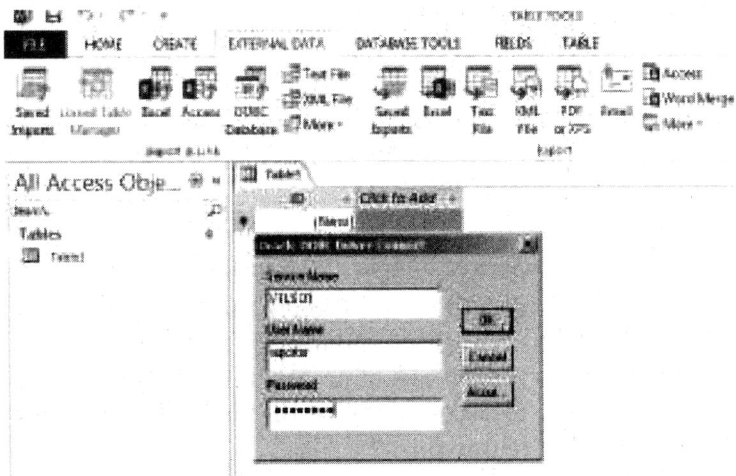

Fig. 5.15. Accessing Oracle Database through MS Access (Screenshot)

- Get the list of tables in database and
  - — Click on selected table 'DBADMIN_BIB_TITLE_V'
  - — Get the table view of bibliographic records
- Options to select tables, filters, queries, forms, reports etc. also as shown in the following screenshots.

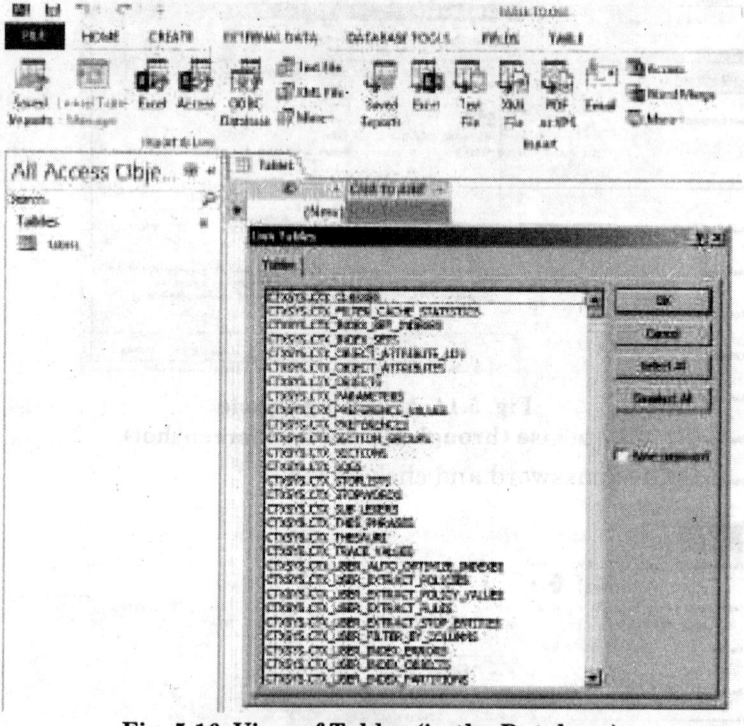

Fig. 5.16. View of Tables (in the Database) through MS Access (Screenshot)

After setting up the connection to the library database (built on Oracle), save the same database as short cut by the file name with an extension of access database (.accdb) on the local system to access/retrieve the data or generate a report whenever required.

Retrieving Bibliographic Data

Control panel
Administrative Tools
Data Sources (ODBC)
Add connection
Select Oracle
Select TNS Service Name
Set USER ID
Set Password
Test the Connection

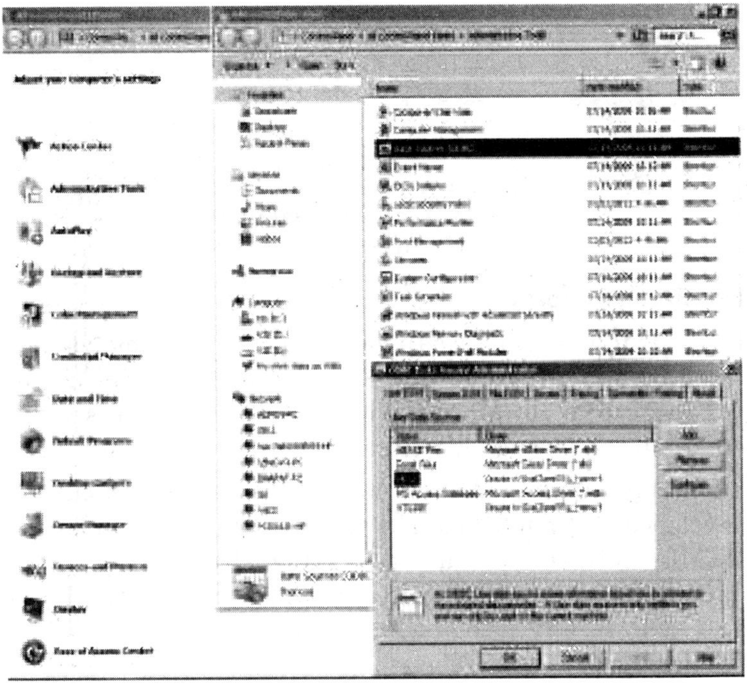

Fig. 5.17. Accessing Database through MS Access (Screenshot)

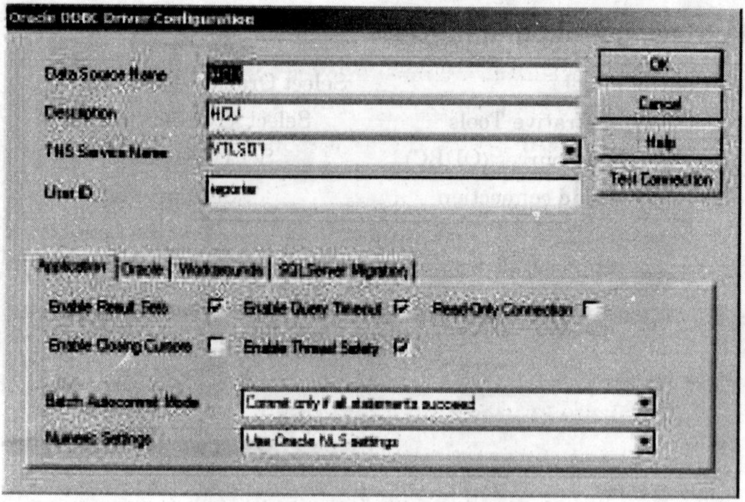

Fig. 5.18. Accessing Database through MS Access (Screenshot)

Obtaining Reports

Oracle Reports can be generated by accessing information at all levels within and outside of the organization in an unrivaled scalable and secure environment through MS Access.

Sophisticated Web as well as paper reports can be developed and published in a variety of formats (including HTML, XML, PDF, Enhanced Spreadsheet, Spreadsheet data, delimited text, delimited data, PostScript, and RTF) and sent to any destination via e-mail, Web browser, WebDav, FTP, Oracle Portal, and file system in a scalable, efficient manner. Integrated reports can be generated by forming a query.

- Select the suitable tables
  - — Select the required fields
    - * Apply filters if necessary
      - * Generate table view
        - * Save the report in the required format (.xls or .cvv or .doc etc.) in the required location in the local PC

Selection of tables, fields filters, queries, forms, reports etc. also as shown in the following screenshots.

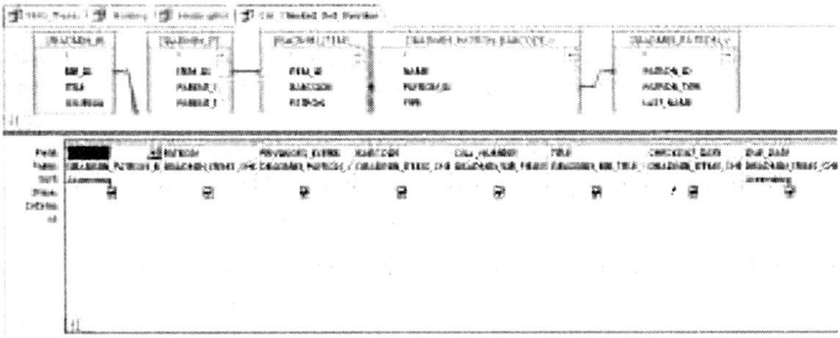

Fig. 5.19. Accessing through MS Access (Screenshot)

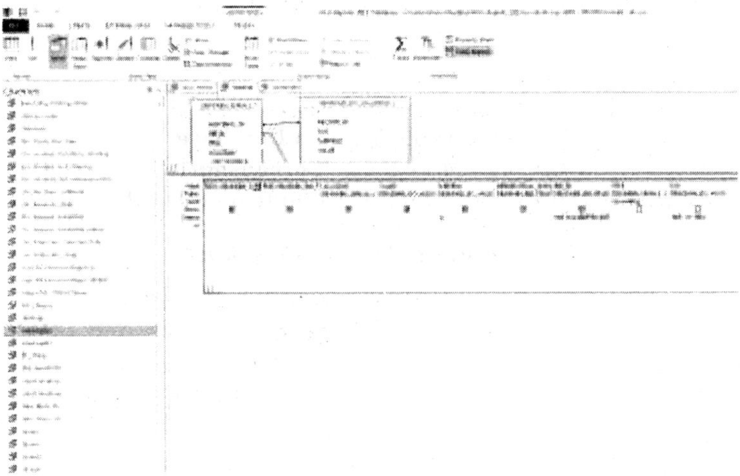

Fig. 5.20. Accessing Database through MS Access (Screenshot)

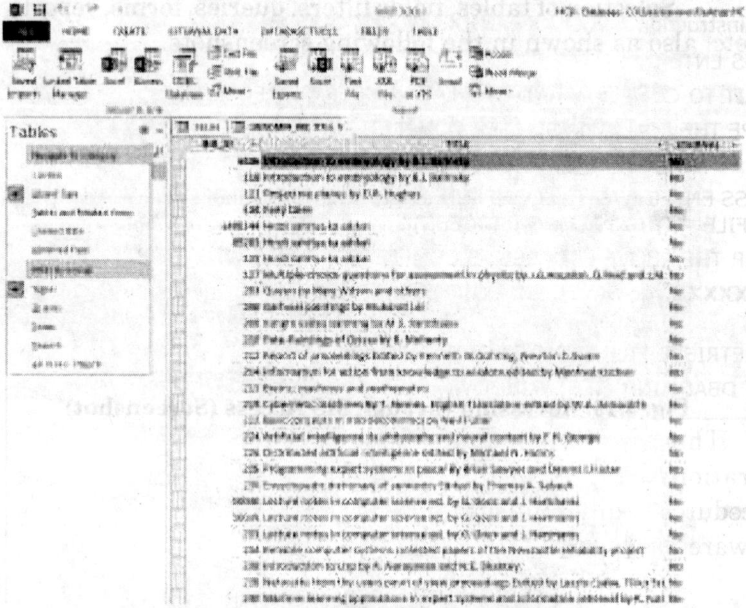

Fig. 5.21. Table View in Database through MS Access (Screenshot) [Records (Rows) and Fields (Columns) or Attributes]

To Retrieve (Bibliographic) Records– (A Case)

Often or at periodical intervals, there will be a necessity of taking backup of the bibliographic records and other records etc. for libraries as a part of data security, while exporting data for sharing purpose and also while migrating from one server to another.

Libraries need to retrieve bibliographic records in MARC format or XML format to share with consortia for making union catalogue. This data can be drawn through FTP software (Secureshell or Putty or Any Ftp Server) installed in a system on network.

(Lower case commands to type as it is and capitals are instructions)

GO TO MAIN MENU = window

- CLICK ON = new terminal in current directory
- LOGIN TO SERVER USING DBADMIN USER

XXXXXXXXXXXXXXXXXXXXXXXXX

Give instruction = **XXXXXXXXXXXXXXXXXXXXXXXXXX**

PRESS ENTER

- WAIT TO COMPLETE AND DISPLAY NUMBER OF RECORDS
- TYPE THE FOLLOWING AFTER COMPLETION OF THE ABOVE PROCESS

write2709.exe <XXXXXXXX> XXXXXXXX.rec –A

(PRESS ENTER WAIT TO COMPLETE & DISPLAY RUN OF RECORDS FORM THE FILE - THIS IS LONG PROCESS)

AFTER THE ABOVE PROCESS IS COMPLETED, A FILE WILL BE SEEN

XXXXXXXX.rec SAVED IN A DIFFERENT DIRECTORY.

usr/vtls/class01

TO RETRIEVE FILE FROM **usr/vtls/class01**

TYPE DBADMIN (VTLS) WINDOW = **/usr/vtls/clas01**

The above mentioned few examples of RDBMS operations can be considered as basis for applying the procedures to different situations or purposes with different software packages.

6

Library Databases

In the current scenario of handling electronic and digital information products along with print-based information material, libraries need to maintain different types of internal databases and several external databases. The modern libraries are providing the visibility of resources as well facilitating access to full text content that the users sought. Libraries acquire their collections through purchases, subscriptions, deposit, consortia memberships or as complimentary.

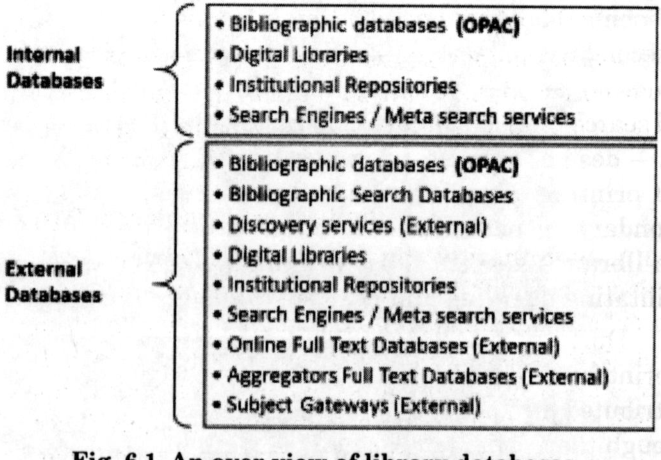

Fig. 6.1. An over view of library databases

6.1. BIBLIOGRAPHIC DATABASES

The file is a set of records in bibliographic databases, containing the bibliographic description of the documents of a particular library which serves as an index to the materials held by the library for serving the user needs with different approaches.

Bibliographic databases containing the description of documents is normally based on a catalogue code like AACR2 or CCC, etc. in MARC format. International Encyclopedia of Information and Library Science (2003) defined the **bibliographic database** as – "a database of bibliographic records, an organized digital collection of references to published literature, including journal and newspaper articles, conference proceedings, reports, government and legal publications, patents, books, etc. In contrast to library catalogue entries, large proportions of the bibliographic records in bibliographic databases describe articles, conference papers, etc., rather than complete monographs, and they generally contain very rich subject descriptions in the form of keywords, subject classification terms, or abstracts."

Libraries or information centers normally build these bibliographic databases as their catalogues, while all other as secondary and tertiary services construct their databases of articles or chapters facilitating different indexes, filters and search engines. In case of libraries, all DBMS operations viz. – design, data entry, generation of indexes, querying and printing are all done locally, whereas in the case of secondary agencies, these functions are carried out by the non-library agencies those are managing databases and facilitating querying and printing to the end user.

During print period, these databases were maintained in print form as card catalogs by libraries, whereas they were distributed through non-library agencies in the form of books. Though these original print forms, were initially published and distributed on CD-ROMs along with or without print, they were later made available to users online through internet. In this context, the Dictionary for Library and Information Science (2004) further explained that – a bibliographic database may be general in scope or cover a specific academic discipline. A significant number of bibliographic databases are proprietary and available by licensing an agreement with vendors or directly from the A & I (indexing & abstracting) service agencies that create them. In the developmental process many bibliographic databases evolve as full-text databases with relevant indexes, abstracts, table of contents. These databases distribute scholarly content by creating completely specialized (disciplinary) information systems with search/browse and user alert applications, e.g. DIALOG, BIOSIS, Mathscinet, Chemical Abstracts, and Scopus etc.

The development of bibliographic databases followed the line of other databases. Prior to the mid-20th century, researchers were depending on printed bibliographic indexes for searching through published literature. During early 1960s computers were used to produce text and reduce the cost as well as time required to publish two American abstracting journals, the Index Medicus of the National Library of Medicine (NLM) and the Scientific and Technical Aerospace Reports of the National Aeronautics and Space Administration (NASA). By late 1960s, such bodies of digitized alphanumeric information were known as bibliographic and numeric databases, constituted a new type of information resource. Online interactive retrieval became commercially viable in early 1970s over private telecommunications networks. The initial services offered as databases or indexes & abstracts of scholarly literature. These databases contained bibliographic descriptions of journal articles that were searchable by keywords from author and title and journal title or subject heading or abstract. The user interfaces of early databases were crude, the access was expensive, and librarians on behalf of 'end users' did searching.

A Database Management System for library bibliographic databases and information products may contain a master file having records of documents those present the description of items. In addition, the DBMS may contain few files having the indexes to the master file, cross-references, data entry screens, etc. All these files in a DBMS form an integral part of facilitating the retrieval of information. The description of the following components forms a better understanding of bibliographic databases.

6.1.1. Bibliographic Description and Record

A document or a set of documents, in any physical form published or issued or treated as an entity and as such forming the basis for a single bibliographic description. A record is a set of fields describing an item. In bibliographic databases, each record gives a complete description of a document fallowing a catalogue code.

The bibliographic databases may be described as a series of linked bibliographic records, where each record contain some components in combinations - document number; title; author; source reference; abstract; full text; key words or phrases; citations or references; source of document or author's address; or both language of the full document local information, example: location, special classification number, etc. In cataloguing, the description of a bibliographic item is divided into the following areas:

- Standard numbers and terms of availability
- Author or Creator
- Title and statement of responsibility
- Edition
- Imprint: Place, Name of the Publisher, distribution etc
- Collation: Number of pages, size, illustrations
- Series
- Notes of useful information which cannot be fitted into other areas

- Added entries
- URL

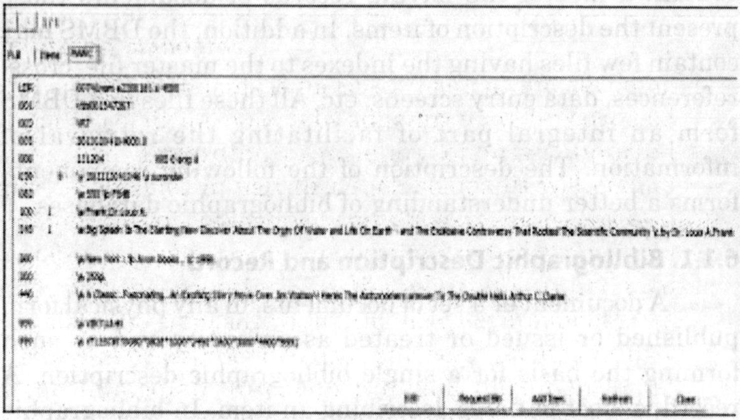

Fig. 6.2. Virtua (VTLS) MARC Record with Fields and Subfields (008 Fixed Field Editor) (Screenshot)

Field (Tags), Subfields and Indicators

A field contains a piece of information about the item. In case of bibliographic databases it can be author, title etc and is normally represented by >TAG code e.g. CCF, MARC or UNIMARC. A field may be subdivided into a number of subfields representing parts of the field. For examples, the author field may be subdivided into: last name; first name; Title and subtitle, etc.

Referencing

Each bibliographic record holds a description for a document represented in the database. These components of bibliographic record or description together can constitute a reference to document. Such of these databases contribute to bibliographic control, by facilitating their records for the retrieval of documents when they are needed. Some of these components are more commonly used as primary retrieval keys such as - author, title, etc. Others may serve as secondary retrieval keys. For example- language, focal information, etc. The remaining information is displayed

mainly to help the user in locating the document or judging its relevance to his search.

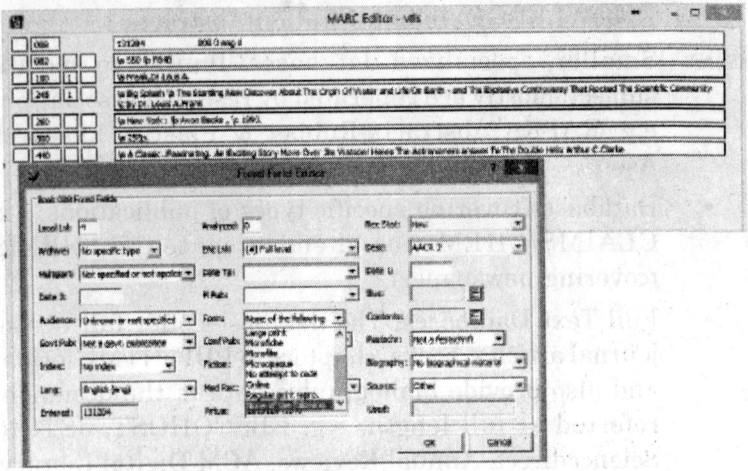

Fig. 6.3. Virtua (VTLS) Record (Library Internal Bibliographic Database) (Screenshot)

Bibliographic Databases Produced by Non-library Agencies

Such database provide references to journal articles in the areas of science & technology, social sciences and humanities. Bibliographic databases containing references also to news, sports, cultural affairs, law and government, business and economics and interdisciplinary fields are also available. These databases invariably include abstract of the document for proper evaluation of content as per users requirements. Depending on the type and size of content, bibliographic databases, bibliographic databases can be categorized as –

- Discipline oriented larger abstracting services/ databases, e.g., BIOSIS (Biological Abstracts), CAS (Chemical Abstracts Services), AMS Mathscinet, Sociological Abstracts and Psychological Abstracts, etc.
- Interdisciplinary databases: The coverage is normally based on key or core broad subjects, SCISEARCH

(Scientific Information), SOCIAL SCISEARCH (Social science information), SCOPUS, WEB OF KNOWLEDGE, Indian Citation Abstracts

- Smaller, specialized databases: limited to specific subject, mostly are generated by research associations e.g. RAPRA Abstracts-Rubber & Plastics Research Assn.
- Databases covering specific types of publications, Ex: CLAIMS/CHEM (for chemical patents), NEXIS (covering newspaper),
- Full Text Databases: The databases offer full text of journal articles, books, chapters in PDF, HTML format and also provide bibliographic data of the document referred at full length, e.g. EBSCOHOST, JSTOR, Sciencedirect, Annual Reviews, ACM Digital Library, IEEE online, American Chemical Society, Cambridge Books Online, etc
- Statistical Databases – e.g. Indiastat presents the statistical data with content as well as bibliographic description
- Images Databases – e.g. ARTSTOR presents images with content as well as bibliographic description

The categorization of description and distinction between bibliographic search, citation and full text/content faded ever since bibliographic search databases were including full text hyperlinks and DOI (Digital object identifier) in their records and full text databases have been giving the entire description of document at full length. Similarly the distinction between library and non-library databases as well as resources are superseded as the level of relating bibliographic records and databases grows with the emergence of new integration technologies and discovery services.

6.1.3. DBMS Features - General vs. Bibliographic

For processing bibliographic data, general DBMS approach is normally taken with a few modifications to make the bibliographic data management more effective.

Generally, a file is defined as a set of similar records. For example, in a salary database, each record contains an employee name, Dept. /Unit, Basic pay, D.A, etc. It is to be noted that here in all the records, the data would be more or less same. However, in the case of bibliographic information, there would be a large number of fields covering the bibliographic description of various types of documents like monographs, conference proceedings, journal articles, patents, standards, etc.

However, depending on the type of document, only a few fields would be filled. Moreover, in bibliographic database, the length of each field greatly varies from record to record. This situation demands that the database designer to declare the field length to a maximum to accommodate all length of titles and leaving a large number of blanks in each field, results in high wastage of disk space.

The bibliographic databases include different kind of fields which are to be treated as one field at the time of data entry and should be treated as separate fields for the purpose of indexing or printing. The author, place of publication fields belong to this category. However, it is quite unpredictable to record and designate the number of authors for each document; to declare fields as author1, author2, author3, etc. So, at the time of searching, the query should be given as - if author1=X or author2=X or author3=X, etc. kind of statement. On the other hand, if all the author names are put together in one field, the database should provide embedded search. Then the author index for printing purpose becomes impossible as the machine can in no way identify authors individually from a string of authors. To resolve this problem, the bibliographic DBMS has introduced the concept of repeatable fields. Here, at the time of database design, author field is declared as one field and at the time of data entry, each author is demarcated by a separator and at the time of index generation and printing, each author is treated as a separated field.

Normally, the general DBMS allows one to create fields with a mnemonic name in a particular language. For example, the field name can be author, title, publisher, etc. However, there would be restriction in the length of the field name and a restriction that it should start with an alphabetic character and so on. However, using alphabetic mnemonic names for fields greatly restricts the use of bibliographic information across networks, as it is language dependent. A good information network should cater to the requirements of users irrespective of the language in which the information is presented. This necessitates that numeric code should be allowed to represent various bibliographic elements. In fact, CCF, UNIMARC provide a numeric code for each bibliographic element. However, the idea of standardizing these tag codes in bibliographic DBMS was greatly taken care by the international agencies/ Associations such as ALA, Library of Congress, etc. by bringing out a standard format covering all languages for entering bibliographic records, for all types of documents, since many standards emerging from every country like USMARC, UKMARC were practically not meeting the requirement.

The above features of bibliographic databases and information retrieval requirements are very distinct from the remaining types. Some of the distinctions of bibliographic databases comparing with other databases are mentioned below.

General Database

- **Bibliographic Database**

Master file contains a set of similar records

- Master file contains a set of records which may be dissimilar, depending of the type of document described.

The number of fields in each record is fixed

- The number of fields in a record may vary, depending on the type of document described. For example: The number of fields for a record describing a monograph will be different from a record describing a journal article.

The length of fields is fixed

- The length of field is variable depending on the actual length of the data. Ex: In one record, the title may be shorter and in another the title may be longer.

Normally, the maximum field length is more than 256 characters.

- Field length can be more than 256 characters, especially in fields like authors, title, notes, abstract, etc.

The length of records is fixed

- The length of records may vary, as the number of fields and the length of each field varies

There is no concept of "repeatable field"

- Repeatable field is essential as fields like authors, ISBN may have more than one element

Field name is used to identify an element in a record

- Tag codes are used to identify an element in a record to overcome the language barrier

Structured Query Language (SQL) is used for querying.

- A search language is used with Boolean operators.

The record structure is designed by the DBMS software developer

- Record structure is based on specified standards such as ISO 2709

Bibliographic Database Management Systems (BDBMS) have become essential to handle large information within the libraries locally by using CDS/ISIS or using any other commercial LIS software and outside by secondary information agencies on CD-ROMs or via online.

6.2. ELECTRONIC DATABASES

The term 'Electronic' according to Oxford Dictionary – is a device operating with components such as microchips and transistors that control and direct electric currents. The word 'Resource' in the context of libraries and information centres can be mentioned for 'Information resources'. Thus e-resources can be basically referred as the documents produced and preserved in electronic medium and distributed through computer operated networks. The terms digital, virtual or paperless or online are used almost synonymously with electronic in spite of holding slightest variations. Library of Congress explained that - "an electronic resource is a manifestation of a work that requires the use of a computer for access. Peripheral devices attached to the computer (such as a CD-ROM drive) may also be required. The manifestation's carrier is accessed either directly (e.g., via CD-ROM, etc.) or remotely (e.g. via the internet). The information in electronic format will be full text, numerical data or graphical models or images or multimedia or in interactive form or in combination altogether. In either way it is requiring computer or any devise to access the electronic product".

The developments in information industry are correlated with several technological advancements in the design of powerful computers; fast random-access storage devices and low cost terminals and also effective telecommunication networks. Online information industry is as recent as 30 years old. Initial use of computers was limited to provide quick, easy access to scholarly Information about the print publications i.e. for typing entries, printing cards or bibliographies, storing bibliographic data, sorting, compilations for Abstracting & Indexing services, CAS and SDI services in print and also other formats. The popular researcher Tenopir of University of Tennessee and others (2003) described the evolution of e-resources in three phases starting from late 1970s.

1. The print journals shifting into electronic format were minimal until early 1990s.
2. With the publishing and distribution of electronic journals over internet and the invention of the World Wide Web in 1993, publishers started massive publication of e-journals on the web in parallel with the traditional printed versions.
3. The advanced a third phase began later from the year

2000, which is characterized by the placement of e-journals in a full digital context, i.e. the searching capabilities and other advanced features were integrated.

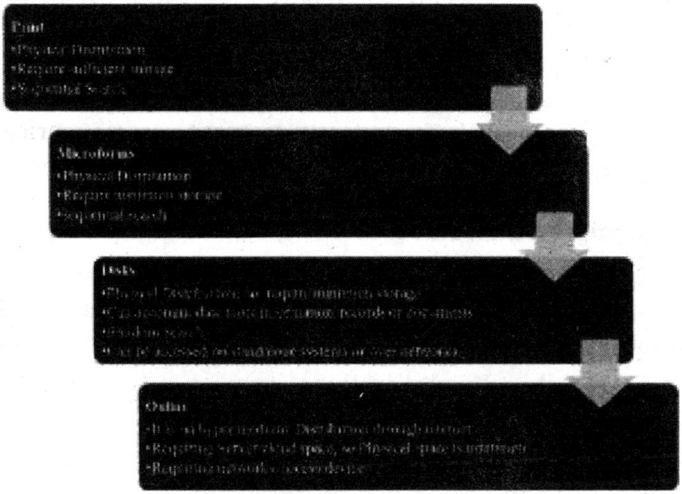

Fig. 6.4. Transformation of Physical Format

6.2.1. Integrated Databases of Information Resources

Electronic databases are the integrated collections of records representing information resources in electronic format i.e., journal articles or journals, book chapters or books, abstracts, statistical data tables, images and multimedia files. Full text databases primarily constitute metadata with hyperlinks to full text documents in HTML or PDF format, while bibliographic search databases provide metadata of the documents with only hyperlinks to full text of the documents and both the databases are facilitating search/browse and advanced search options. Full text /full content access to institutions these databases are subject to their license agreements with publishers. Similarly, document delivery services also could be possible because of the integration of articles from several institutions, offering a minimum of search/browse functions.

These databases though initially were facilitating the exchange of bibliographic data and functioning for reference purpose later evolved incorporating back files and personalized features for users. These developments were replacing gradually CAS Current awareness services SDI services. E-resources are delivered on FTP (File Transfer Protocol), Electronic mail, Disk (CD/DVD/Blue ray) or Online through Internet.

6.2.2. Optical Disk Databases

Optical disks can store various forms of electronic files – full text, numerical, multimedia, images, and searchable records, search programs or inbuilt integrated search engine.

- Easy to handle physically
- Comparatively low cost media and highly durable
- High information storage capacity: ranging from 700 MB to 50 GB
  - CD-ROM (Compact Disk Read only Memory) can store up to 700 MB;
  - DVD (Digital Video Disk) (4.7 to 8.4 GB),
  - BD (Blu-ray) stores up to 25 GB for single layered disks to 50 G.B. for dual layered disks
- Easy to access the data (random access) and also to transfer
- Searchable and user friendly interfaces
- Data protection / Data security
- Able to access offline and online (intranet)

Fig. 6.5. Optical Disk Drives

Types of Disks : The optical media and optical storage, an optical disc drive (ODD) or optical disk is any storage media that holds content in digital format and read using a laser assembly is considered optical media. The "Optical data storage" techniques that use optical means are to read, write and/or erase data. These disks are direct access storage devices that are written and read by light is said to be Optical Disk.

Fig. 6.6. Optical Disks

- **Read-Only :** Read-only discs are pressed from a master at the time of manufacture and cannot be erased. Music CDs, CD-ROM, DVD-ROM, DVD-Video and BD-ROM (Blu-ray)
- **Write-Once (Burnable) :** Write-once discs are recorded in the user's environment but cannot be erased. CD-R, DVD-R, DVD+R, BD-R (Blu-ray), WORM, MO (magneto-optic) discs
- **Rewritable (Phase Change and Magneto Optic) :** Rewritable discs can be written and re-written number of times. CD-RW, DVD-RAM, DVD-RW, DVD+RW and BD-RE (Blu-ray)
- **Magneto-optic (MO) disks :** are extremely robust (see magneto-optic disk). DVD, holographic storage, ISO 13346, multilevel optical disc and legality of optical storage

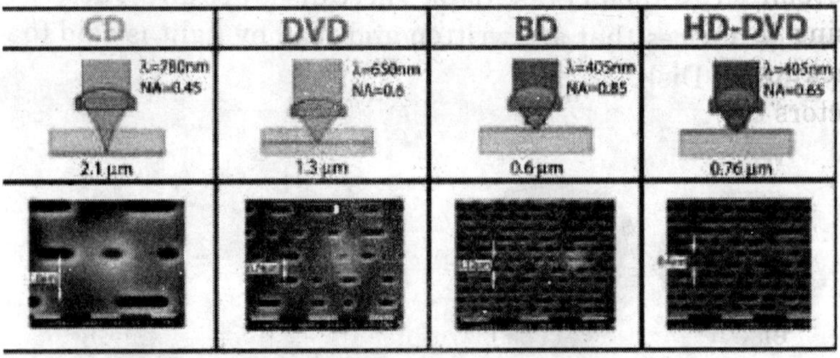

Fig. 6.7. The "Optical data storage" techniques to read, write and/or erase data

Library Applications : Though the disk media emerged from the necessities of music recording companies improving the clarity, durability, storage and distribution of their recordings, it was the information world that utilized the technology for disseminating their products safely, easily meeting the storage space needs. The features were helpful for vendors of information products in distributing the bibliographic search databases; full text databases; bibliographies, directories, document delivery services, union catalogs etc. It was also useful for libraries to maintain the information in larger quantities in lesser space at lesser cost, while it became a valuable tool for library to search retrieval of information through the programs / applications or search engines. Further this information in the form of disks were also used for the-

- Exchange of bibliographic data easily
- The efficiently handling reference services and tools
- Promoting CAS/ SDI - Current awareness services among researchers
- Securing the precious library data by preserving in disks, which is called back up data and Archiving

Limitations : Though initially most of the information services were rendered using optical media to disseminate their content, now due to the prominence of online dissemination of the products, only fewer publishers are using this medium especially for supplementing online or backup or archiving the data. Additionally the following factors contributed for decreasing the dependency on disks

- Wear and tear
- Limited storage capacity ranging from 700 MB to 50 GB, whereas the information is unlimited
- Investment on intranet equipment is an additional or else it remains accessible through standalone personal computers
- Accessing devices also need to be updated to maintain the compatibility
- Constant updates are necessary and possible only by means of replacing the disk with updated one.
- All the publishers/vendor will not be following same standards and retrieval interfaces
- Chances of missing disks in transit

The above limitations set aside the disks for exclusive purposes of information dissemination and backup while paving the way for online information systems.

6.2.3. Online Databases

The Online Information Systems are considered advantageous as the data, content or information generated from all the divisions is well integrated among the divisions and flows over the network of all communication channels. They are designed to work as a coherent entity. Their search interfaces provide information to users from within and also beyond the system. However such a significant system requires primarily the resources electronically generated by the learned societies, academic institutions, commercial publishers, government departments, non-government or private agencies, non-profit agencies, associations and individuals. The system further requires -

- Random access storage devices
- Electronic data compilation, Computer timesharing
- Interactive information retrieval software
- Internet connectivity and network components - Modem, Routers, Hub, Cables, Switches, Wi-Fi, Data card, Communication (FTP) software
- Computer Terminals to access (PCs, laptops, tablet PCs, Smart mobiles etc.)
- Peripherals – word processors, printers, flash drives
- Provision of online access – subscription, open

Lancaster (1995) defined E-Journal as "the one created for the electronic medium and available only in this medium . .". E-Book can be explained as "an electronic book is a book-length publication in digital form, consisting of text images, or both, readable on computers or other electronic devices". Van Damm stated that it is "an electronic version of a printed book "... the ability to store text in electronic form and subsequently retrieve it through the use of a computerized device". Watkinson (2001) mentioned that Reference book/s made available in electronic form, whereas e-monographs are books, which are records of primary research. In (certain) disciplines such work represents the main channel for communication of research. The E-resources are packaged and distributed as -

- Individual titles
- Publishers Databases
- Aggregator's databases
- Collections (databases)
- Bibliographical search databases
- E-prints, preprints, post prints, as single files
- Special Collections
- Customized Collections

E-resources can be accessed by way of subscribing directly with the publisher/aggregator or through vendor or by being member of a respective consortium or wherever openly available. Access is usually authenticated to institutional IPs as per site wide multiple user's licenses or simultaneous single, two or three user licenses or even according to FTE (Full time equivalent) counts of the institutions. For accessing resources in institutions, password authentication (login/password) is rare; however password authentication is compulsory for administrators to download usage metrics and registered users to realize personalization features. Open access is free of subscription does not require any user/administrator's password authentication.

The initial online systems were IBM STAIRS in 1973 and the activity was triggered around 1990 when computer storage technology made it possible in a economical way. The initial abstracting and indexing services were turned into full text databases in later years integrating with full text content of journal articles, books and other documents, while scholarly publishers started migrating their full text publications to web editions facilitating search and other user centric features.

ProQuest's Dialog online information service was acquired from Thomson Reuters in mid-2008. Dialog was the first online information retrieval system used globally and developed from Dialog system in 1966. In 1980s a low-priced dial-up version a subset of Dialog was marketed to individual users as Knowledge Index including INSPEC, MathSciNet, over 200 other bibliographic and reference databases, as well as third-party vendors who would go to physical libraries to copy materials for a fee and send it to the service subscriber.

The early projects such as EIES (Electronic Information Exchange System) and the BLEND (the Birmingham Loughborough Electronic Network Development) to publish the refereed, edited, copyrighted electronic journals during 1980s lead to the success of e-journal publishing all ovèr the world, but both the experiments were not successful and discontinued after one or two issues. Turoff and Hiltz in 1982 outlined the initial forms of electronic journals, later evolved as -

1) An informal newsletter
 = electronic newsletters or 'Zines',
2) An un-refereed 'Paper Fair' = preprint servers
3) An electronic form of print journal = e-journals
4) 'A highly structured inquiry-response system'
 = listservers/electronic conferencing

The electronic journal publishing began accelerating during 1990s with the active publication initiatives of academic institutions, i.e. Universities of Houston, Virginia Polytechnic Institute and State and North Carolina State etc. 'Online Journal of Current Clinical Trials' was the first peer-reviewed electronic full text e-journal with graphics launched in Oct. 91 as a joint venture of OCLC (Online Computer Library Center) and AAAS (American Association for the Advancement of Science). Some more titles were added subsequently to this program by scientific societies like American Chemical Society (ACS), Royal Society of Chemistry (RSC), American Institute of Physics (AIP), Institute of Physics (IOPP), and academic publishers -MIT

Press, John Hopkins University and Oxford University Press etc. those initiated providing free online access to print subscriptions. Even the commercial publishers such as - Elsevier, Wiley, and Sage have joined in e-publishing activities and began distributing e-journals at additional price of 5% to 12.5% over the print journals, while some publishers like Springer, World Scientific, etc. have been offering free web editions with print. The technological advancements and innovations in networking, World Wide Web, and portal technologies including the hypermedia enabled the federation of e-resources, formation of collections or databases, and the development of consortia, gateways, digital libraries etc. brought transformation in scholarly communication. Further, the electronic publishing brought speed, economy, user-centric applications and the value to the scholarly communication while expanding the range of information products services to academic and research community.

The principle stakeholders in the creation and distribution of information generated in electronic format are – authors, publishers, vendors / aggregators, intermediaries those performing searches for users, libraries facilitating resources and the end users.

According to the depth and nature of content, these online resources can be grouped into general and scholarly. The scholarly information resources can be peer-reviewed and also non peer-reviewed.

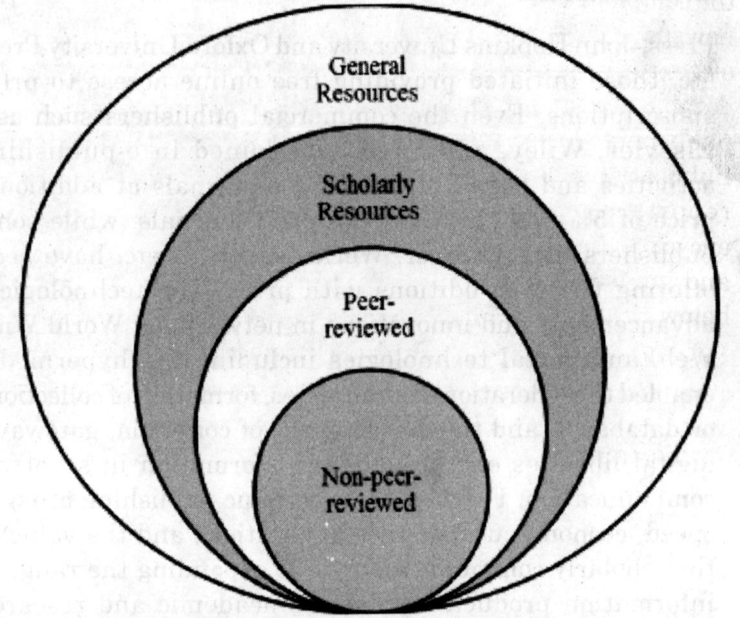

Fig. 6.8. Online Databases - Content

The main constituents of the electronic resources presently contains -

- Article Full text, Abstracts
- Current issues as well as Archives (Back files)
- Table of contents
- Images, Graphics, Models
- References, Reviews
- Citations
- Hyper Links to related articles
- Search interface with 'Basic search'; Advanced search options and Tips for searching
- Filters to minimize irrelevant retrieval
- Indications as articles for subscribed / unsubscribed / open access
- Pricing options for purchasing unsubscribed article/s

Full Text Databases : A full text database contains

the complete text of scholarly articles in journals, magazines, newspapers, books, dissertations, reports or any other kinds of textual documents. The popular publisher's full text database portals form a platform to host content of other publishers. These full text databases cover journals, serial Publications, books, theses / dissertations, patents, annual reports, technical reports and reference material - encyclopedias, directories, handbooks, prospectus, calendars, and guidebooks. Some of the popular databases are given below

- Elsevier's Sciencedirect: (Elsevier, Academic Press, Cell Press etc.) Journals, Books, Reference books etc
- Emerald for journals, books, management content
- Springer Link (Springer, Kluwer and other publishers full text content)- Journals, Books, Lecture note series, protocols)
- Cambridge Journals Online
- Oxford university press journals, Books,
- Project Muse – John Hopkins University Press
- HeinOnline - Research product with legal history available in an online, fully-searchable, image-based format.
- Project Euclid – Cornell University Library licensed publications of other publishers
- Taylor and Press – Multidisciplinary full text database for journals, books
- Wiley Digital Library (Multidisciplinary Books, Journals, Protocols etc)
- Popular scientific societies such as - AMS, ACS, RSC, IEEE, ACM, SIAM, AIP, APS, SIAM, IOPP
- JSTOR - Back files of Full-text periodicals covering a wide range of disciplines
- EBSCO (aggregators database)
- ABN/ Inform Complete (aggregators database)

- ProQuest - Dissertations and Theses
- U.S. Patents Full text databases
- Indian Journals.com

Majority of full text databases are currently highlighting authors identities and affiliations contact details, purchase options, recommended articles, related articles, citing article, metrics of articles, Feedback etc as illustrated vide Screenshots

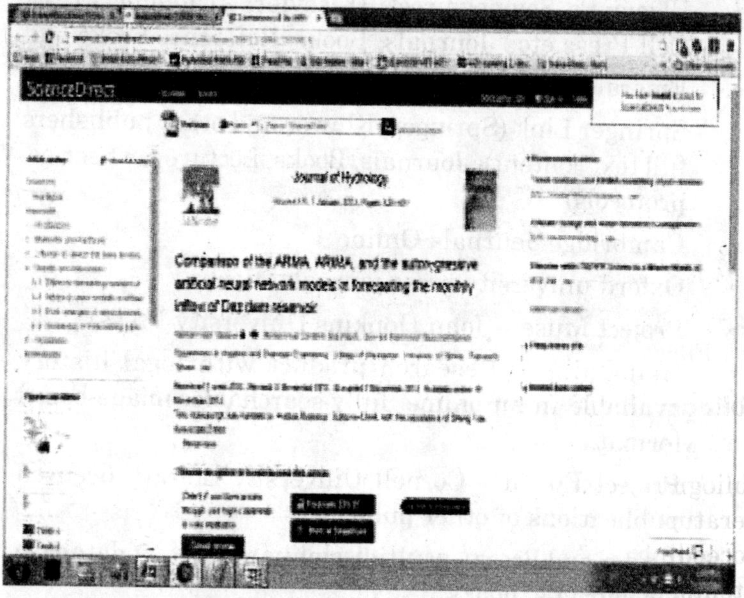

Fig. 6.9. Sciencedirect Article Record (Screenshot)

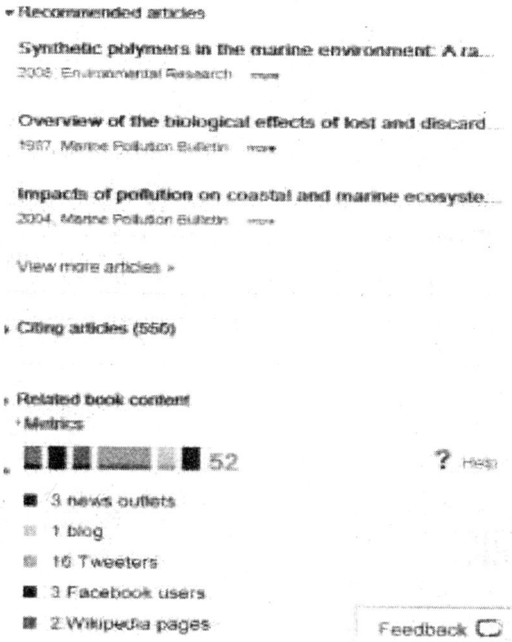

Fig. 6.10. Sciencedirect Article Record (Screenshot)

Bibliographic Search Databases

A bibliographic search database is a collection of bibliographic records containing references to published literature i.e. journal and newspaper articles, conference proceedings, reports, government and legal publications, patents, books, etc. Most of the bibliographic databases are proprietary, available by licensing agreement with the creators (indexing and abstracting services) or vendors, e.g. Chemical abstracts.

Until mid-20th century, researchers were depending on printed bibliographic indexes for scholarly literature search. These databases were highly expensive contained bibliographic descriptions of journal articles that were searchable by author, title, journal name or subject headings. The early online user interfaces were crude, the access was quite costlier and searching was done by librarians for users'.

These databases provide the bibliographic data of each document listed along with hyperlinks to full text documents as shown in Screenshot of ERIC database

- Web of Knowledge – Thomson Reuters
- ERIC - Education Resources Information Centre
- Mathscinet - American Mathematical Society
- RSC Abstracts -Royal Society of Chemistry
- SCOPUS - Elsevier
- Chemical Abstracts Service - SciFinder Scholar, STN database
- Indian Citation Abstracts

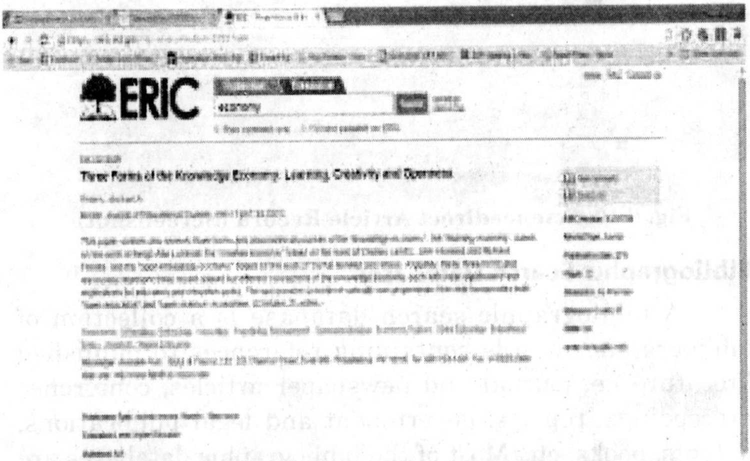

Fig. 6.11. ERIC Article Record (Screenshot)

Statistical Data (categorized data)

- Censes Databases
- Manupatra's range of online information products legal research in India encompasses traditional and new media formats including - Online Databases, CD-ROMs, Journals, Manupatra Law Reports

- CMIE economic outlook - A Product by Centre for Monitoring Indian Economy Pvt. Ltd. Industry Outlook | Prowess | CapEx
- EPWRFITS India Time Series Database
- IndiaStat - Statistics and Socio-economic data
- Government / Non-government Websites

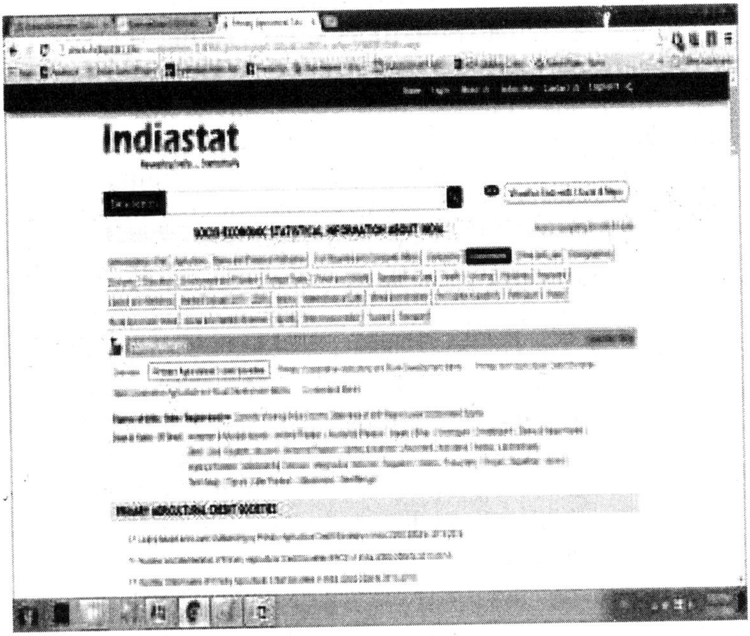

Fig. 6.12. Indiastat statistical data Record (Screenshot)

Multimedia Databases (categorized data)

Multimedia computing and access began dominating all facets of human life significantly in academic ventures. Multimedia can be defined as "a combination of different media i.e., text, pictures, sounds, video, animations, etc. used to present multimodal information in conjunction with computer technology". The data of media files are stored in binary strings of zeros and ones, and are encoded according to file type – i.e. media file. With development and integration of GUI technology the task of storing text for getting media effect has become complex. There is great variance in the quality and size of storage of still images on the basis of resolution, size, complexity and compression scheme used to store image.

The digitalized videos are the most space consuming multimedia data type especially 3D objects and videos. They are forming part of educational, training and research resources of the current time, transforming the teaching strategies and students learning styles. However, the huge amount of multimedia data and information could also challenge educators to efficiently search, browse, access, use, and store the data for their classroom teaching. "Digital media provide excellent opportunities for creating engaging learning environments, and help students acquire creative, communicative, and collaborative skills. New media, including Web 2.0 applications such as social networking, blogs, wikis, YouTube, and podcasting have become pervasive and are becoming an integral component of learning environments. The growing popularity of these new media suggests that educators need to understand these new possibilities of emerging technologies and incorporate them into the teaching and learning environment" (Yu and Brandenburg, 2011).

A multimedia database is a database that hosts one or more primary media file types such as video, audio, radar signals and documents or pictures and animation sequences and composite multimedia i.e. a combination of two or more of the above date in various encoding. The popular image formats are jpg, png, bmp, and tiff. 'These media files are - Static media images and handwriting); dynamic media (time-dependent, i.e. video and sound bites); dimensional media - 3D games or computer-aided drafting programs- CAD (Manoj, 2013). Media is also categorized as - continuous (audio and video) and discrete – i.e. time independent still images and graphics. Primarily these media files consists of special data structures and formats to store and display the information about multimedia objects and also to provide access to the real object. The multimedia database applications differ from conventional databases in the way they are stored, data is maintained and retrieved. They are multidimensional and characterized by its high volume space requirements, temporality features, lacking specific structures and a different logistics requiring compression algorithms etc. Though these databases are complex in nature, the data is used for class room teaching, demonstrations, learning and also considered as a source of self –help for librarians in implementing several ICT applications for the benefit of working environment and refining the users' services.

Other Resources

Electronic Mails, Blogs; Electronic Forums; Subject Gateways; Online Directories; Online service portals.

After several decades of the invention of printing, technological advancements in Information Communication Industries brought tremendous developments in information generation, document production, and dissemination of information.

Advantages and Limitations

Libraries can be more secured since problems related to print media will not be there with electronic information material such as

- Unlike print, their subscription is more economical, since the content is usually supplied for multiple years and printing costs or distribution expenditure is not involved.
- They are cost beneficial, cost effective since the one subscription to database/s are providing many titles in their collections
- Open access material links can be collected and used.
- Storing and maintaining of databases as well as

archival collection is very easy in CD ROM or DVD formats or through intranet servers with less space that avoids the building construction expenditure and man power.

- Institutions can be integrated to form online consortium or resource sharing networks to share the resources.
- Further it is possible to link several journals of a single publisher, e.g. ACM Digital Library or aggregations of many publishers e.g. EBSCO to form databases or collections
- Saving stack space, its maintenance (organizing, shelving, dusting, binding, spine labeling etc) and theft/ tear of pages / damage
- There is no delay in getting the material, neither issues will be missing in transit and no claims and also Libraries need not physically circulate resources among users.
- Speedy document delivery (across network)
- The usage of e-resources can be monitored
- Information updates will be available
- Standardized interfaces and services, make it easy to learn, use and manage

Users prefer e-resources due to advantages

- Users can immediately refer e-resources after publication
- Users can see related and cited articles
- Can view citations to their own articles
- Several value based facilities like multimedia, search interface that provide basic as well as advanced search across the journals over the period. Further it provides simultaneous and multi user access.
- E-journals are presented with hyperlinks to references or other related documents, citing articles etc.

- Users can register with their e-mail and topics of their interest, so they can get e-mail alerts regarding the publication of articles and also searches as well as search results
- They can purchase access to unsubscribed articles

Limitations : unlike print, Libraries can never own the content. Institutions can only access the content provided to them. Therefore, it is not possible for -

- Libraries to retain subscribed content after the expiry of the subscription period
- Preserve back files or archive online content for future use
- Document delivery
- Posting on public websites or blogs or public networks

Further, the

- Failures in electricity, access speed, network structure, virus, firewall etc. will hamper the use of e-journals by academic community.
- Frequent changes in display format of bibliographic data or user interface cause disturbance in accessing the content easily.
- The excessive use or unfair practices of online access to licensed content by the users interrupt the publishers service for violating the fair-use terms and license terms & conditions.
- Users require regular orientation
- Libraries require skilled manpower

After several decades of the invention of printing, technological advancements in Information Communication Industries brought tremendous developments in information generation, document production, and dissemination of information. The emergence of the digital computers, e-publishing, invention of Internet and the World Wide Web, etc. have vigorously transformed the media of scholarly communication and laid a great impact on the library's perspective of information resources, maintenance of library collections by redesigning of information retrieval systems and tools.

7

Information Retrieval Systems and DBMS Approach

The need for information arises in any abstract form. Information is recorded in the form of text, numerals, digits, images, and multimedia and exists in documents. The library database consists of bibliographic records of books, periodicals and other materials, whereas publishers catalog contains records of their publications; and electronic databases constitute the records of electronic resources provided by publishers/aggregators. Institutions need to handle data in huge quantities, consisting of several designated elements. The large amount of data has to be organized in convenient manner so that the needed piece of information can be retrieved from any part of the database as and when required. The information retrieval (IR) is a challenge in itself in getting efficient retrieval with precision against the query. Information Retrieval System is designed with an objective of representing information for efficient retrieval and the creation of possible approaches as per user's requirements.

7.1. INFORMATION RETRIEVAL SYSTEM

Since, the computers are used to process, manipulate,

store to retrieve data, the information retrieval systems are referred to as Computer Based IRS or computerized IRS. The term Information retrieval has several definitions giving different dimensions, however primarily referring to the function of finding the sources of information with a query. Random house dictionary defined the term Information Retrieval as - the systematic storage and recovery of data from a file, card catalogue or the memory bank of a computer'. McGraw-Hill dictionary described IR as "the technique and process of searching, recovery and interpreting information from large amounts of stored data". World Book encyclopedia referred it as a system for locating facts in a central information storage area, whereas the encyclopedia for computer science meant IR as a "concern with the structure, analysis, organization, storage, searching and dissemination of information'. Information retrieval systems deal with the design of integrated information system, which deals with recovery of particular data from a store through an efficient mechanism of search.

7.1.1. Objectives

The main objective of an IRS is to provide information or information about resources against specific queries from the respective database/s (collection of information records). In the context of library and information services, the objective refers to the ability of the system to retrieve the bibliographic references or documents to satisfy the user's information need. Further, the IRS will be able to:

1. Have a means for creating, modifying and organizing data to achieve the general goal
2. Produce a correct representation of users' needs and match the need with the information in database
3. To reduce the unwanted retrieval of information by applying filters and be able to provide appropriate displays of information entities which match the need
4. To relate the information available through different types of sources

5. Allow the above steps to be repeated until the satisfactory results are obtained

7.1.2. Components of IRS

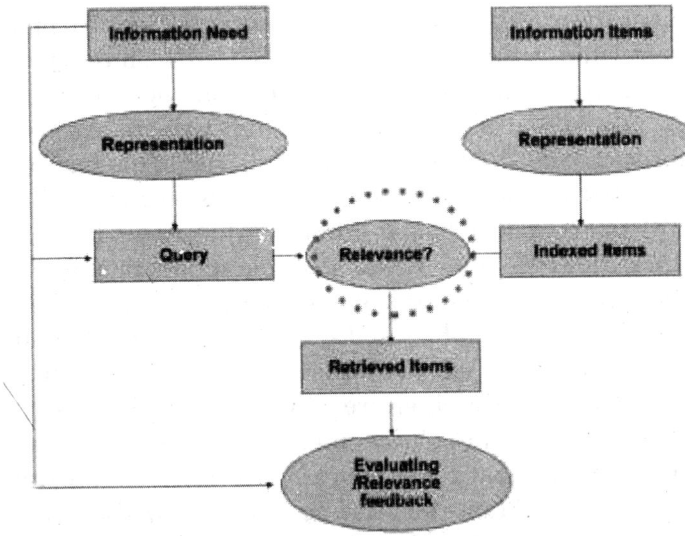

Fig. 7.1. IRS Components

Information retrieval systems functionally encompass the whole range of activities from putting together information to its dissemination and then to incorporate changes into the system, based on the feedback given by the users of the system. Thus, IRS system is encircled in the entire activity from the stage of acquisition of documents, recording the data, storage, process, dissemination and feedback and modification. Accordingly the components of the IRS system of a central collection or a database includes-

- A module for in-putting, editing and updating facility
- A module for dissemination (manual or automatic)
- A search interface for users to handle the query and retrieval of information through display or output
- A module for incorporation of feedback
- Scope for redesigning the system

The information retrieval systems were developed with the pioneering efforts of MEDLARS, DIALOG, H.P. Luhn during 1960s and 70s. The early systems of library computerization did not have in-built character representation until the General Electric's Gas Turbine Division, Ohio, USA initiated with IBM-704 computer on US Naval Ordnance Test Station (NOTS) applications. The system printed out a report with author, title information and abstract, but GE system permitted the use of the Boolean 'AND' in search logic. Further MEDLARS was the major attempt in computer based bibliographic databases for searching Index Medicus. It was also operational in machine searching of a large file of journal article citations for the generation of bibliographies and search outputs on-demand. The system could support the Boolean logic with terms 'and', 'or' 'not' and could search entire citation file, wherein each record is marked by the subject descriptors. This has become model for other database producers and later for hosting them on online systems for easy access. The DIALOG was the landmark in the development of IRS. This was the first online retrieval system. In this users key-in their queries from remote terminals using dial-up connections over telephone lines. Chemical abstracts was next important initiative in 1961 using KWIC (Keyword-in-context) index to the titles of articles. KWOC (Keyword-out-of-context) index listed keywords separately with full titles. Both KWIC and KWOC indexes were used to provide multiple access to documents listed in current-awareness publications. SDI (Selective dissemination of information) services (Haravu, 2004).

7.2. IRS - FUNCTIONAL FEATURES

Bibliographic data of the items is the basis of any resource sharing or information networks. Theoretically and functionally, the information processing is marked with two distinct processes in the design and development of IRS for bibliographic databases. The first process for such a system would be regarding the data/document representation and the second is the modes and methods of storage of data, i.e. the problem of automating storage, manipulation and retrieval of data. The end objects the various formats of data exchange available and standards for data exchange. For example, a document databases and a user's databases are two databases in any library, with an inbuilt mechanism in the respective DBMS for cross referencing, search and matching the documents and users profiles.

7.2.1. Bibliographic Item Representation

The identification of an item from a large information store by means of document and content (subject) representation is an important aspect of IR. Representation of documents in terms of various data elements – creator of the document, title, publisher location etc and the subject (content) descriptors – subject headings, keywords, etc. helps to locate the reference in a larger bibliographic database/s. These keywords along with context provide the necessary semantics to derive the thought content of the document to be represented. Various models of indexing and the features of indexing languages tackle the problems regarding this approach to IRS. The problem of representing documents arises when searching through the whole collection for an information source is not physically possible because of the size the collections. To make things simpler, information is processed and stored as an indicator of the sources in the collection in terms of keywords or descriptors. These keywords along with context provide the necessary semantics (meaningful) to derive the thought content of the document. Various indexing models and the features of indexing languages tackle the problems regarding this approach to IRS.

The variation in the pattern of user information requirements necessitates restructuring of document representation. The choice of the different bibliographic elements needs to be provided to users to represent the query in syntax or search language apart from structuring the entire information in database into smaller units or elements to represent the ideas. This is the approach followed in the DBMS, since our problem on hand is exactly the same as the objectives of DBMS that are adopted to handle the bibliographic data

7.2.2. Automation of IRS – DBMS Approach

In any case, the information is structured into many fields. Each field is filled in with well-defined data elements. A collection of such fields forms a record. A collection of such records together forms a database. Often, there is a need to compile more than one database for an integrated information resources or services. Thus, the database management system (DBMS) aims at organizing data in a structured way for easy and efficient access and retrieval. Out of various DBMS models, the relational model is the most suitable to build an integrated information management system for maintaining the bibliographic databases (BDBMS) for libraries. They are designed to take care of automating processes such as data entry through inbuilt forms and retrieval by highly defined search interfaces. Therefore, the database forms the central focus and all the related functions and applications required for users. For example, bibliographic records form the centre of any library database, which would be comprising of document description in terms of the various data elements like author, title, publisher, year of publication etc. IRS, thus deals with the whole range of activities ranging from collection, storage, search and retrieval. Now the functions related to this database are designed according to the functions within a library.

- Any DBMS essentially would have the facility to input and store data.
- The database forms the central focus and all the related functions. For example, the bibliographic records of the library database would be the document description

in terms of various data elements like - author, title, publisher, year of publication, ISBN/ISSN etc. Accordingly, the functions related to this database are completely designed for the library such as - printing a catalogue card as per the code of cataloguing, Circulation control where the functions are loaning documents to users as per the library lending policies.

- System design takes care of the internal requirements to handle the specific tasks.
- Peripheral or support programs are built into the system to tackle the specific activities.
- The information would be disseminating through various information services and OPACs.
- Bibliographic data is the basis of any resource sharing or networking.

Thus, the trend is to structure the information in the collection into smaller units and then represent the ideas into a whole. The same approach is followed in DBMS to handle the bibliographic data.

7.2.3. Scope of IRS (Print Through Online)

Information recorded in documents flows in informal channels such as invisible college. Thus, the focus of IRS would be on the recorded information irrespective of the format it holds whether it is print, magnetic tapes, microfilms, optical disks or online through internet. Conventionally, the libraries have standard practices of maintaining catalogs for displaying their holdings related to print collections viz. the books and journals and acquiring sophisticated indexing/abstracting tools to assist in the search of scholarly information or published literature to the researchers.

Information is Structured	*Information is Retrievable*
• Searchable terms or keywords	Document/ content descriptors
• Relational words	Author/s,
• References	Title or series,
• Cross references	Subject headings and
• Punctuation marks etc	Keywords, phrases etc.

International Standard Bibliographic Description (ISBD) provides standards for documents description from time to time to catalog library books and other information material, whereas subject representation has been taken care through standard subject headings like LC, Sears etc. These standards facilitate consistency in bibliographic representation, and content representation while indexing designates order (i.e. syntax) to these description terms - alphabets, numerals, symbols, characters etc. The ISO 2709 format standard prescribed standards for exchange of data of bibliographic sources.

The types of file systems, nature of indexing the data elements and ultimately the methods of organization of information, files or documents in the information storage system, decide the method of retrieving the information or documents. Earlier systems ran in batch mode using magnetic tapes as storage medium were rather slow, wherein multiple (added) entries, reference and cross reference entries were helping to satisfy the user's multiple search approaches, e.g. Library catalogs or other publisher/vendors catalogs, reference tools and bibliographic search tools etc. in print/tape formats consist of sequentially arranged records or information. The random access file structures in automated integrated information systems made it easier for locating entries from lengthy and heavy files at a minimum search time. Technological innovations in information storage and random access methods multiplied the information storage and the access speed largely while increasing the recall value and precision in retrieval.

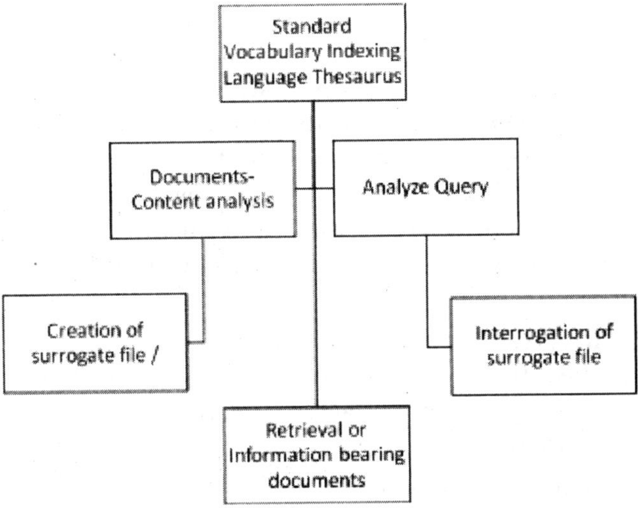

Fig. 7.2. Information Processing and Retrieval Process [*Source* : Documentation and Information – Guha]

7.2.4. Retrieval, Recall, Relevance and Precision:

Retrieval, Recall, Relevance and Precision: are important concepts in Information Retrieval process, which are widely used to measure the performance of IR System.

In an information retrieval scenario, the given a search term results in return of a set of relevant documents; that categorize the entire documents as - “relevant” and “not relevant”.

The term “relevant” refers to the “relevant” category, whereas ‘Recall’ is the number of relevant documents retrieved through a search, divided by the total number of existing relevant documents.

$$\text{Recall} = \frac{\text{No. of relevant documents retrieved}}{\text{Total number of existing relevant documents}}$$

The precision is defined as the number of relevant documents retrieved through a search, divided by the total number of documents retrieved by that search.

$$\text{Precision} = \frac{\text{No. of relevant documents retrieved}}{\text{Total no. of documents retrieved}}$$

In the context of information retrieval, 1.0 means a perfect precision score i.e. every result retrieved by a search was relevant (but says nothing about whether all relevant documents were retrieved) whereas a perfect recall score of 1.0 means that all relevant documents were retrieved by the search (but says nothing about how many irrelevant documents were also retrieved). Alan Gilchrist has identified the following factors to achieve maximum recall and precision.

- RECALL – synonyms control, word form control, classification including hierarchies, lattices, facet analysis, semantic factoring and clusters
- PRECISION – coordination, links, roles, weighting and relational indexing

Further, the libraries also need to operate beyond these conventional practices for accommodating complex electronic documents or digital collections into their collections by adopting the newly emerging standards and metadata formats.

- Standards such as International Standard Bibliographic Description (ISBD)
- The Anglo-American Cataloguing Rules (AACR 2)
- MARC 21
- Dublin Core (a small set of terms that can be used to describe web resources such as -video, images, web pages as well as physical resources such as books or CDs, and objects like artworks)
- The latest RDA (*Resource Description and Access – the standard for cataloguing) etc.

These standards and formats are providing instructions and guidelines on formulating data for resource description, discovery and retrieval. However, these standards and formats were primarily intended for the use by libraries and other cultural organizations such as museums and archives to provide bibliographic information about their resources. Initially the publishers of abstracting agencies have widely applied standard formats to attain consistency in the metadata and to increase precision in the retrieval of information. In the era of wide spread electronic or digital resources, the journal/book publishers also have been adopting these formats, standards and technologies for organizing the ever exploding concepts in world wide web and indexing them in a way retrieving the relevant information with utmost precision from their databases.

7.3. ONLINE INFORMATION RETRIEVAL SYSTEMS

The rapid growth of information resources in electronic format and the varied sources over networks have become extremely unmanageable for leading libraries and publishers/providers with the existing IRS models and technologies.

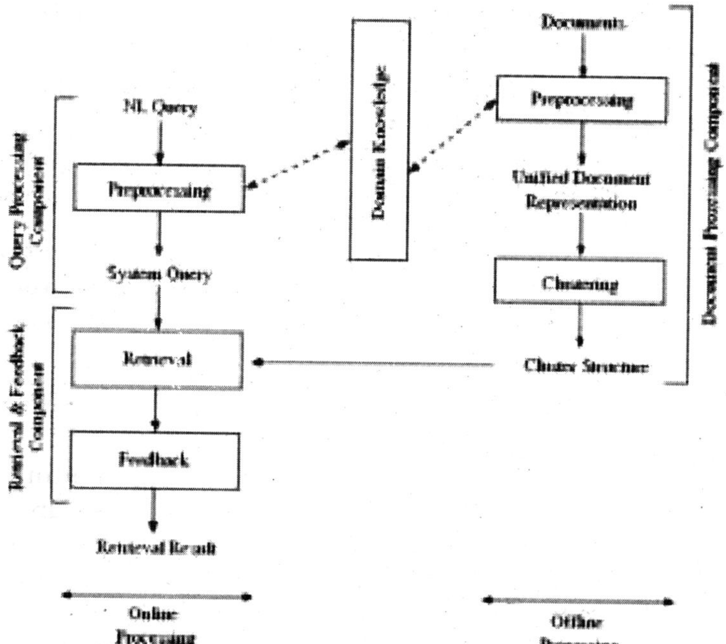

Fig. 7.3. Online Information Retrieval Systems

The publishers, as the most significant stakeholder of the information cycle have been taking active part in this transformation of information generation, dissemination over the public or authenticated networks. They have been more innovative ensuring visibility and authenticity of their resources, by utilizing the emerging technologies, opportunities for their marketing through e-commerce applications to reach these products to a wider range of information users. The situation demands new information seeking systems emphasizing on individual users' needs including personalization, collaboration, and distributed facets. Currently, web users rely on autonomous information systems, where the 'dataset' is very large and heterogeneous with respect to content, structure and quality.

The Internet and WWW have made the approach and access to information much easier also faster, but the problems of finding exactly what is wanted to user/s could not be resolved. The initial support of computer technology could manage the organization as well as of indexing of complex information available through libraries, information centres and abstracting agencies. The aim of online information services initially was to deliver the information or documents directly to the user's desk instead of users approaching the library or source, later the several online information systems based on intellectual effort, technologies and intelligence tools began creating several meaningful approaches to online users for retrieving the information covering the entire document.

Limitations and Issues

The information retrieval systems are tailor made for the needs of libraries and users. However, the results of information retrieval depend on -

- The nature of different sources (targets) connected
- The retrieval system that connects the resources and various sources
- User interface

- The modifications often done by each of the provider system to improve the performance of information sources
- Construction of the query
- Input of the data

Haynes (2004) identified two issues in retrieving information in the context of internet.

- Lack of precision – internet searches often result in the retrieval of too much material, that could be mostly irrelevant
- Low recall – relevant material is missing because the search is not comprehensive enough or the resource is hidden in the deep web and the search is not complete.

Relevance is much reducing while retrieving web documents/information as –

- The user's key in metadata does not appropriately match with those obtainable from the content of the web document. This happens due to lack of representations of (semantics) relations between terms.
- The sources are heterogeneous (different) with regard to the characteristics and functionalities of search interfaces. For example in the case of CD-ROMs or online information systems, there are various interfaces each with its own search language and syntax. It is rather difficult for a user to learn each one of them.
- The heterogeneous character of information or data occurs due to syntax (data format; structure); different attributes such as homonyms, synonyms in databases and semantics (the meaning of terms in a special context of application).

The limitations of meta-search services perceived by Walker (2010) with regard to speed, quality of search and retrieval and the stability are discussed hereunder.

1. Search Speed : Search engines such as Google have

a set of user expectations and sub-second response times that are expected from library search engines. The presentation of the results set, meta-search engines are dependent on the speed of response of the target systems and wait for the slowest resource to respond (subject to a system timeout). Some meta-search engines address this challenge by presenting results from each target resource as soon as they receive them. However, such practices are not effective, as it does not allow merging and de-duplication of results.

2. Search quality : In order to offer a single query interface, the search functionality is reduced to facilitate a common approach across all resources.

3. Stability : Meta-searching relies on the capability of the engine to adapt the user's unified query to the search protocol and syntax of each of the search targets (sources or connectors), and then convert the results obtained in a unified format. As the information providers regularly change their interfaces, such connectors require constant maintenance. Though the meta-search providers usually update such changes, the delays if any are affecting the results in retrieval.

The above issues concerning information retrieval through meta-search interfaces have been paving way for the emergence of new schemes of organizing concepts in WWW, indexing methods, integrated discovery services and tools that ensure comprehensive access to the entire collection of information resources including library's as per the expectations of the current generation users.

7.4. ONLINE IRS - TECHNOLOGIES

LIS field has been all through exploring ways and means of organizing, mapping the ever exploding concepts, types of documents, application of technologies, evolution of techniques and tools for meeting the information needs of users.

In the current context of electronic information world, the word 'information' or 'data 'is referring to the content or sources of information available through various storage devices like the hard disk, floppy diskettes and optical disks and World Wide Web. It is also a fact that CD-ROMs are compact, handy and comprising of larger information sources and also proved as useful application for disk based information services. The capacities of these small optical disks were equivalent to a whole shelf of books was quite attractive to the library users. Subsequently a number of online applications were developed for users to browse / search, retrieve and access the required information from web such as – Online Public Access Catalogs, search engines, meta-search engines, the search interfaces in full text databases, bibliographic search & citation databases, discovery services etc. The libraries generate OPAC to display their collection, while assisting users in accessing the other non-library services. Thus the library collection has gone beyond the purview of traditional catalog services or even web OPAC as they were designed for displaying library holdings and services are limited to specific library/ or a group of libraries. Therefore, getting the comprehensive view is harder during the retrieval because –

- The information generated in varied digital data formats
- The information is often distributed across multiple information systems or sources
- The access to information is mostly restricted in network protocols.

In the present context of maintaining hybrid libraries (containing the collections of print information material and networked information resources and digital documents), it is required that information and these resources needed to be displayed with unified search. Therefore, the user interfaces should be able to bring these diverse information sources together highlighting the hidden relations among aggregated sets of information. The ability to retrieve relevant information is very important aspect of research development, disciplines and industry. Thereby users are automatically directed to relevant information enhancing their abilities. Dempsey (2003) identified the extension of information services especially when users retrieve information or documents from World Wide Web.

- To provide the cross-searching or meta-search services, that hides the differences in search interfaces and searches across several sources and present the combination of results.
- To provide 'views' or sets of resources based on individual preferences. In each case, the focus has been on accessing the bibliographic resources, catalogs, abstracting and indexing services, e-journals, and locally developed databases, as well as openly available scholarly resources.

7.4.1. Integration of Resources

The integration of resources forms a centralized solution for managing e-resources and facilitating collaboration, extensive support for consortia needs and sharing of e-resources. Ex Libris, the library automation vendor was providing a complete solution for managing the wide spectrum of library materials and processes as part of an integrated system. Libraries can offer a single user interface for searching all material types— electronic, digital, and print. Users get the most up-to-date collection of journals and e-books available from their institution. Users also search via a single, intuitive interface for e-resources from a wide range of information providers. Users can immediately view full text, citations, and other retrieval options and services provided by their institutions. The main library can share the resources through cloud based services. Rules and regulations of the library and ILL facilities can be put on the cloud and shared by libraries making it more convenient for the users.

7.4.2. Federated Technologies

The ideal solution is to facilitate one search to users through several sources (targets). The meta-search services provide users with a unified interface that is connected to the diverse and discrete information environments and therefore library does not require storing, indexing or updating the full data of the target resources hosted by all publishers/vendors. The terms -integrated searching, meta-searching and cross-database searching etc. are used to describe the mechanism that connects the search engine, to licensed and free resources. This mechanism also broadcasts the query to each database simultaneously in real time and displays the results at once. The features of federated search technology are explained by the providers of federated search technology, WebFeat clearing some of misconceptions prevailing regarding federated search.

1. Federated search engines leave no stone unturned : Although many vendors claim to offer federated search engines and most of them search through Z39.50 and free databases, but cannot search the databases, under subscribed licenses and IP authentication, particularly for remote users.

2. De-dupe really works : Federated search engines cannot present de-duplicated results because in principle this technology does not support download of all the results to sort and index again to de-duplicate.

3. Relevancy rankings are totally relevant : for the similar reason, the relevancy rankings are inaccurate.

4. Federated searching is software, is software, and also a service. A federated search engine searches databases that update and change an average of 2 to 3 times per year. This means that a system accessing 100 databases is subject to between 200 and 300 updates per year almost one per day! Subscribing to a federated searching service eliminates the need for libraries to update the software almost daily so that they can avoid disruptions in service.

5. We don't make your search engine. We make your search engine better : The federated engine does not enhance the native database's search interface, but translate a search into the way federated engine can understand. But it's restricted to the capabilities of the native database's search function. Moreover, it reflects almost similar capabilities of the connected database's search function. Federation searching cannot improve on the native databases' search capabilities, but can only use them for better functioning.

The term federation is also used when describing the inter-operation of two distinct, formally disconnected, telecommunications networks that may have different internal structures. Solomon (2004) differentiated the term 'federated searching' from integrated searching as a system's ability to post-process the retrieved results to rank, cluster or categorize them.

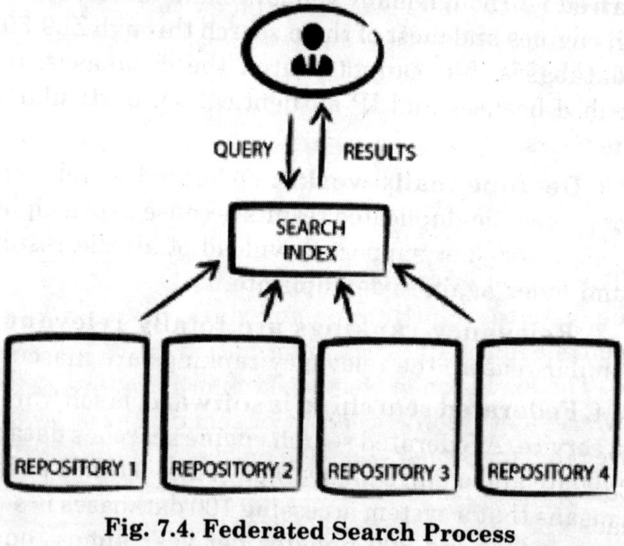

Fig. 7.4. Federated Search Process

All the products connected offer similar functionality to users including resource discovery, querying multiple databases, retrieving and displaying results. The librarian customizing through vendors can configure these connections. The results vary depending on the retrieval process, resources connected in case of querying multiple databases and the amount of customization.

WebFeat, was the provider of federated search technology to more than 900 public, academic, and corporate libraries, including more than half of the top 10 U.S. public libraries. In a move to consolidate the federated search sector of the library automation market, WebFeat has been acquired by ProQuest and later merged into Serials Solutions. The addition of WebFeat to ProQuest results in a major consolidation in the federated search arena—narrowing the number of choices available to libraries.

ProQuest was part of Cambridge Information Group, which owned R.R. Bowker. Although Cambridge Information Group's strategic focus has been on publishing and electronic content, the company has increasingly become involved in the search technology. WebFeat and Serials Solutions were the two top competitors in the federated search arena. Federated search has been the primary focus of WebFeat throughout its business history, whereas Serials Solution offers federated search as one of the components for providing access to electronic content. This acquisition of WebFeat essentially doubles the size of the federated search component of Serials Solutions' business.

7.4.3. Semantic Web

The advent of World Wide Web in the mid-1990s has created greater challenges for data or information management in the libraries, information centres and even beyond. The explosion of web based information paved way for new arena of web i.e. concept of semantic web which is conceived by Tim Berners Lee, the head of W3C (World Wide Web Consortium). A semantic web is intelligent, understands and reads web pages. The technologies that support semantic web are – eXtensible Markup Language (XML), semantics based languages such as RDF (Resource Description Framework) and ontology languages like (Web Ontology

Language). Since the security of web operations has become the main concern, controlled access to documents is considered mandatory. XML layer of the semantic Web, XML schemas, RDF and ontologies are the main components to be referred for securing the web operations.

7.4.4. XML (EXtensible Markup Language)

XML is a software- and hardware-independent tool. It was designed to store and transport data, which is human- and machine-readable. W3C recommended XML for web development. XML does not convey any information regarding its display. It works as a complement to HTML. HTML is applied for the display of format and data, while XML stores or transport data as separate XML files. The XML files can be read with JavaScript code and update the data content of any HTML page. These advantageous features made XML more significant for applying to libraries, since it enables to search and share resources in different formats easily.

Catalogs are designed to provide access to physical resources that are under direct control of the library, whereas providing electronic access to remote resources such as journal articles, books, news items, data etc. and dynamically updated web pages has become challenging to libraries for getting them to their patrons.

Though bibliographic records are created applying international standards and formats like MARC, unless the structure is encoded in a meaningful way, the uniform retrieval will not be possible. Libraries have been maintaining encoded bibliographic records and sharing them to reduce the costs and to improve services, but not every information that the patrons want to access i.e. remote electronic resources is not feasible through the same MARC. However, the information stored in XML is making possible to share and integrate data in several meaningful ways that would not otherwise be possible. XML sets rules for defining new formats and provides structure for storing information, in this sense, it can be considered as a grammar than as a language. For effective use of XML other technologies Document Object Model (DOM), which is an interface between programs and an XML document and also allows programs to do useful things with XML such as finding, sorting, manipulating, and displaying information. This does not require serious programming skills, but forms as universal language that integrates all information resources. Baneree (2001) mentioned that like other powerful technologies such as relational databases, the SQL, WWW, and HTML, XML is also a tool, describing the useful applications in developing larger databases with web-based specific resources e.g. news services, journal database, online catalog, building of archives and retrieval aids.

The University of California Berkeley library in 1993, developed a method for encoding archival materials in XML. The project was named as the Encoded Archival Description (EAD) standard. It was later maintained by the Library of Congress. Oregon State University in 1998 developed an automated interlibrary loan the free application called InterLibrary Loan Automated Search and Print (ILL ASAP). It will automatically search interlibrary loan requests and print request forms sorted by location, call number, complete with availability information, scanned Ariel / shipping labels and customized billing data according to borrowing library or consortium.

The Washington Research Library Consortium developed a system using XML known as ALADIN (Access to Library and Database Information Network) to provide access to a combination of commercial, open source, and locally developed platforms i.e. subscription databases, digital collections, materials requested via interlibrary loan, and library catalogs. This also involves critical tasks such as patron authentication using XML messages transmitted between user applications over the Web. The Library of Congress announced an official specification for representing MARC data in an XML environment in 2002, MARC XML.

It can combine MARC data (e.g., the online catalog) with non-MARC resources also (e.g. a locally maintained database or special collection).

The Open Archives Initiative (OAI) has developed a protocol for Metadata Harvesting (OAI-PMH) making it easy to send a query to a database over the web and receive the results in XML. It is an application-independent interoperability framework. Through this protocol the data providers (repositories) represents structured metadata, while the service providers make requests to harvest that metadata. Basically the record format that is containing the specific metadata returns to XML-encoded byte stream in response to a protocol request to disseminate a specific metadata format from a constituent item. The XML-encoding of records are constituting with parts: 1) header — contains the unique identifier of the item and properties necessary for selective harvesting i.e. the date stamp — the date of creation, modification or deletion of the record; zero or more set Spec elements — the set membership of the item; and, an optional status that attributes with a value of deleted items, if any; 2) Metadata — a single manifestation of the metadata from an item. The OAI-PMH supports items with multiple manifestations (formats) of metadata. 3) About — an optional and repeatable container to hold data about the metadata part of the record, which must conform to an XML Schema. (http://www.openarchives.org/OAI/openarchives protocol.html)

7.4.5. Concept of Ontologies

The information or data is heterogeneous in nature, mostly occurring due to - syntax (data format; structure); different attributes such as homonyms, synonyms in databases and semantics (the meaning of terms in a special context of application). For retrieving web documents through search engines or the search interfaces designed in the publisher as well as aggregator's portals, users supply metadata i.e. the terms (keywords) that will be matching

with those obtainable from the content of the web document. The process is facilitating the retrieval without much relevance to the context. The ontologies are relied on while retrieving the relevant information because they represent relations between terms. In the context of libraries, information science and computer science ontologies are considered as thesauri in which the basic meanings of word fields and their relations to one another are depicted in computers. Stuckenschmidt and Harmelen (2005) discussed the way the problem to be solved by ontologies as "information sharing". This encompasses the integration of heterogeneous information sources and results. The problem of information sharing can be solved by giving the machine a better access to the semantics (meaningful or related terms) of the information. Not only that it is needed to store metadata such as its authors, title, creation date, etc., but also make the important concepts in the documents, the relation terms to these concepts with those in other documents are also accessible in a machine.

Krause (2008) stated that the heterogeneity of the ontologies are again creating problem in sharing the information across the networks, since the information domain utilizes its own vocabulary and develops ontology (the multiple ontology approach). There is no arrangement regarding a common vocabulary or a minimal global ontology. He also described the approaches of handling semantic heterogeneity issue in two projects 'Vascoda' the German science portal and the social science portal 'sowiport' developed at the GESIS Information Centre in Bonn, Germany. Vascoda is the major project in the field of scientific information in Germany, merged 40 collections to integrate high-quality information by using search engine technology (FAST) and new concepts technically, while solving the problem of semantic heterogeneity. To reduce the semantic complexity in heterogeneous digital libraries, Mayr et al (2008) proposed models by combining heterogeneity components in a project- 'Competence Center Modeling and

Treatment of Semantic Heterogeneity', devising the three structural value adding methods for the information retrieval process - query construction, search and ranking and re-ranking. In the context of the latest developments in artificial intelligence; web ontologies; and the semantic web, the Indian information scientists from DRTC Prasad and Devika (2008) suggested to reexamine the context-sensitive pre-coordinate indexing methods such as PRECIS and POPSI. In these indexing methods, the words are represented along with their semantic context to achieve greater precision in the retrieval of information from the web or digital libraries.

7.4.6. Web Mining / Data Mining:

Data mining is the computational process of exploring patterns in larger data sets to extract information and structure in a specified format for further use. The mining operations are applied to larger databases as well as the database systems combining different kinds of technologies, solutions, techniques, statistics, linear algebra, algorithms and also the data structures. The 'Intensive Working Group of ACM SIGKDD Curriculum Committee' has identified the following core components mentioning that – 'the core endeavor in data mining is to extract knowledge from data; this knowledge is captured in a human-understandable structure'. The data mining concept of computer science discipline has been gaining importance due to its real value applications in mining the ever exploding data and also in information in industry, science, engineering and government. Libraries and information centers have been adopting the latest available technologies and tools to handle the information or data as per the user's current expectations. Further library managers need concrete data or information to identify lapses in the existing processes and systems to take appropriate decisions.

The data mining techniques associated to extract data has been gaining exclusive attention of library managers in this electronic and digital era, since it refers to the capability

to discover data from the web, analyzing the content and presenting the information in useful form. Nicholson and Stanton coined the term bibliomining synonymous to data mining referring to both data mining concept and bibliometric technique to the data generated from library operations to achieve set objectives of the library system or to provide specific services or to resolve management issues while helping in taking important decisions for the betterment of the library. Web mining is the application of data mining techniques to discover patterns of information or data on the Web. Data on web constitute files in varied formats linked through hyper-medium. Web mining aims to discover useful knowledge from hypertext, hyperlinks and usage log. The web mining tasks are three main types: Web structure mining, Web content mining and Web usage mining.

Libraries manage large stores of different types of data generated from the computerized library activities, integrated automation of their operations apart from acquiring web resources to facilitate online access to their users. Libraries are also as well providing portal based services through their networks. The data generated from library automation activities and portal services etc. will be usually stored in the library/institutional or publishers servers. Moreover, the libraries are involved in the creation and maintenance of digital libraries, institutional repositories and ERMS, ERAMS, which leaves log data.

Thus, data mining or web mining is the process of putting queries and extracting patterns from large quantities of data. The significant use of mining operation is analyzing the web logs and audit trials. This can establish whether any unauthorized patrons are intrusions are attempted or queries posed etc. The process may be used to detect the unusual data patterns and retrieval behaviors and possibly prevent cyber-attacks and trace virus threats.

7.5. CONCLUSION

In view of the digital library architectures, information systems should be designed as user centric models for providing solutions to the issues associated to information retrieval and built in tune with the user specific services. Several information retrieval tools/resource discovery devices are being developed by vendors based on the evolving technologies in the context of proliferating web based information resources and electronic documents. These tools and technologies enable the publishers as well as libraries to enhance the users search performance, minimizing their retrieval time.

Information Retrieval Systems encompasses the entire range of activities from acquisition to dissemination of information. In computerized web environment, it involves automatic text entry, data processing, manipulation of data through database management systems and the dissemination of information is through library networks, disks which is retrievable through online information systems. However, the objective of the IRS is the information query, whatever be the form and the format of the information, the type of storage and the method of dissemination.

8

Approach to Online Information (Strategies and Tools)

"A user's access to information is limited by his or her ability to articulate the question"

(Borgman, Christine L et.al, 1984 referring a classical idiom of librarianship)

8.1. ONLINE INFORMATION SEARCH

In the current scenario of electronic and digital resources, the web is considered as the potential source of getting the needed information on any topic. The scholarly information is scattered in published articles, journals, books, and research data and also in unpublished form. The web publishing has become very quick and easy process, but the information systems have become more complex, in spite of automation of integrated library operations and the advancements in data management systems; data formats (as per international standards); speedy networks; integration & federation technologies; indexing / sorting techniques and the semantic web applications etc. Moreover, the differential practices, formats, sources (information targets) with heterogeneous user interfaces, varied technologies, tools and approaches, have been making the information retrieval more complicated. The automation of integrated library operations, excessive increase of disk storage, the data file structures that allow random information access made it easier to locate entries from lengthy and heavy files at the least search time. However, the computerized information systems designed to match the users request for information (query) with relevant document/s, are failing to provide entirely precise information to researchers. The underlying reason for getting exorbitant retrieval is basically the explosion of scholarly information resources and also free text indexing systems that facilitate search of all the terms from abstract of the document or even full text.

Therefore, it requires knowledge about the information need, data structure, data sources, tools to search as well as to retrieve the information and a search strategy that covers the logical approach (steps to follow), search construction and handling the user interface etc.

8.2. SEARCH STRATEGY

The term 'Search' refers to the intention to find specific item with a definite purpose using prescribed vocabulary or a specific term. Though the terms 'browsing' and 'navigation' are used synonymously with searching, they are varied in the sense that – 'browsing' is casually referring to some major sources. In this process required entities may also be found though not looked with a definite purpose. Navigating refers to finding one's way according to the directions indicated.

In general sense 'Search strategy is a detailed plan or strategy applied to find some information, some solution or an answer. Search strategy in the context of Information Science, is an inbuilt program or set of programs for processing the request for information and obtaining the retrieval with maximum relevance, whereas, in connection with electronic resources, it is an inbuilt program to retrieve the most precise information out of numerous. 'Search strategy' is the method of search or the technique applicable in searches and also the steps followed in searching. The search strategy helps user -

- To get information according to the user's choice
- To get authentic and reliable information from standard resources
- To improve the utility of the data as the search process showcases the hidden (unknown) resources also
- To improve the precision in retrieval
- To save the time, cost of the searches
- Facilitates the search through multiple resources, databases across several years of literature or websites.

Ultimately, the objective of search strategy is to obtain optimum relevance and precision while retrieving information. The search strategy lays down 3 questions reflecting logical approach to information.

1. What to search?
2. Where to search? and,
3. How to search?

Thus, the information search logically begins with 1) the translation of information need into query terms, i.e. the formulation of query, 2) selecting the search source and 3) applying search technique. Figure 8.1 briefly explains the basic components of logical approach to information.

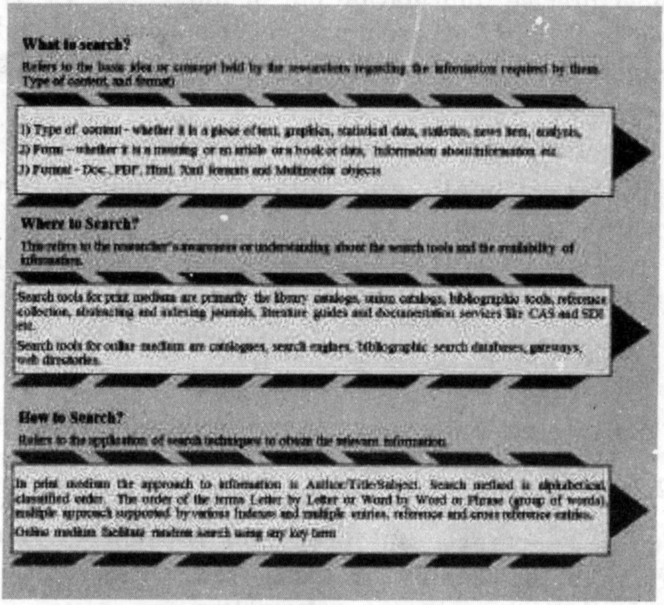

Fig. 8.1. Search Strategy – Basic Components

8.2.1. Formulation of Query

'Query' means posing a question about anything or a request for information. This is the basic approach for seeking information. Ever since the online search services are made available to institutional users under campus wide licensing users are able to handle the query process on any user known interface without requesting librarian. The role of librarian has transformed from an information searcher to a facilitator, instructor or educator or counselor etc.

'Query' is the translation of information need into request in searchable terms. This is requiring coordination of two or more distinct concepts or terms those are representing the document or content.

The classical idiom of librarianship "a user's access to information is limited by his or her ability to articulate the question" (Borgman, Christine L et.al, 1984) holds valid not only in the manual searches of the period, also the web searches of the current time. The formulation of search/query, constitutes –

- A clear understanding of information need in terms of specific subject topic i.e. selection of specific topic, including the language of the content, with chronological and geographical specifications
- Knowledge about the type of information required - Definition, Formula, Graphics, Abstract, Review or Citation or Article Full Text , Census or Statistical Data or Bibliography
- Analyzing the specific subject topic into keywords
- Identifying the main as well as related concepts, synonyms, alternate spellings, or variant word forms of these concepts

8.2.2. Selection of Information Source (s)

If the reference or citation is readily available, the resource can be directly approached by locating it. Or else, the appropriate source of information (search tool) should be explored through a search engine, meta-search cngine and bibliographic search database to obtain link or resource or articles. Further the subject directories, gateways can be approached to find the concerned resource. The information sources or search tools are discussed in section 8.5

8.2.3. Search Techniques

The search techniques imply the methods to follow for searching the required information i.e. basic search or advanced or federated search methods. The search methods are explained in section 8.3.

The construction of search string is significant in search strategy in the light of advancements in information retrieval programs like - keyword searching, phrases, truncation, Boolean operators and filters etc. Section 8.4 deals with techniques to be applied while constructing the search string in query process.

8.3. SEARCH METHODS

Depending upon the user's requirements and their knowledge, their approaches to information is broadly categorized as 3 types - basic or simple search, advanced or powered search and federated search etc.

8.3.1. Basic Search (Keyword)

Basic search is common feature of all the databases, catalogues, directories or gateways. Along with the basic search interface, these sources often provide browsing function to access author-wise, title-wise and subject-wise lists of resources. A simple term keyword can be used for searching. The keyword can be author, or title or abstract or content or subject either exactly same word/s or part of the string. Using spaces helps to separate keywords in simple keyword searching.

Fig. 8.2. Basic Search (JSTOR) (Screenshot)

8.3.2. Advanced (Power) Search:

It enables the user to operate 'filters' and refine their search results to get higher precision. User can exercise various options like - region, scope (full text or abstract), sites, type of document/s, title of the document/journal, duration or period, specific subject data, author publisher, etc. Apart from the regular features of search interfaces provided by the catalogues, databases and each one source developed different search strategies for advanced search.

Figure 8.3 depicts the advanced search interface page of Sciencedirect database. In addition to the regular search interface for using keyword, with author and journal/book title, volume/number/year, the interface shows all the searchable fields associated with Boolean operators. It includes the selection of material type – journals or books or reference works or images or all. The results can be refined by selecting collection, setting the period of publishing the material. Licensed users can even filter the retrieval using 'my favorites', subscribed publications or guest users even choose to search through 'open access content'

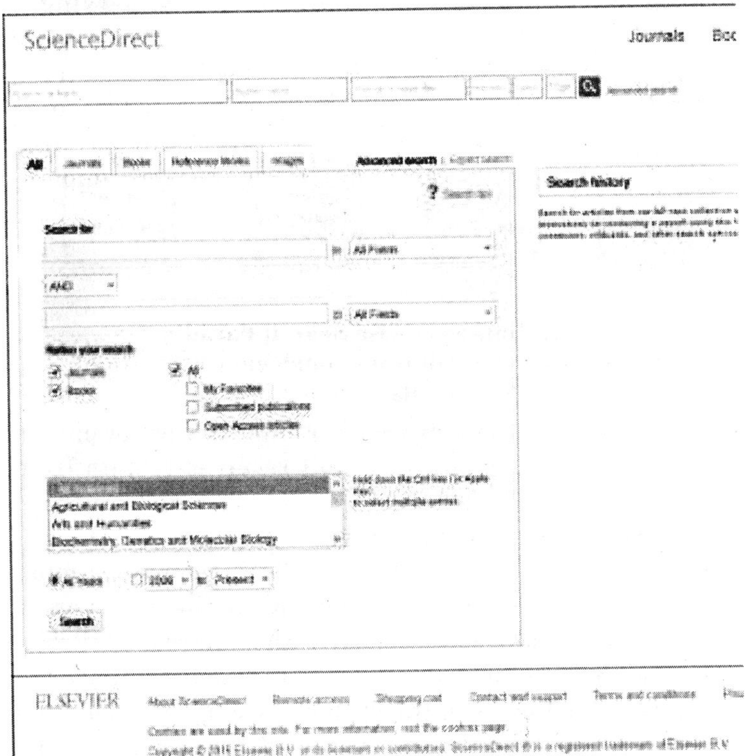

Fig. 8.3. Advanced Search (Sciencedirect) (Screenshot)

8.3.3. Federated Search

Searching online information or data or a piece of text or image has been a complex process since there were numerous individual resources and databases on the web.

To search information, users need to tap all the possible databases or resources. These sources are heterogeneous as per their interfaces, search features and strategies etc. the users often need to select their database/s until federated search technique evolved. The old search paradigm in figure 8.4 illustrates database-wise search paradigm in conventional search system, wherein each database is a unique search tool.

Fig. 8.4. Database-wise Search Paradigm
http://assets.serialssolutions.com/legacy/promotion/ centralsearch.asp

In a federated search, the user enters a word or phrase into a single search interface and receives results from multiple "targets" - i.e. other search engines, commercial information services, or internal as well as external databases. To implement the capability, companies must install a federated search program on their server or subscribe to an information service that allows the use of such a program. Figure 8.5 indicates the federated search model developed by Serials solutions, when it merged with ProQuest, that has already acquired this product from WebFeat.

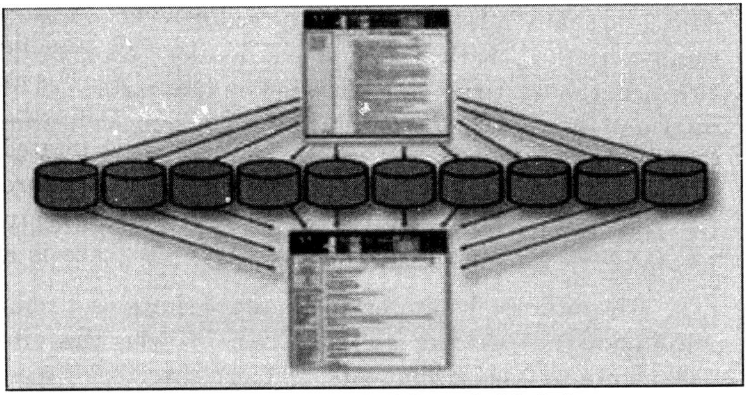

Fig. 8.5. Federated Search Model
(Source: http://www.serialssolutions.com/promotion/centralsearch.asp)

The federated search cannot extract records from authenticated databases. It can neither de-duplicate nor offer accurate relevancy rankings, but enhances the quality of searching, thereby paving the way for the development of a variety of discovery services.

8.4. SEARCH CRITERIA AND CONSTRUCTION

In the initial days online search services, searches were usually undertaken by the libraries or information centers since the cost of the databases were expensive and each search was counted. Few libraries only could afford to provide search services to their users and also to multiple institutions at a price. The librarians could access the bibliographic search databases through their password authentication (login) and taking care of the query process in view of the heavy costs incurred in literature search. The process was including the professional discussions with users about their information needs, subject topics with chronological, geographical specifications. Further librarians translate the information need into searchable terms selecting the search resources and also presenting the search results to users.

In the search strategy, the available content can be retrieved online using different search criteria – Author/s, title, and many other fields of the record such as - series, publisher, ISSN/ISBN, year of publication, book/journal titles, database title, classification number, form of the information, physical format and subject or subject heading. Obviously the subject will be the prime approach to any researcher. Almost all the portals and search engines support free text search which can be a keyword or a phrase or subject headings, title, abstract, full text content.

The internet facilitates the search of citations, through which journal article authors can browse the cited documents, related documents. Subject Directories aid in searching using subject options to cover a broad range of information. In the conventional card catalogue files it is possible to find information by searching on the author, the title, or the subject, whereas through online catalogues it is possible to search applying many more parameters.

In spite of using standard formats for inputting the data, inconsistencies occur due to variations in spelling or rendering, especially when document or content representation is not done uniformly. Thereby, the search results might miss many relevant documents. The following techniques in general be applied for constructing the search string to increase the relevance in retrieval and reducing the unwanted documents.

8.4.1. Truncation of Words

Almost all the portals and search engines support free text search which can be a keyword or a phrase or subject headings, title, abstract, full text content. The following example of author search reveals the rendering variations of the term "Radhakrishnan, S"

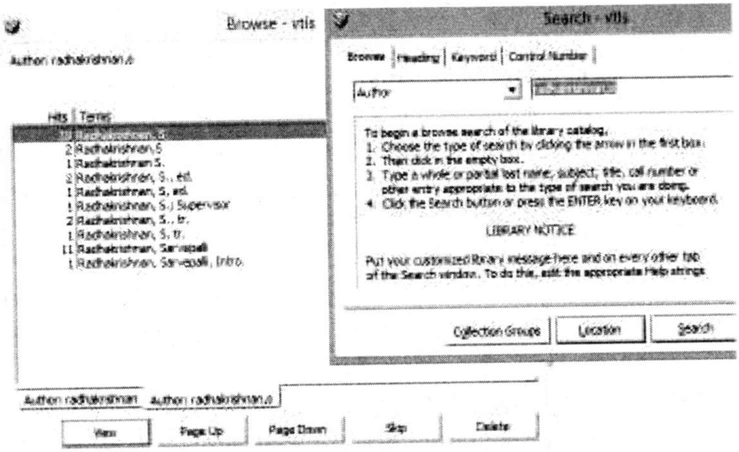

Fig. 8.6. Rendering Variations of Author Search (Screenshot)

To expand the range of search, the truncation mechanism will help to retrieve all the forms of search word whether this is author or title or subject or any keyword. Borgman (1984) refers the word "Truncation - as the ability to request all the forms of entry which include a specified series of characters". It is a search program for retrieving all the variations of a search term or part of word with symbol *. Truncation symbol is entered after the search word. The most commonly used symbol is the asterisk (*) at the end of a word provides retrieval for all variants of the word. However, the truncation may even include irrelevant items in its retrieval, about which researchers need to cautious. Some examples of truncation are given below.

Table 8.1. Truncation in Searching

Search Term	*Retrieving Words*	*Relevance*
educat*	retrieve - educate, educating, education, educational, educator, educators, etc	Included the variations
wom#n	woman and women	
child*	child, children	Included the variations
femini*	feminism, feminist, feminine	Included the variations

pollut*	pollution, pollutants, polluting	Included the variations
classif*	classification, classifying, classifiers	Included the variations
classif	classification, classifying, classifiers, reclassification, declassification	Increased the range of variations
parent	parents, parenthood, parental, grandparents, parenthesis, transparent	Increased the range of variations. Retrieval is alarming as it includes the unwanted retrieval / reduces the precision

8.4.2. Phrase Searching

PHRASE is more than one Keyword, searched exactly as keyed (all terms required to be in documents, in the order keyed). This is as simple as keyword searching and can be searched through any tool. It requires terms to appear exactly in the order they were entered. e.g.

- To enclose the phrase in double quotations " ". E.g.: "affirmative action", "world health organization"
- Capitalizing initial letters enable the phrase search, e.g. World Health Organization

8.4.3. Boolean Search

When necessary to search information on more than two related concepts, it is essential to understand the type of relation among them, i.e. combination of concepts (e.g. Vitamin C and Common Cold), all concepts together (e.g. Vitamin C or Common Cold) and elimination of certain concepts from retrieval (e.g. Common Cold but not Vitamin C). The results of each situation are diagrammatically represented in the following figure.

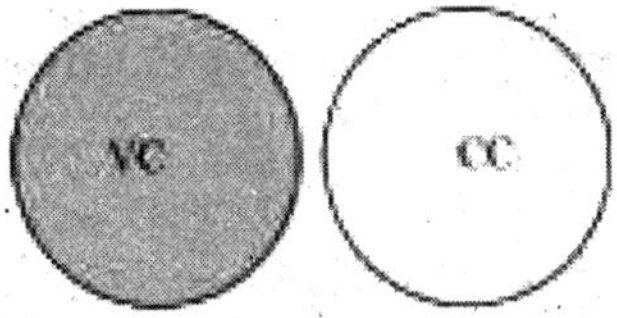

(a) Individual Concepts

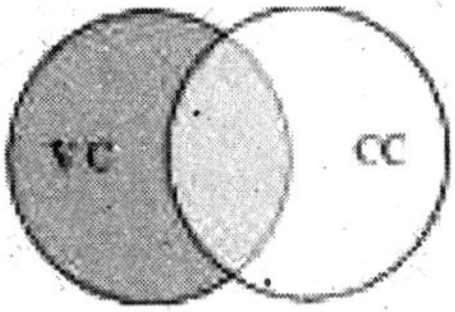

(b) Combined Concepts ('and')

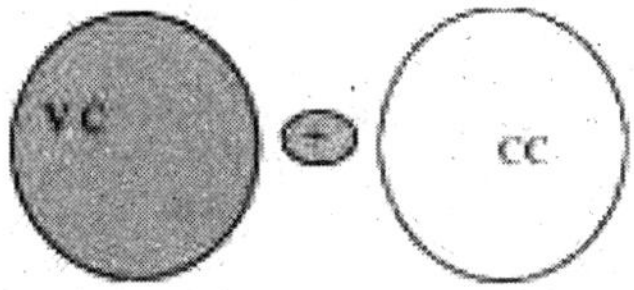

(c) All Concepts together ('or')

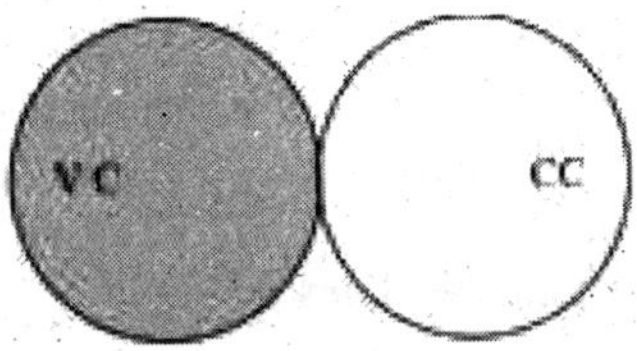

(d) Concepts on Elimination ('and not')

Fig. 8.7. Relations between Concepts - Results

In the above example, each concept represented by keyword or a phrase results in the retrieval alarmingly more as unwanted information or documents or data will be included. It reduces the relevance and precision. Thereby, it consumes more time to search and assess the relevance which leads to stress. Searching concepts (two or more with distinct terms) with Boolean operators AND, OR, AND NOT increase relevance in retrieval excluding the irrelevant results. Boolean Operators (combining and excluding /eliminating words) help in making the search precise and eliminate unnecessary junk in retrieval.

Table 8.2. Searches using Boolean Operators

Boolean operator	*Search Examples*	*Retrieval and Relevance*
AND (combined topics)	water AND pollut*	Enhance the precision in retrieval while using combined concepts.
OR	Pollut* AND (water OR sea* OR river*)	enhance the range by enabling to search through all synonyms of water - sea and river
AND NOT (eliminate the topic)	Pollut* AND (water OR sea OR river) NOT sewage	To exclude sewage from pollut*

Search interfaces, search methods, use of symbols might differ from one information system to another. However, search tips associated to the search interface will guide the user for getting results effectively and precisely.

8.4.4. Application of Filters

Another feature of search interfaces of recent databases or search engines or discovery services and even online is to narrowing the search results by customizing the search or applying 'Filters' (built-in indexes). This application functions through a well built structured database, where certain identified keys are indexed e.g. authors or journal title or publication name, years of publication, images, collection, concepts, publishers or even database. These filters automatically refine the retrieval according to search requirements, until the user achieves précised results. It also enables to refine the results by exercising options to select – full text or abstracts; books or journals or all; material – print or online or print plus online; subscribed or open or all etc.

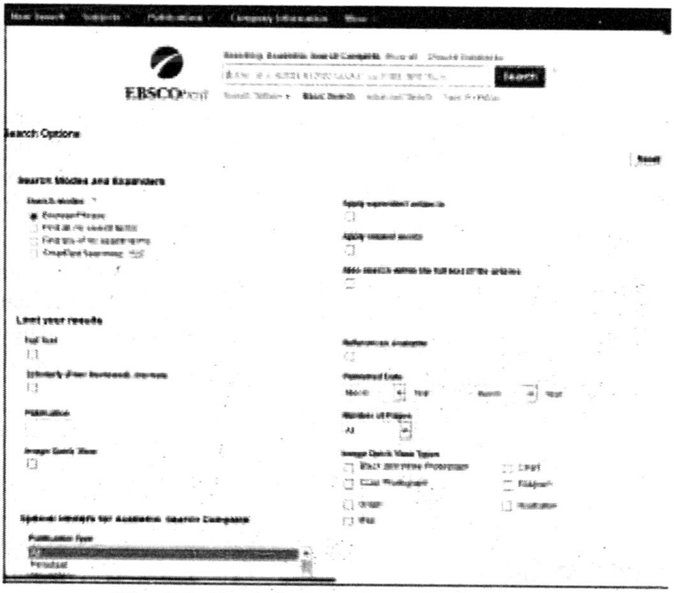

Fig. 8.8. Search Interface in Database (EBSCOHOST)-Application of Filters (Screenshot)

Fig. 8.9. Search Interface in Database (JSTOR) (Screenshot)

Citation databases even provide search options – journal-wise, author-wise, institution-wise, year-wise, subject-wise and provide results in the form of lists as well as analytics from the referencing data. Usage reports or Admin modules of online databases provide formatted usage reports through administrators, authentication from the data accumulated in publishers/aggregators' servers.

Majority of the databases cover text, images, charts, tables etc. These databases provide filters to specify items or together all most all above search / retrieval applications. However, certain databases exclusively focus on specific type of data e.g. statistical data, bibliographic records, citations or images or media files or full text and all together. The features of different search applications or tools are described in the following section.

8.5. WEB SEARCH

All the web resources whether articles, databases, full text file or only abstract or bibliographic search, or websites, search engines/meta search services, web directories, catalogues or web documents, research gateways, any web based services will have a precise location or address of the document /information resource called URL (Universal / Uniform Resource Locator). Web based information or documents can be accessed through internet, only when the respective location (exact URL) in web is known. Though different types of data is available in web at an identified unique locators URL (or its location in web) it is difficult to get the required information or document, because web resources are numerous, unlimited, uncontrollable and not indexed in any standard manner.

- The most common way is to note down the URL from the references collected.
- Guessing organization's URLs from the appropriate domain for websites - The nature and structure of the organization provide some clue about the URL of the Web site as shown in table 8.3. However, URLs of

specific information or web documents are lengthy, filled with several types of characters, numerals and text. It is difficult to guess or note down or remember except pasting in browser.

Table 8.3. Organizations Domains Headings

Domain endings	*Organization*
.com	Commercial
.net	Networks, but can be used by anyone
.edu	U.S. higher education
.org	Other organizations but can be used by anyone
.mil	U.S. military
.gov	U.S. federal government
.int	International organizations established by treaties
.state.XX.us	U.S. state governments,
.biz	Businesses
.coop	Co-operatives
.info	Open for anyone
.name	Personal pages
.museum	Museums

- Search for URL of the organization or database or document through online search tools, web directories, search engines / meta-search engines or subject gateways.
- The present day web browsers support the search by any key word i.e. term, name, acronym, or brief name of the organization. It can be skipped mentioning http:/ / or even www.
- Each database provides its own unique search tool (interface) supporting both basic as well as advanced searches with tips.
- In view of the exploding resources and developing information retrieval technologies most of the databases are providing filters to get precise

information. The filters are included for narrowing down the results until user gets the precise results.

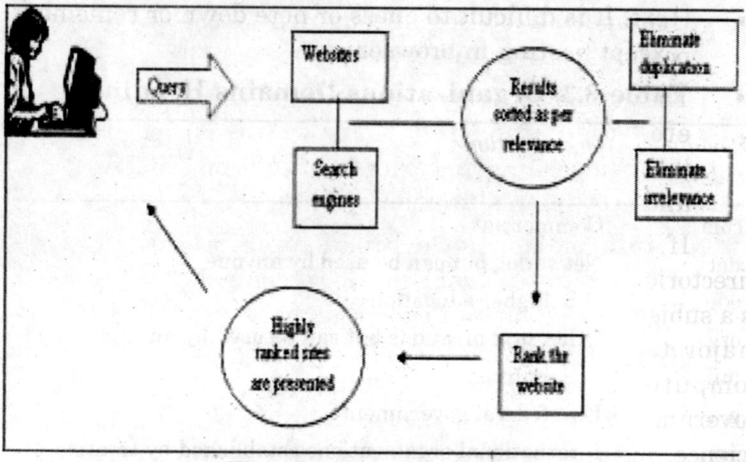

Fig. 8.10. Web Searching

Successful searching is possible with the selection of appropriate source and a smart use of web directories, search engines and advanced discovery services. Further it is needed to

- Add more words to focus results
- Use "phrase searching" and unique words as much as possible
- Use directories (Yahoo, Google) for broad, general topics
- Use of multiple step approach can be several clicks to an answer
- Among links some standard websites need to be selected, such as .edu or .gov., because they provide the most authoritative information at free of cost or at nominal price
- As far as possible ecommerce sites to be excluded, because majority of them are commercially priced and also quote non-standard prices
- Standard sources to be selected to maintain the quality

- Focus results more by subject, because in majority of titles subject is implicit
- Use specialized search engines for news, use net postings, phone numbers, etc.
- The databases, search engines, directories or gateways etc. keep updating their features in view of technological advancements in information retrieval and growing requirements of users.

If information on a broad topic is needed Web directories are to be consulted. Google or Yahoo directories is a subject-tree style catalogue that organizes the Web into major topics, including arts, business and economy, computers and internet, education, entertainment, government, health, news, recreation, reference, regional, science, social science, society and culture etc. Under each of these topics is a list of subtopics and under each of those is another list, and another so on, moving from the more general to the more specific, example to find out about Web page publishing from Yahoo, we need to select the Computers and Internet Topic, under which subtopics are found on Wide World Web. Selection of any of these subtopics eventually takes to Web pages that have been posted precisely for the purpose of giving information.

Primarily for print medium, the search tools are library catalogs, union catalogs, bibliographic search tools such as abstracts, indexes, reviews, literature guides and documentation services like CAS and SDI etc. The organization of search terms is mostly alphabetical or subject – alphabetical either LETTER BY LETTER or WORD BY WORD or PHRASE (group of words). The need for multi-faceted approach is met from several indexes and entries, reference and cross reference entries. Unlike print, the electronic medium (Computer, CD/DVD or Online) has much wider scope for the user to search and retrieve the information than through print due to the availability of various types of tools ranging from online catalogs, bibliographic search databases, directories, and search / meta-search engines A-Z tools. Furthermore, many libraries are attempting to provide a unified interface by subscribing bibliographic search databases since they are covering bibliographic records of all most all disciplines, publishers, types of resources and even meta-search services that explore the content from different sources.

Features of these online tools are discussed hereunder in the context of information search and retrieval. These services facilitate users to download, print, save items, reviewing and annotating them.

8.6. ONLINE SEARCH TOOLS

Currently libraries are handling enormous quantity of e-resources coming through consortia networks; direct subscriptions or purchases; open resources; and also the digital resources of their own institutions and other institutional repositories. So they are now applying different devices or tools such as WebOPACs, library websites, digital libraries for providing bibliographic search, information about the resources and also the full text links to their users.

The emergence of internet facilitated a number of online tools for searching information from different locations in World Wide Web. In the context of library and information centers and related services, the online library catalogue has distinct place since it is the users first and foremost approach to locate the required item within the library collection. For literature search, several indexing & abstracting services in this internet era have transformed as their conventional secondary sources into online e.g. Biological Abstracts (BIOSIS), Scifinder Scholar (Chemical Abstracts). The integrated technologies enable the publishers like Elsevier to develop bibliographic search services like SCOPUS. Exclusive databases have emerged for specific type of information such as citations (e.g. Web of science, Indian Citation Index), document delivery services, e.g. JCCC.

Apart from the databases, search engines also playing key role in retrieving information in the required form whether it is free or priced from any location in WWW. The recent developments in information search and retrieval processes are the emergence of discovery services. These tools not only support the unified search but also help in discovering the underlying relations between the concepts and also automatically generate results against the users query.

8.6.1. Online Library Catalogues

Publishers, distributors or book seller's catalogs are containing the records of books that are readily available with them for sale, whereas the library catalogue is the inventory of library material designed for locating documents in the library. Online catalogs are popularly known as OPAC (Online Public Access Catalogs) or Web OPAC (Online Public Access Catalogs). An Online Public Access Catalog (OPAC) is a database of all bibliographic items hosted by library/ groups of libraries situated at several physical locations in a network.

The following definitions reflect the characteristics of OPAC services. ALA Glossary defines OPAC as, "a computer based and supported library catalog (bibliographic database) designed to be accessed via terminals so that library users may directly and effectively search for and retrieve bibliographic records within the assistance of a human intermediary such as a specially trained member of the library staff." ODLIS (Online Dictionary for Library and Information Science) defined OPAC as — "a database composed of bibliographic records describing the books and other materials owned by a library or library system, accessible via public terminals or workstations usually concentrated near the reference desk to make it easy for users to request the assistance of a trained reference librarian. Most online catalogs are searchable by author, title, subject and keywords and allow users to print, download, or export records to an e-mail account".

The online dictionary has differentiated WebOPAC (WEBPAC) as 'an online public access catalog (OPAC) that uses a graphical user interface (GUI) accessible via World Wide Web, as opposed to a text-based interface accessible via Telnet'. Husain & Ansari (2006) described the OPAC as 'an interactive search module of an automated library management system. Any record is searched directly from a node within a database of the organization or remotely through national and international networks'. They mentioned the features and limitations of first two second generations OPACs with regard to information retrieval as–

- The first generation OPAC systems have no scope for browsing and no keyword searching and also cannot find variations in spellings. Users can search with only the limited parameters that were available in the traditional card catalogue. On the whole they were just primarily book finding lists with few bibliographic details.
- The second generation OPACs emerged in late 1980s were marked with improved user interfaces, keyword searching, use of Boolean operators, enhancing the search capabilities with truncation, wild card support and browsing capabilities, use of full MARC records, interactive search refinement, and also subject access to items. Second generation OPACs are also provided with greater manipulation of search results and a better help systems.

The limitations of first two second generations OPACs with regard to the retrieval of information and their incompatible features lead to the exploration for next generation interfaces

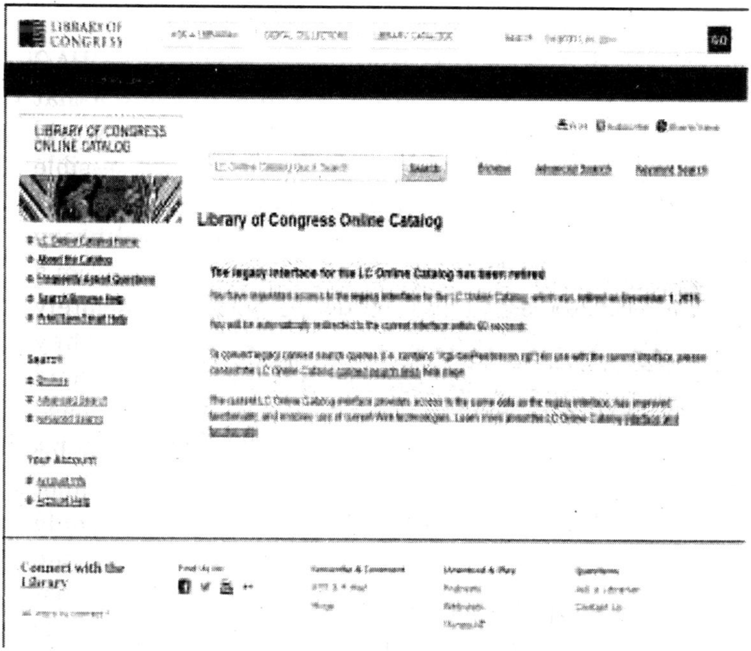

Fig. 8.11. Search Interface of Online Catalogue (Library of Congress) (Screenshot)

Further developments of Web OPACs are featured with advanced search functions, GUI interfaces, Z39.50 compliant systems, created a search environment that enhances the efficiency in search processes and provide better results, e.g. Webcat, Voyagar, The following few examples of next-gen systems that included the discovery features were mentioned by Walker.

- The eXtensible Catalog, sponsored by the Andrew W Mellon Foundation
- Encore (Innovative Interfaces)
- Primo (Ex Libris)
- WorldCat Local (OCLC)
- Visualizer (VTLS)
- Summon (Serials Solutions)

The OPAC 2.0, the application of Web 2.0 to online

catalogues is also referred to as next generation or third generation or twenty-first century catalogues. The OPAC 2.0 is the extension of library 2.0 and web 2.0 kind of advanced user centric services enabling the user participation, feedback and social networking for libraries. The OPAC 2.0 enhanced the searching experiences by showing relevance ranking, subject tagging, clustering or faceting for filtering and expanding search results, suggestions for additional searching based on authority headings, indexing of data from several sources, spelling corrections using the catalogue database contents and community/user reviewing or tagging. Majority of the integrated library system (ILS) vendors are including these Web 2.0 applications to the OPAC to transform the user experience for improving the catalogue's usefulness and usability.

8.6.2. Bibliographic Search Databases

A bibliographic search database is a collection of bibliographic records containing references to published literature i.e. journal and newspaper articles, conference proceedings, reports, government and legal publications, patents, books, etc. Most of the bibliographic databases are proprietary, available by licensing agreement with the creators (indexing and abstracting services) or vendors, e.g. Chemical abstracts.

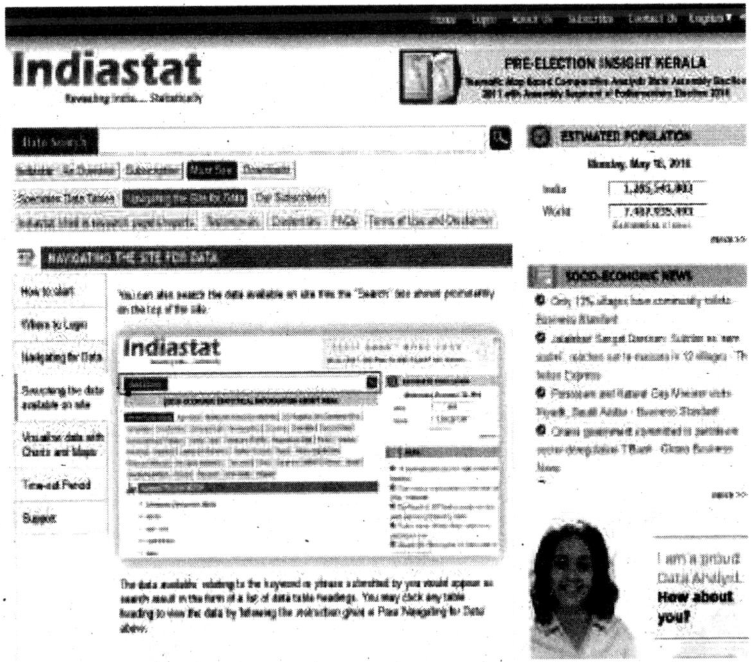

Fig. 8.12. Statistical Database Layout with Search Interface (Screenshot)

Though these databases provide all most all the data elements required to retrieve the information, they may differ in visible format and layout of the other links. Specialized databases such as Indiastat provide information exclusively regarding the content they specialize i.e. Statistical data. The figure 8.13 presents the screenshot of an image database layout for ARTSTOR with search interface, browsing and sharing options etc.

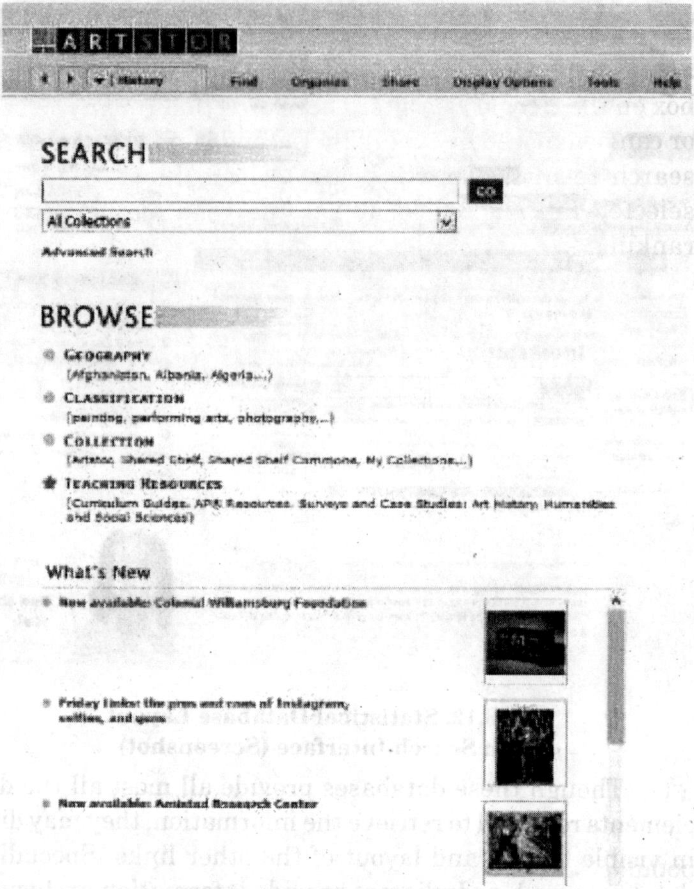

Fig. 8.13. ARTSTOR Search Interface Layout (Screenshot)

8.6.3. Search Engines and Meta-Search Engines:

Searching on the internet is the prime activity of search engines. Search engines crawl and index billions of pages from web documents, portals, directories in their databases and attempt to find information almost from entire Web. Mostly the proprietary websites, authenticated content and associated text with multimedia products, intranet files, and pages omitted by robots cannot be covered by these search engines.

The following search engines are working for Internet

Google : Searching with Google is easier because it auto-directs the user as soon the term is input into the search box on the Google web site. These directions might be useful or can be ignored by typing the second word. Further actual search results also will begin to load. It will review the selected link or article. It has the good features of page ranking.

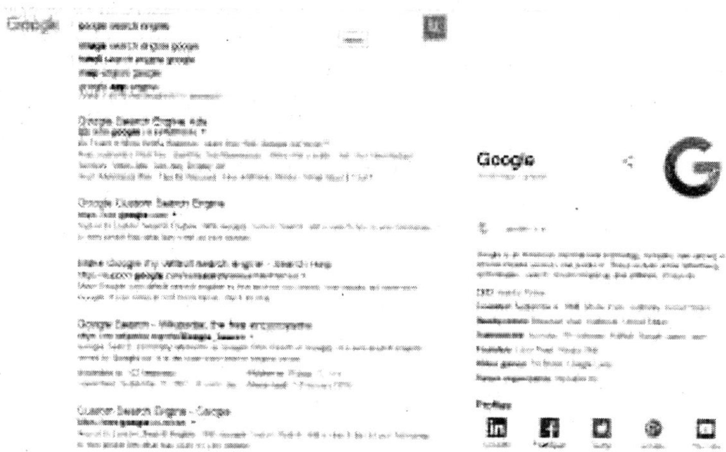

Fig. 8.14. Google Search Engine Functionalities (Screenshot)

Bing : Microsoft's search engine is the second most popular search engine in the world

Quora : As Google gets better and better at answering more complicated questions, it will never be able to match the personal touch available with Quora.

Ask.com : A question and answer type search engine.

SlideShare : Founded in 2006 and it is now part of LinkedIn. It is comprising a database of presentations with content from topmost experts to share. Through the search engine the best presentations can be explored. It is a common platform for uploading presentations, infographic, document or videos.

There were subject specific search engines such as SIRUS (for STM Literature), which later merged in SCOPUS bibliographic search database. Metasearch services searches all through search engines to present their results.

Web Search specifies - standard search interface, standard vocabulary for search terms, syntax, standard database/s management systems with specified indexing operations, use of expanders, limiters or filters etc.

Metasearch engines are the tools those search across search engines and collecting data from them. They consolidate the results from the connected search engines and display them to the user. The most popular metasearch engines are – Search.com; Info.com; PolyMeta.com; Mamma.com etc. Users are assured of the most refined results.

Fig. 8.15. Metasearch Engine (Search interface) (Screenshot)

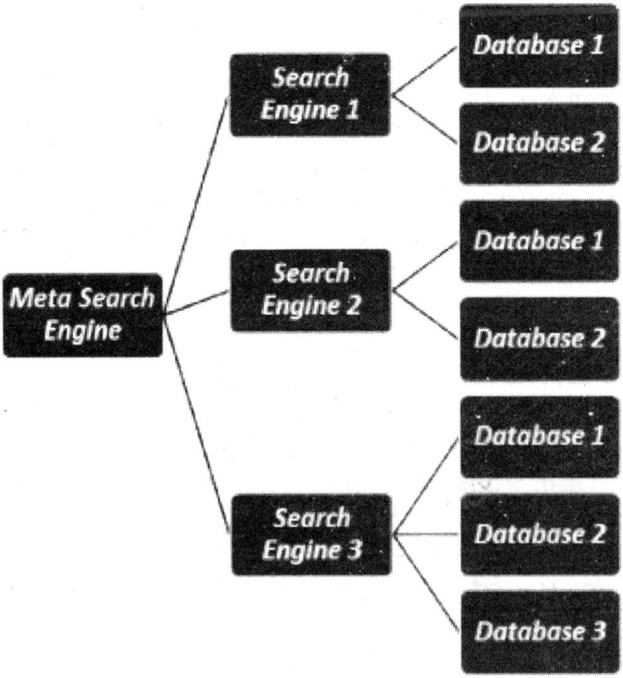

Fig. 8.16. Metasearch Engine (Architecture)

8.6.4. Directories

AOL, Bing, Google, and new are getting added by online directories encyclopedias etc such as yahoo, Amazon, eBay, Wikipedia. Directories though not give as many references as a search engine will, but provide comprehensive information on the topic. Web directories usually come equipped with their own keyword search engines that allow us to search through their indices for the information we need. Search engines and Web directories are being integrated in useful ways. For example, if we use the Google search engine and one of the results happens to be found in the Google's Directory, Google will offer us a link to that section of the directory. Meanwhile, if we conduct our search *in* the Google directory, Google will order the results according to Page Rank, which is Google's all-important measure of "link popularity."

8.6.5. Document (Search and) Delivery Tools

JCCC (J-gate Custom content consortium) has been popular in providing the bibliographic information about the subscribed resources of member libraries, now evolved as J-Gate an electronic gateway to global e-journal literature, including good number of open access journals. It was launched by Informatics India Limited, Bangalore, India supports several groups of academic and research institutions. J-Gate also supports the online subscription of journals, electronic document delivery, archiving and other related services. E.g. the J-gate functions as a common interface for all the publishers' content subscribed or even not subscribed by the UGC-INFONET Digital Library Consortium and the journals (print and e-journals) subscribed by 26 document supply centres. Thus provides a list of hyperlinked articles on users search so that a user can select the article and access/ download those articles which were already licensed (through subscription/ consortium) to the home university. The journal articles that are not accessible to a searcher from home university, the interface facilitates semi-automatic generation of a document supply request directing users to the INFLIBNET Centre or to one of the document supply centres as the case may be. J-gate collects the journal subscription information from all the document delivery centres and also the articles published in open access journals to list them in their portal, so that they will be visible to all university users when they search for journal articles.

The search functionalities of the J-gate home page gives various search options such as quick search, advanced search and browse journals. The user can choose to search by author, title, authors' address/institution, keywords, etc. Quick search allows users to search for articles using Boolean operators such as AND, OR and NOT.

8.6.6. Citations Databases

A citation index is a kind of bibliographic database,

containing citations reflecting the continuation of research and later documents cite. In 1960, Eugene Garfield's Institute for Scientific Information (ISI) introduced the first citation index for papers published in academic journals, first the Science Citation Index (SCI), and later the Social Sciences Citation Index (SSCI) and the Arts and Humanities Citation Index (AHCI). The first automated citation indexing was done by CiteSeer in 1997. Other sources for such data include Google Scholar. ISI (now part of Thomson Reuters) publishes the ISI citation indexes in print and compact disc. They are now generally accessed through the Web under the name Web of Science, which is in turn part of the group of databases in the Web of Knowledge. Elsevier publishes Scopus, available online only, which combines subject searching with citation browsing and tracking in the sciences and social sciences. Indian Citation Index covers peer reviewed journals published from India in major subject areas - scientific, technical, medical, social sciences, arts and humanities.

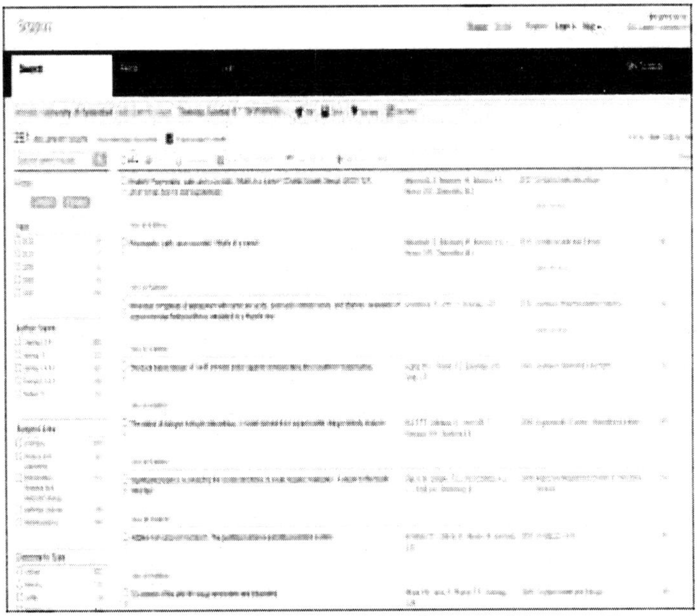

Fig. 8.17. SCOPUS Bibliographic Search Database Layout with Citations (Screenshot)

8.6.7. Discovery Services

Presently most of the LIS software vendors, and the enthusiast publishers and aggregators of full text as well as bibliographic search databases serving the library market, are now actively involving in developing and marketing tools to provide integrated resources and unified search. Walker described the features of the discovery services included in University of Rochester eXtensible Catalog as an example of a next-gen interface.

- User interface that accommodates library users at varying levels of proficiency, helping them to gain access to diverse library collections
- Grouping of results consistent with the concepts of FRBR (Functional Requirements for Bibliographic Records)
- Support for multiple metadata schemas integration with meta-search applications integration with local ILS (integrated library system) implementations
- Integration with external environments such as learning management systems

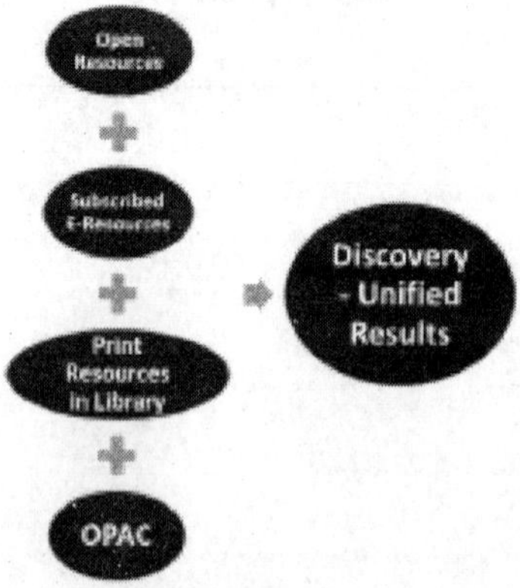

Fig. 8.18. Mechanism of Discovery Services

Discovery Services are the most comprehensive collection of searchable data comprising the Abstracts, indexes, full-text databases with unified search facility. Serials Solutions discovery 'Summon service' is built around a single, unified index that returns a single, unified set of results allowing users to search and navigate effectively across almost all accessible resources including the libraries. The Summon® web-scale discovery service provides researchers with advanced tools that facilitate single, unified index and unbiased relevancy ranking features.

EBSCO Integrated Knowledge Base includes e-journal access license information and historical details specific to the subscribing institution forms the largest and most customized source of e-resource data to libraries. EBSCO Information Services, USA has been developing comprehensive as well as subject specific databases, tools and customized services to libraries, viz. EBSCO A-to-Z Complete e-resource listing service; EBSCO LinkSource — Powerful item-level linking solution; EBSCOhost Integrated Search (EHIS) is extending the reach of the discovery solution by including external resources; EBSCO's Discovery Service (EDS) is the most comprehensive collection of searchable data comprising the base index, abstracts, indexes, full-text databases, EBSCOhost databases and also library's subscriptions. Its discovery solution provides users with a unified search and access to an institution's entire collection via a single, customizable interface. Another example of discovery service from GIST is Knimbus with similar centralized search facilities of library catalogue and adding subscribed as well as unsubscribed resources and also the open resources.

The published content is no longer limited to that stored within the library walls or servers, and the libraries are much more than book depositories; they are very large information centers, offering access and navigation to vast number of articles, technical papers, patents, poetry, photographs, and more. Moreover, the type of content required by users often can't be cataloged by most libraries. So the catalogue information is insufficient and cannot form as library's primary source of information.

In the light of growing impact of semantic web applications in extracting the hidden relations among concepts and the electronic commerce initiatives in several major information retrieval systems/projects, the larger electronic databases are containing rich information projecting the analytics regarding their content and usage. Thereby the full text, bibliographic records or analytics data are coming up together articulating latest technologies, tools to retrieve information from web resources supplementing the catalogue data or even merging into them.

9

Emerging Trends in Data Management in Libraries

9.1. OVERVIEW

Data management is a continuous process for the libraries, whether they acquire, organize the resources and disseminate the information creating their own ICT environment or using the services as well as infrastructure through outside agencies. The emerging trends in maintaining hard/software, RDBMS database model, MARC standard data formats, the SQL, integration processes, data warehousing, web / data security technologies, semantic web applications are moving their services much beyond the comprehension and the range of physical libraries.

The recent trends of building multimedia databases, temporal databases, Geospatial Information Systems, digital libraries, mobile applications, development of integration among several published sources, emergence of analytic data etc. The scholarly information in the form of e-resources and databases floating through electronic, digital and virtual environments, are accessible through smaller devices such as - iPad or tablets and even mobiles to the users of desktops, laptops.

9.2. CLOUD SERVICES

Cloud computing is one of the recent technologies supporting libraries in preserving the digital documents, archiving, records, maintaining web services, etc. Libraries are also at advantage by utilizing the cloud computing services by getting the upgraded services at cost effective manner, ability to integrate to web 2.0 tools, connecting to the resources published in the latest formats. The new cloud libraries model are gaining significance with the explosion of information resources, rising cost of resources as well as the infrastructure building as the model can support the development of digital libraries, shared activities of cataloguing, acquisition and storages and also sharing the resources on virtual library environment on the web.

The cloud computing is a model for enabling convenient, on-demand network access to a shared pool of configurable computing resources (e.g., networks, servers, storage, applications, and services) that can be rapidly provisioned and released with minimal management effort or service provider interaction. The cloud services for libraries includes – building digital libraries/institutional repositories, website hosting, automation of library integrated operations, e.g. Polaris, File storage, searching the library data, as well as searching scholarly content.

The present day library data management is very complex requiring the establishment of hardware/software, maintaining computer, networking and LIS professionals, bearing the cost, risk of data loss, virus threats encountering security issues etc. The cloud computing is one step solution to the library managerial issues in connection with latest ICT environment. Further there were many free as well as commercial slots available for storing the digital documents which will organize the content for easy retrieval. OCLC World Cat is the best example for making use of this service for sharing the library data over the years enabling the search. Now discovery services are also being placed on Cloud, e.g. Knimbus, etc.

However feasible the cloud services are, it is necessary to exercise a bit of caution while entrusting the entire library data for preserving, monitoring and retrieving purpose by maintaining a backup in any convenient form or an assurance from the service providers.

9.3. SPECIALIZED DATABASES

A temporal database is formed by compiling and storing temporal data. This dimension of data is associated with time. Wikipedia defines 'a temporal database is built in support for handling data involving time, being related to the slowly changing dimension concept' e.g. history. It contains time-varying data, which is important to real world computer applications to represent day to day operations in banking, reservations, medical records etc. The relational data model and an object-oriented data model, objects/attributes are indicating time wherein the ordinary data has two time values attached to it, a start time and an end time to establish the time interval of the data. Such data will not be available when the data is modified or deleted. Thus, by associate time with data, it is possible to store the different database states.

Time can be interpreted as valid time or transaction time (when data was entered into the database). In many instances of library integrated transactions, the archived data is crucial to note the history of circulation transactions of the loaned item or a member or by a date etc. The design of temporal databases is different from conventional ones and posing challenges to DBMS designers to incorporate the temporal element.

9.3.1. Multimedia (Resources) Databases

Multimedia databases comprising of different media i.e., text, pictures, sounds, video, animations, etc. have become part of the latest library information material and their applications in education in classroom teaching, learning and applying have become highly significant.

However, the huge amount of multimedia data and information could also challenge educators to efficiently search, browse, access, use, and store the data for their teaching. A multimedia database is a database that hosts one or more primary media file types such as video, audio, radar signals and documents or pictures and animation sequences and composite multimedia i.e. a combination of two or more of the above date in various encoding. The popular image formats are TIFF, BMP, PPT, IVUE, FPX, JPEG, MPEG, AVI, MID, WAV, DOC, GIF, EPS, PNG, etc. The multimedia databases differ from conventional ones in the way the data is stored, maintained and retrieved. They are multidimensional and characterized by its high volume space requirements, temporality features, lacking specific structures and a different logistics requiring compression algorithms etc.

Libraries have been acquiring these multimedia resources individually in CD/DVD format and along with books and other material and they need to be organized in a different location in the library and make it visible to users through library catalogue distinctly identifying as CD/DVD or DISKs in the MARC record. The physical format can be indicated in MARC via 300 Tag and 008 fixed field Tags, while the contents of these disks can even be made available to users over intranet if they are placed on CD Servers and linked through 856/u Tag to respective MARC record. The CD/DVDs can be arranged physically in classified order according to 'Call Number'; or in the 'Accession Number' sequence indicating their availability to users through catalogue.

Apart from those multimedia resources freely available through YouTube and other social networking websites, the educational multimedia material are made available through most of the online databases, search engines (e.g EBSCO, Google). The dedicated database like ARTSTOR presents the collections of two/three dimensional images, art pieces from the world popular art galleries, etc. on subscriptions.

These multimedia resources or information about them can be retrieved from internet conventionally through catalogues and search engines, search interfaces of the database. The information about multimedia can be obtained through three approaches, - keyword-based, feature-based, and concept-based approaches (Johnson, 1998) with due content representation in free text or suitable tags in the catalogue or concerned record.

1. Keyword-based approach : The multimedia content is described by the user through annotations.

2. Feature-based approach : A set of features can be used for representing and retrieving the multimedia data. Many multimedia databases allow users to query a database by specifying keywords and/or image characteristics. For example: general information like colour, texture, shape, speed, position, or particular applications like fingerprint recognition or medical images.

3. Concept-based approach : Concepts are subsequently used to interpret the content of the data and to retrieve the data itself. "This is usually an application domain specific process and occasionally requires the intervention of the user"

Information retrieval or querying process in a multimedia is different from other conventional textual, numeric databases as the free text searching does not arise unless there is appropriate content representation. Queries based on the input of multimedia objects by the user may not yield the best matches but on the degree of similarity as indicated by Grosky (1997), while Yoshitaka & Ichikawa (1999) suggested a query-by-example approach for content-based representation i.e. specifying a query by giving examples. For example, an image object is retrieved by the shape of objects, by specifying colours and their spatial distribution in the image, or by a specific pattern appearing in an image.

Thus the latest data kind of multimedia are posing

challenges for librarians in creating content representations for easy retrieval of objects.

9.3.2. Geospatial Information Systems

Geospatial Information Systems comprises the wide range of modern tools contributing to the geographic mapping and analysis of the Earth and human societies. These technologies have been evolving through maps making, drawings, prints together with aerial photography as early cameras sent on balloons, pigeons, airplanes during the 20th century over the period. The photographic interpretation and map making took new dimensions with satellite images of Earth's surface and human activities storing in computers in digital form. "Computers allowed storage and transfer of imagery together with the development of associated digital software, maps, and data sets on socioeconomic and environmental phenomena, collectively called geographic information systems (GIS)" (Geospatial Technologies Project, AAAS, 2016 http://www.aaas.org/content/what-are-geospatial-technologies). This requires high quality hardware and secured networks and now the data is made available to academic, research personnel, decision makers in universities, corporations, and non-governmental organizations regarding the topics such as industrial engineering, biodiversity conservation, forest fire suppression, agricultural monitoring, humanitarian relief, and much more. The noted applications of GIS are - Remote Sensing, Global Positioning System (GPS) and Internet Mapping Technologies

9.3.3. Mobile Database Applications

Mobile applications are becoming highly popular not only in wireless communications but also in information technology. Due to the recent advancements in portable and wireless technology led to mobile computing, a new dimension in data communication and processing emerged enabling several publishers, providers develop mobile enabled apps for the eacy access to information in smaller computing devices like notebooks, tablets and mobiles. Mobile database allow the exploitation of database applications enabling relational database function in devices, with their corporate cellular networks, download data, work offline or online to synchronise with the corporate database. However, there were some mobile relational database systems mainly concerning with RAM oriented constraints but the latest devices are overcoming the issue by enabling the users to handle files transfer, emergency response, emergency calling etc.

9.4. ABOUT DATA

As described in chapter I, libraries need to handle data comprising of text, numerals, images or multimedia mostly in electronic or digital form which either in library servers or getting through the publishers/aggregators or providers. The data is disseminated to users via catalogues, databases, portals. The other type of data that the libraries need to handle for managerial purpose is - usage data, big data etc. varies from the conventional data in format, source and application.

9.4.1. Digital Libraries

Digital libraries vary from their traditional libraries in the acquisition, preservation, maintenance, organization of digital material and facilitating access or remote access to users. The magnitude of these data collections as well as their diversity and multiple formats provide challenges on a new scale. The future progression of the development of digital libraries is likely to move from the present technology of retrieval via the internet, though net searches of indexed information in repositories, to a time of information correlation and analysis by intelligent networks. Techniques for collecting information, storing it, and organizing it to support informational requirements will provide the baseline for development of approaches appropriate for digital libraries.

9.4.2. Usage Data

Libraries, publishers, aggregators and other providers of database formats the log data accumulated in their servers according to the COUNTER and SUSHI standards. This formatted data will be supplied to the institutions or data access is provided to the institutional administrators for exercising decisions about the renewal of databases or to refine the user services to promote their usage. Regular monitoring of usage data becomes compulsory for the librarians to track the usage of expensive e-resources and also to create user centric services in the library.

9.4.3. Big Data

The internet transactions, emails, video, clicks on hyperlinks, multimedia and digital sources, searches by the registered users through many devices yield log data in larger quantities. This data gets accumulated aggregated and stored from the devices of Individuals with smart phones and on social network sites and multimedia. The present e-commerce trend to analyse this exploding data in large pools and making use by projecting to the users with helpful suggestions regarding the related products, which are otherwise unidentified to users. Organizations age supplementing their databases with data receiving from diverse sources - social media, video, smart mobile devices, and other sources. This big data is advancement in technology and also an added advantage for making decisions apparently in the selection of books and other material required for the libraries and also refining user's services. It is undoubtedly a different and difficult effort for libraries to build such an architecture to capture the user's activities, yet the commercial publisher's or aggregators databases are facilitating these analytics to their registered users in broad scale. However, in an integrated library automated environment, LIS software packages can build the necessary architecture to integrate big data during user searches, recommendations for books and other materials.

9.5. CONCLUSION

The data management in libraries has been continually evolving with the technological advancements in hardware/ software (servers, OS, RDBMS or ORDBMS, LIS Application software) communications and accessing devices. The crucial issues revolving around the data management need to be kept up to date with the latest trends and developments of database technologies, new data types, standards, formats, metrics, integration of concepts following the discovering information patterns in retrieval and data security applications. Furthermore, when the external applications are used by libraries for their data management and for facilitating the easy and precise retrieval of information by users, the core link between input and retrieval need to be invariably monitored by the libraries concerned. Though, most of the applications related to the data production, maintenance and dissemination of scholarly information has gone beyond the range of libraries, the librarians are one way connected to external applications and to users as facilitators, trainers, educators, counsellors etc. for the efficient functioning of libraries.

Bibliography

REFERENCES

1. Banerjee, K. (2002, September). How does XML help libraries? *Computers in Libraries, 22*(8). Retrieved April 19, 2016, from http://www.infotoday.com/cilmag/sep02/banerjee.htm
2. Borgman, C. L. (1984). *Effective online searching: a basic test.* New York: Marcel Dekker.
3. Burton, B. and others (2009, October-December). History of Database management systems. *IEEE Annals of the History of Computing, 31*(4), p3-5. Retrieved December 10, 2015, from ., Volume 31, Number 4, Retrieved on http://muse.jhu.edu/journals/ahc/summary/v031/31.4.grad.html
4. DBase: http://www.dbase.com/
5. DBase: http://www.manmrk.net/tutorials/database/dbase/IntrodBASEIIIPlus.htm
6. DBMS: http://dbms.ca/concepts/evolution.html
7. Dictionary for Library and Information Science (2004): Retrieved from http://www.abc-clio.com/ODLIS/odlis_A.aspx
8. Doke, E. R. (1991, Winter). Software maintenance revisited; a product life cycle perspective. 4 (1). Winter 19991 p.8-11. *Information executive*, p.8-11.
9. File Maker: http://www.filemaker.com/

10. Grosky, W. (1997). Managing multimedia database: Information in database systems. *Communications of the ACM, 40(12), 73-80., 40*(12), p.73-80.

11. Guha, B. (1983). *Documentation and Information: Services techniques and systems.* Calcutta: World Press.

12. Haravu, L. (2004). *Library automation; design principles and practice.* . New Delhi: Allied.

13. Haynes, D. (2004). *Metadata for information management and retrieval.* London: Facet Publishing.

14. Hane, Paula J.: phaneCcdinfotoday. com

15. Hoffer, J. A. (2002). *Modern database management. 6th edition. Delhi, Pearson Education, 2002.* (6, Ed.) Delhi: Pearson Education.

16. IBM DB2: http://www-01.ibm.com/software/data/db2

17. Information Today, Vol. 20 No. 10 — Nov./Dec. 2003 available at http://www.infotoday.com/it/oct03/hane1.shtml (accessed on 29.3.2014)

18. International Encyclopedia of Information and Library Science. (2003). Abingdon UK: Taylor and Francis.

19. Johnson, R. (1998). Internet multimedia databases. *Multimedia Databases and MPEG-7,(IEE Colloquium on January 29, 1999) . Ref. No. 1999/056*, pp. 1/1 - 1/7. . IET. Retrieved from http://ieeexplore.ieee.org/stamp/stamp.jsp?tp=&arnumber=755821&isnumber=16371

20. Kochtanek, T. R. (2004). *Library information systems: from library automation to distributed information access solutions.* Westport: Libraries Unlimited.

21. Krause, J. (2008). Semantic heterogeneity: comparing new semantic web approaches with those of digital libraries. *Library Review, 57*(3), p. 235-248.

22. Kujani, T. D. (2013). Review Paper on Multi-dimentional Data Structures . *Indian Journal of Computer Science and Engineering (IJCSE)* , *4*(2), p163-167. Retrieved from http://www.ijcse.com/docs/

INDJCSE13-04-02-090.pdf

23. Kurtz, M. and others (2010). Usage Bibliometrics. *Annual Review of Information Science and Technology-Section 1 Metrics: Chapter 1, 44*(1), p.1–64.
24. Lancaster, F. (1995). The evolution of electronic publishing. *Library Trends, 43*(4), p.518-525.
25. Laney, D. (n.d.). *3D Data Management: Controlling Data Volume, Velocity and Variety.* Retrieved February 13, 2016, from http://blogs.gartner.com/doug-laney/files/2012/01/ad949-3D-Data-Management-Controlling-Data-Volume-Velocity-and-Variety.pdf
26. Lavagnino, M. (1997, May). Networking and the role of the academic systems librarian: an evolutionary perspective. *College & Research Libraries, V.58*, p.217-231.
27. Lightenna on ER diagrams: http://www.lightenna.com/book/export/s5/111
28. Microsoft Server: https://www.microsoft.com/en-us/server-cloud/
29. Moen, Willium E. Resource Discovery using Z39.50: promise and reality. www.unt.edu/wmoen/Z3950/papers/MoenZ3950.htm
30. MS Access: http://www.quackit.com/microsoft_access/microsoft_access_2013/tutorial/adding_data.cfm
31. NewGenLib: http://www.verussolutions.biz/technology.php
32. Nicholson, Scott (2003), "using data mining to discover web-based scholarly research works", *Journal of the American Society for Information Science and Technology*, 54 (12):1081-1090.
33. Open Archives Initiative Protocol for Metadata Harvesting http://www.openarchives.org/OAI/openarchivesprotocol.html
34. ORACLE http://docs.oracle.com/html/A73172_01/output/bawor_si.htm#1010716

35. ORACLE http://docs.oracle.com/cd/B28359_01/nav/portal_4.htm#clients_for_database_administration

36. ORACLE LEARNING LIBRARY - https://apex.oracle.com/pls/apex/f?p=44785:141:0:::141:P141_ PAGE_ID, P141_SECTION_ID:6,18

37. ORACLE TUTORIALS http://www.oracletutorial.org/forms-and-reports/forms-and-reports.php

38. Pankaj Kumar, D. S. (2010). A Data Warehouse for Mining Usage Pattern in Library Transaction Data. *Assam University Journal of Science and Technology, 6*(2), 125-129. Retrieved from http://www.inflibnet.ac.in/ojs/index.php/AUJSAT/article/view/194

39. Prasad, A. and others (2008). Faceted infrastructure for semantic digital libraries. *Library Review, 57*(3), p. 225-234.

40. Praseeda, M. (2013, February). Emerging Database Models and Related Technologies. *International Journal of Advanced Research in Computer Science and Software Engineering , 3*(2), p.264-269. Retrieved from www.ijarcsse.com

41. Postgresql: http://www.postgresql.org

42. RPM Package Manager: http://www.rpm.org/

43. Satzinger, J. W. (2006). *Systems Analysis and Design in a Changing World, 4th Edition. Course Technology* (4 ed.). Boston, USA: Course Technology.

44. Schulz, G. (2006). Top 10 ways to secure your stored data. *Computerworld.*, August. Retrieved from http://www.computerworld.com/article/2546352/data-center/top-10-ways-to-secure-your-stored-data.html

45. Serials Solutions http://www.serialssolutions.com/en/services/webfeat

46. Serials Solutions http://www.serialssolutions.com/promotion/centralsearch.asp

47. Sharma, P. (2009, March). Advanced Applications of Data Warehousing. *DESIDOC Journal of Library &*

Information Technology, Vol. 29, No. 2, 29(2), 61-66. Retrieved from http://publications.drdo.gov.in/ojs/index.php/djlit/article/viewFile/242/152

48. Sowa, J. and others (1992). Extending and formalizing the framework for information systems architecture. *IBM Journal, 31*(3), p.590-616.
49. Stuckenschmidt, H. and others (1998). *Information sharing on the web.* Berlin: Springer.
50. Techopedia on Database model: https://www.techopedia.com/definition/6762/database-model
51. Tenopir, C. and others (2003). Patterns of journal use by scientists through three evolutionary phases. *D-Lib Magazine, 9*(5). Retrieved February 12, 2016, from http://www.dlib.org/dlib/may03/king/05king.html
52. Thuraisingham, B. (2008). *Building trustworthy semantic webs.* NewYork: Auerback Publications.
53. Todd Miller: tmiller@webfeat.org
54. Turoff, Murray and Starr Roxanne Hiltz (1982). The electronic journal: a progress report. Retrieved 27.6.2012 from http://web.njit.edu/~turoff/Papers/ElectronicJournal.html)
55. Tutorials Point on Data warehousing http://www.tutorialspoint.com/dwh/dwh_overview.htm
56. Tutorials point on MySQL: http://www.tutorialspoint.com/mysql/
57. Tutorialspoint on Data warehousing: http://www.tutorialspoint.com/dwh/dwh_overview.htm
58. Tutorialspoint on ER model: http://www.tutorialspoint.com/dbms/er_model_basic_concepts.htm
59. Tutorialspoint on MySQL: http://www.tutorialspoint.com/mysql/
60. Walker, J. (2010). New resource discovery mechanisms in the E-Resources. In *Management Handbook – UKSG* (pp. p.1-11).

61. Watkinson, A. (2001), Electronic Solutions to the Problems of Monograph Publishing, The Council for Museums, Archives and Libraries
62. W3C (World Wide Web Consortium) https://www.w3.org/Consortium/
63. Webopedia on Data: http://www.webopedia.com/TERM/D/data.html)
64. Wikipedia on Data: https://en.wikipedia.org/wiki/Data#cite_note-].
65. Wikipedia on Database design: https://en.wikipedia.org/wiki/Design
66. Wikipedia on Visual FoxPro: https://en.wikipedia.org/wiki/Visual_FoxPro
67. Yale University: http://codex.cs.yale.edu/avi/db-book/db4/b.pdf
68. Yale University: http://codex.cs.yale.edu/avi/db-book/db6/appendices-dir/d.pdf
69. Yoshitaka, A. &.-9. (1999). A survey on content-based retrieval for multimedia databases. *IEEE Transactions on Knowledge and Data Engineering*, p81-93.
70. Yu, C., & Bradenburg, T. (2011, February). Multimedia database applications: issues and concerns for classroom teaching. *The International Journal of Multimedia & Its Applications (IJMA).*, *3*(1), p.1-9.

GENERAL READING

1. Date, C. (n.d.). *An Introduction to Database Systems: The Systems Programming Series.* Addison-Wesley Publishing Company. Reading, Massachusetts.
2. Dempsey, L. (2003). The recombinant library: portals and people. *Co-published simultaneously in Journal of Library Administration, 39(4)*, p.103-136. (S. B. Lee, Ed.) New York: The Haworth Press. Retrieved from http://www.oclc.org/research/staff/dempsey/recombinant_library/

3. Doyle, L. B. (n.d.). Information Retrieval and Processing. Los Angeles: Melville Publishing Company.

4. Feather, J., & Sturges, P. ed. (2003). *International Encyclopedia of Information and Library Science* (2nd ed.). London: Routledge.

5. Fosket, A. (1996). *Subject approach to Information* (5th ed.). London: Facet Publishing.

6. Gaydasch, A. (1988). *Effective Database Management*. Engle wood Cliffs, NJ: Prentice Hall.

7. Gopinath, M. A. (Ed.). (August 1994). Teaching, Research and Practice in Classification and Indexing. *DRTC Annual Seminar*. Bangalore: DRTC.

8. Harrod, L. M. (1984). *Harrod's Librarians' Glossary* (5th ed.). Hants: Gower Publishing Company.

9. Ingersoll, P. and others (2004). *Managing information technology; a handbook for systems librarians* . Westport: Libraries unlimited.

10. Intensive Working Group of ACM SIGKDD Curriculum Committee. (2006). *Data Mining Curriculum*. Retrieved March 2, 2013, from ACM SIGKDD: http://www.kdd.org/curriculum

11. Kemp, A. (1988). *Computer Based Knowledge Retrieval*. London: ASLIB.

12. Martin, J. (1976). *Principles of Database Management*. Englewood Cliffs: Prentice Hall Inc. .

13. Pujari, S. (n.d.). *Database: Six Important Types of Databases*. Retrieved January 30, 2016, from Your article library: http://www.yourarticlelibrary.com/database/database-six-important-types-of-databases-business-management/10375/

14. Reitz, J. M. (2004). *Bibliographic database. Dictionary for Library and Information Science* . Westport, Connecticut: Libraries Unlimited.

15. Rob, P. and others (2003). *Database systems design,*

implementation and management (5th ed.). Singapore: Thomson Asia.

16. Rowley, J. (1990). *The basics of System Analysis and Design for Information Managers.* London: Clive Bingley Ltd.
17. Rowley, J. (1996). *The Basics of Information Systems.* London: Library Association Publishing.
18. Ullman, J. D. (1992). The Relational Data Model. In *Foundations of Computer Science.* W.H.Freeman. Retrieved from http://infolab.stanford.edu/~ullman/focs.html#pdfs
19. Van Rijsbergen, C. (1979). *Information Retrieval* (2nd ed.). London: ButterWorths.
20. Vickery, B. C. (1970). *Techniques of Information Retrieval.* London: Butterworths.
21. Waiters, C. (1982). *Dictionary of Information Science and Technology.* Boston: Academic Press Inc, Jovanorich Publishers.